W9-DFO-208

The First Century
of New England Verse

The First Century of New England Verse

BY

Harold S. Jantz

New York

RUSSELL & RUSSELL

1962

PUBLISHED, 1962, BY RUSSELL & RUSSELL, INC.
BY ARRANGEMENT WITH THE AMERICAN ANTIQUARIAN SOCIETY
L. C. CATALOG CARD NO: 61—13764

PRINTED IN THE UNITED STATES OF AMERICA

The First Century of New England Verse

BY HAROLD S. JANTZ

Acknowledgments

This study is indebted immeasurably to the directors and librarians of our great historical societies, to a number of other historians, and to several colleagues, all of whom contributed most generously of their time, and knowledge, and wisdom, to bring unknown material to my attention, to guide me to other possibly fruitful sources, to add to my information from their more specialized knowledge. The list of them is far too long to print here, and those individuals and institutions whom I here single out, are simply those upon whose time I have made the greatest demands and from whom I have received permission to publish material included in this study.

Mr. Clarence S. Brigham and Mr. Clifford K. Shipton of the American Antiquarian Society particularly have nursed along this work from its infancy and shared sympathetically in all its growing pains. With certain materials unavailable to me at this distance from New England, Mr. Shipton had to devote much time at the final completion to filling in blanks and checking details, and he has been most patient and forebearing when completion was delayed farther and farther beyond the original date-line. Mr. Allyn B. Forbes and the staff of the Massachusetts Historical Society have furthered the work at numberless points, and I have received gracious permission to publish several of their most important pieces in the appended anthology. Mr. S. Foster Damon, curator of the Harris Collection of American Poetry at Brown University, put the resources of that splendid collection and of his wide understanding at my disposal; the publication of the important Fiske manuscript from this collection adds a new poet and a new poetic technique to our literature. The Samuel Sewall commonplace book at the New York Historical Society is one of the most important single collections of our early verse; for permission to publish the unknown or incompletely known poems from the manuscript, I am deeply indebted to that Society. I am grateful to the Boston Public Library and to the Historical Society of Pennsylvania for permission to publish two important little sets of verses. Mr. George E. Duckworth, of the Department of Classics at Princeton, most patiently unravelled for me many a passage of baroque, unclassical Latin. My two assistants, one at the beginning and one at the end of the work, ably furthered it at the critical times when otherwise its progress would have been almost imperceptible. My most especial gratitude goes to my best, severest, and kindest critic, not only for her able assistance but for her noble forbearance while this work was being rushed to (or rather beyond) its date-line.

Princeton University

I. Introduction

TO BEGIN with, it was rather an advantage than otherwise that this study originated as a by-product of totally different investigations, for much of the newly discovered verse came to light almost without extra effort in the course of search through various manuscript collections and old libraries for material in another field. This illusion of ease tricked me into consenting to read a paper on my new findings before the American Antiquarian Society. Since the fortunes of war had made it impossible for me to continue with my main project, I thought it might be amusing to find out in my spare time just what there was to our seventeenth-century verse.

In my fathomless naiveté I was not content simply to present the new discoveries; I felt I needed to find out all that had hitherto been known about our early verse, so that I could see the new parts in their proper setting and perspective. The results were disastrous for my spare time and made necessary a thorough revision of my leisurely plans, for it soon became apparent that previous surveys and bibliographies were unacquainted not only with the unpublished verse but also with a large part of the printed verse. As a result, many of the literary judgments and general conclusions were almost worthless, since they left out of account so much of our finest verse (some of which flatly contradicts their material and critical statements) and gave undue emphasis to certain well-known poems which are strictly mediocre or worse.

The list of previously known Puritan poets was compiled in an amusingly haphazard fashion more than a century ago. An anonymous reviewer in the *American Quarterly Review* of December, 1827, wrote the first survey of Puritan verse which I have been able to find, including whatever had come to his attention. Leaning heavily on this article, but expanding its contents, Samuel Kettell two years later made the second survey in the introduction to his *Specimens of American Poetry*, and there we had the almost immutable canon of thirty-odd writers, impartially chosen from among the good, indifferent, and bad versifiers of the period, on which no one has tried to improve except by reduction or by occasional single additions. Moses Coit Tyler's noted *History of American Literature*, 1878, added not one new name of the slightest importance (though his critical examination is on a far higher plane), nor did the *Cambridge History of American Literature* of over forty years later, nor any of the lesser surveys. Even the surveys and bibliographies specifically concerned with the early verse added very little.

In other ways, however, important new contributions were made. First there were the all-too-rare studies of certain individual poets: from the edition of Anne Bradstreet in 1867, through that of Richard Steere in 1907, of Benjamin Tompson in 1924, John Wilson and Samuel Danforth in 1927, to that of Edward Taylor in 1939—not to forget Winslow's *American Broadside Verse*, 1930. Second and fully as important is the verse widely scattered through the various proceedings of historical societies, other historical periodicals well known and obscure, local histories, genealogies, and even newspapers of the eighteenth and nineteenth centuries. With the persistently wretched indexing, "buried" is a more accurate word than "published," and scholars will no doubt continue to come upon items comparable to the Michael Wigglesworth poem (otherwise unknown) which is safely tucked away in one of the lesser periodicals. Several privately printed items are so rare that they seem to have remained virtually unknown.

This state of affairs made it necessary first to compile a critical bibliography, an agonizingly difficult task, since more than four-fifths of the material (much of it from unpublished manuscripts) had to be newly assembled, and the remainder had to be cleared of errors of every description: misattributions, confusions, bad texts, wrong dates, and so on. Under the circumstances, anything like perfection is still a remote and unattainable ideal, and the best that can be hoped for is that finally enough of the pertinent material has been gathered and arranged in such a way that the individual poems and poets can be seen in fairly correct perspective and that reasonably valid conclusions can be drawn. From this point onward it is hoped that other students of the period will contribute corrections and supplementary material in order to bring the work to a reasonably definitive state. It is planned to publish such additions and corrections in subsequent volumes of the *Proceedings*.

Aside from the lack of the basic factual knowledge, perhaps the most serious barrier to our understanding of the early Puritan verse has been the traditional critical premise that it is provincial, awkward, dull, and often involuntarily funny—this in spite of the fact that verse of true quality and originality has long been known and more has recently been brought to light. One reason for our patronizing attitude has been the misapplication of the critical standards of eighteenth-century smoothness and nineteenth-century romantic lyricism to seventeenth-century Baroque verse which had no interest in being either smooth or romantic. The poetic intent, the artistic will of the time was simply different from our own, and, as we shall see, poetic techniques were used with which we are no longer familiar.

A tentative approach toward understanding the early poets has been to regard them as belated conceptists, fifty or more years after the decline of that poetic fashion in Europe. But here again we must distinguish; there are, it would seem, three different (though overlapping) periods of seventeenth-century Puritan verse, each in its turn containing several age groups: the groups of the early Baroque including the founding fathers, those of the high Baroque including the younger immigrants, and those of the late Baroque including the native poets and later comers. In Restoration England the transitions from high to late Baroque were overlaid and diverted to a considerable degree in the "upper class" poetry by the influx of French classicism via the exiled court; the old poetic traditions were submerged and did not come to dominance again until the latter part of the next century. New England, however, with its strong anti-French, anti-Catholic, and anti-aristocratic prejudices, and with its already crystallizing indigenous tradition, took belatedly and reluctantly to the new influences and standards, preferring instead to continue along a normal course of development into late Baroque poetry, though of course traces of the new influences are to be found from the very first. Only in the eighteenth century was it drawn back again into the English orbit. It can thus be very misleading to look only to English poetry for analogies and comparisons; we need also to look to the Baroque verse of the Dutch, German, and Swiss pietist groups, who were always closely akin in tradition and sentiment to the Puritans.

Once the poetic work of the century lies before us in all its richness and we have learned to understand it from its own point of view, it becomes possible to outline its development in all its greater and lesser mutations, a task which the first part of this study, the historical survey, attempts to perform. The panorama that unrolls before us is a surprisingly full, varied, and interesting one. The writers of high quality now occur with sufficient frequency to make them natural parts of a total development and no longer isolated, exceptional phenomena. The lesser writers too find their proper place in the historic sequence, give background and fullness to the whole, and also help to place and interpret the greater writers. Out of the mass a number of minor figures stand forth, not so much for literary excellence as for intrinsic interest and as representatives of the rather high cultural level of the populace. On the other hand, many once prominent mediocrities, who have long enjoyed the specious prominence of scarcity, recede into the background, blending almost indistinguishably with their many newly found brethren.

Exigencies of space have made it necessary to cut out most of the illustrative quotations from the survey and also much of the general critical and aesthetic discussion, and thus to shift the emphasis to the historical even more than was originally planned. This may be all to the good, for if the verse can first be seen in something like its correct historical inter-relations and sequences, the critical understanding of it will have a better chance to develop naturally and in its due time. There will unquestionably be reversals of judgment and shifts in perspective in the course of years, but these will have to be based upon a knowledge of the whole. In a first survey it is, of course, necessary to devote a larger amount of space to previously unknown poets than to old familiar poets of the same importance.

Later when all are better known, it will be possible to give to each the space called for by his quality and interest.

In the second part of this study, the publication of newly discovered verse, the historical principle also weighs more perhaps than the purely literary, though a number of the poems have respectable literary merits, and a few will add new stature to our literature. Again for reasons of space several of the larger bodies of newly found verse (e.g. Philip Walker's, the younger Peter Bulkeley's) will have to await later publication. Further plans are underway to make the early verse better known and more easily available. First of all, from a purely literary point of view, an anthology of the best and most enjoyable of the early verse needs to be published. Later from time to time it may be desirable to publish the collected works of several of the better poets, such as William Bradford, Nicholas Noyes, and John Danforth, whose separate poems are so widely scattered that it is almost impossible to study them in their entirety.

Upon looking over the development of this study from its accidental inception to its present tentative completion, one cannot help wondering whether similar investigations would show that there is as great a discrepancy in the other fields of early American literature and thought between what we now know and what can be known. Do we perchance know only a haphazard fifth of the verse of our Middle and Southern Colonies? Have many of our best prose writers also remained unknown? Is our knowledge of eighteenth-century verse and prose equally inadequate? To judge from notes which I have collected incidentally in the course of my work, there seems to be good reason to suspect that this is indeed the case and that the results of the present study are typical rather than exceptional. In that event, we may be confident not only that some of the finest single discoveries still await us, but that, after arduous labors, we may have the satisfaction of connecting all the puzzling, scattered fragments of our present knowledge into a full, coherent, true picture of our American origins.

II. The Patriarchs

The three oldest poets of New England, Percival Lowell, Thomas Dudley, and Nathaniel Ward, were born in the 1570's and are thus exact contemporaries of Ben Jonson and John Donne. An even older versifier, Stephen Bachiller, actually born three years before Shakespeare, cannot rightfully be included, since, to our knowledge, he wrote no verse after coming to America.

Thus the poetic Nestor among the early settlers of Massachusetts Bay was probably Percival Lowell (1571–1664), a wealthy merchant of Bristol, who came over to New England in 1639 at the age of 68 and settled in Newbury. Ten years later he wrote a "Funeral Elegy" on the death of Governor John Winthrop. The elegy shows him to have been a man of solid classical attainments who adhered to the popular old English measures and wrote verse which is still readable though hardly of high poetic excellence.

Next in age to Lowell was Thomas Dudley (1576–1653). As early as King James' reign he wrote a poem "On the State of Europe" which was commended by the king. Another long poem "On the Four Parts of the World" inspired his daughter, Anne Bradstreet, to her most ambitious efforts in verse on the four elements, humours, ages, seasons, and monarchies. To judge from one line in his daughter's dedicatory verses,

> Yours did contest for wealth, for Arts, for Age,

the old governor's poem was cast in the ancient form of a disputation among the four continents for preëminences and excellences, and would no doubt be of greatest interest to us on the subject of America, giving us one further ray of light on the concept of America in the minds of the early Puritans. But unfortunately all of Dudley's verse seems to have been lost, except his last testamentary poem, which has been consistently misinterpreted. It is interesting and significant that his inventory of books included (in addition to those in history, his favorite field of study) the only known copy in early America of Langland's *Piers the Plowman.*

About two years younger than Dudley was Nathaniel Ward (1578–1652), whose *Simple Cobbler of Aggawam* with its hobnailed verse is so well known, and the rest of his verse so little known. At its best it has a memorable epigrammatic quality:

> When States dishelv'd are, and Lawes untwist,
> Wise men keep their tongues, fools speak what they list.
>
> A peace well made, is likeliest then to hold,
> When 'tis both dearly bought and dearly sold.
>
> The world's a well strung fidle, mans tongue the quill,
> That fills the world with fumble for want of skill,
> When things and words in tune and tone doe meet,
> The universall song goes smooth and sweet.

Among the most whimsical are his verses prefixed to Anne Bradstreet's *Ninth Muse,* where Mercury and Minerva bring du Bartas' and Anne Bradstreet's books for judgment to Apollo, who is represented as an old pedant. He is baffled until they tell him to put on his spectacles:

> They bid him Hemisphear his mouldy nose,
> With's crackt leering glasses, for it would pose
> The best brains he had in's old pudding-pan,
> Sex weigh'd, which best, the Woman, or the Man?
> He peer'd and por'd, & glar'd, & said for wore,
> I'me even as wise now, as I was before.

This is true early Baroque conceptism, which shares with the late Renaissance a tightly packed form, broken line, and telescoped imagery. Note, as we procede, how different this is from the over-rich, but generously disposed imagery, and the curvilinear but continuous and freely flowing line of high and especially of late Baroque.

The choicest Wardian tidbit, probably the earliest preserved piece of bantering social verse of New England, has remained unpublished till now. It was addressed to his good friend, John Wilson, and rallied him about his ever-ready fondness for making anagrams on every name and occasion. Its earthy good humor and robust end twist are not at all contrary to Puritan character:

We poor Agawams
are so stiff in the hams
that we cannot make Anagrams,
But Mr John Wilson
the great Epigrammatist
Can let out an Anagram
even as he list.

After these few ancients who kept alive their spirit of physical adventure beyond its normal span, we encounter a group, born in the 1580's and early 90's, still in the full vigor of manhood but with enough years upon them to assume a position of seniority in this young society. Oldest of the group is Peter Bulkeley (1583–1659), pastor and founder of Concord. His poetic production seems to have been extensive, much of it still preserved at the end of the century, as Cotton Mather remarks, but nearly all of it since lost. Mather printed a few of his Latin epigrams, as well as excerpts from his Latin elegies on Thomas Shepard and John Cotton, all of them exhibiting the fine virility and trenchant phrase so characteristic also of his prose. His only

English poem known to be preserved is his elegy on Thomas Hooker; it exhibits, with an occasional awkwardness, a practiced poetic hand, a knowledge of European elegiac tradition, and an ability to give new life to old traditional materials:

> The hour of thy decease when Sun went down,
> When light turn'd dark, when heavens began to frown.

Hooker's remarkable preaching he characterized in an expressive line:

> Each Ear that heard him said, He spake to me.

John Cotton in neither his prose nor his poetry has quite the immediacy of striking image and appeal that we find in what remains of Bulkeley's verse, though he has qualities of his own which should not be overlooked. Though his elegy on Thomas Hooker is inferior to Bulkeley's, it does have a certain intellectual polish about it, as does also the poem addressed to Samuel Stone. His verses on the death of his daughter Sarah are simple and beautiful, though the verses that follow on Roland and those on both children lapse from poetic grace. Decidedly his best, among the few poems that have been preserved, are two in John Norton's life of Cotton. The one is a touching expression of his homesickness for Old Boston in England:

> When I think of the sweet and gracious company
>   That at Boston once I had,
> And of the long peace of a fruitful Ministry
>   For twenty years enjoy'd:
>
> The joy that I found in all that happiness
>   Doth still so much refresh me,
> That the grief to be cast out into a wilderness
>   Doth not so much distress me.

The other poem, "A thankful Acknowledgment of God's Providence," has hardly a single distinguished line, and yet it is as a whole a minor work of art.

John Wilson's preserved verse is now easily accessible in Kenneth B. Murdock's *Handkerchiefs from Paul.* The only omissions are Wilson's anagrams and verses on himself, possibly the anagrams concluding the commendatory verses prefixed to Anne Bradstreet's *Tenth Muse*, which sound very much like Wilson, and a recently found poem in his autograph, written in praise of Claudius Gilbert's *The Libertine School'd*, 1657, which the author had sent him from Ireland. It is typical of Wilson's verse, taking as its point of departure an anagram of Claudius Gilbert: "Tis Braul I Cudgel"; this is used as the two-part theme of the poem, the first dealing with the brawling of the Ranters and Quakers, the second with their cudgeling by God's holy word—a theme not very acceptable to a modern reader, though from the formal side effectively handled. His verses to Peter Stuyvesant, written when that enlightened Dutch governor was making yet another effort to establish harmonious relations with the neighboring colonies, seem to have been lost, and we know of them only through the verses which Henricus Selyns, the New Amsterdam pastor-poet, sent to Wilson in grateful response.

Wilson was a rather uneven writer, though not nearly as bad as is generally believed. Even the modern reader who is unacquainted with the underlying principles of Wilson's poetic art will find the elegy on Abigail Tompson really satisfactory verse, particularly in the nearly faultless version to be found in the Roxbury church records. However, once Wilson's technique (the use of the anagram as a theme developed contrapuntally through the poem) is fully understood, a much larger body of his verse will be esteemed at its true value. This technique will be discussed more fully in connection with John Fiske, who achieved a higher perfection in it than did Wilson.

Plymouth Colony also added a notable writer of verse to this group, William Bradford, but before we examine his works, a word at least should be said about a quiet sojourner in Plymouth during its first years, William Morrell. In 1625 he published the poetic fruits of his stay, his *New-England*, a Latin poem together with an English version. Even in his short stay at Plymouth he was able to catch and express something of the essence of the new country:

> Blest is this ayre with what the ayre can blesse;
> Yet frequent ghusts doe much this place distresse . . .
> Thus in exchange a day or two is spent,
> In smiles and frownes: in great yet no content.

In Plymouth the most prolific writer of verse was probably William Bradford (1590–1657). The earliest known verses attributed to him are those of 1626 on the death of John Robinson the previous year. His autobiographical, topographical, and monitory verses have all been published, but there remains unpublished his longest and in some ways most important poem, on the heresies and the Congregational way in New England. For some inexplicable reason Bradford's authorship of the poem has been doubted (by a man who had obviously skimmed rather than read through it), though every bit of the external and internal evidence points to him as author. After a long and interesting review of the various heresies and an eloquent defense of the right Congregational way, he concludes the poem with expressions of hope for peace and unity and with exhortations to the brethren to stand firm in the truth. Several lines of the concluding passage seem to reecho the sentiment and rhythm of Luther's "Mighty Fortress," which Bradford may have learned to know in Holland. Europe is speaking to New England:

be not dismayed; but doe Goe on
in this Good work your selves alone
God will you helpe as you shall see
Though you of me Rejected bee
Yea let the world fome & fret
in the end theirby will nothing Get
for God his truth; will advance high
when all errours; in the dust shall Lye.

In his "Word to New Plymouth" Bradford exhibits a deep pride in his community which opened up a new land for the exiled and distressed, when war and persecution again engulfed Europe. However, Bradford was also greatly concerned with what the future might bring to New England. In his other long poem, "Some observations on God's merciful dealing with us in this wilderness," after recounting the miraculous preservation of the small band of settlers in the wilderness among savages who could easily have wiped them out, their gradual rise from famine and poverty to prosperity, the settlement of a learned ministry and wise magistry among them, he turns to a grave consideration of certain tendencies and the future they forebode: the founders dying off, true godliness and fervent zeal declining, "Security and the world on men do creep." This is the eternal theme song of the Puritan from John White's *Planter's Plea* through Cotton Mather and beyond, that the greatest dangers to a Christian commonwealth and the fastest sources of degeneration are prosperity and security, and they had not misread their history. Bradford also saw with remarkable clarity the coming of a terrible war with the Indians as an inevitable result of the greedy and shortsighted policy of equipping them with arms in the furtherance of a profitable trade. Much of all this is indeed not poetry, particularly not the passages enumerating the various agricultural products, or the economic aspects of cattle raising and of gun-running to the Indians. His final poem of thanks for his life, which he called "Epitaphium Meum," is strikingly similar in tone and feeling to John Cotton's, and again, though there is not a distinguished phrase in it, it is true poetry.

Perhaps the most learned man to settle in Plymouth Colony, at Scituate, was Charles Chauncy. In England he had a high reputation as a classical scholar and as a writer of Greek and Latin verse while he was still teaching at Trinity College, Cambridge. It now appears that he continued writing verse in New England. While he was still at Scituate the deaths of Hooker and Winthrop occurred, the first great losses to the new church and state. In commemoration he wrote a brief, carefully wrought Latin elegy "Novae Angliae Lamentatio." Much later, when he was president of Harvard and nearing the end of his long life, a satirical anti-Catholic poem was published on the last page of John Richardson's *Almanack* for 1670, and signed "Incerti Authoris." Apparently the author was not so "incertus" to the undergraduates of the day, for one of them, Samuel Sewall, some ten years later quoted the last couplet in a letter to his brother and attributed it to "Mr Chauncy President." It is one of the sharpest anti-Catholic satires of early New England, lacking the smoothness and amenities of the classical school, but intellectually brilliant, packed with double meanings and triple connotations, so that it would require an elaborate commentary for a present-day reader who is less well versed in church history, though at the time its implications were no doubt quickly perceived and enormously relished.

Another highly learned man who lived for a while in Plymouth Colony, at Taunton, and then settled permanently at Dorchester as schoolteacher and town clerk, was William Pole (1593–1674). Like Chauncy he had written

Latin verse at College and saw it officially published by the university. In his case we know of only one poem, an Epithalamion upon the marriage of Princess Elizabeth to Frederick the Elector of the Palatinate (the unfortunate "Winter King"). Pole's only known New England verse is the striking epitaph which he wrote for himself, though it seems rather possible that several of the other excellent Dorchester epitaphs of the day may be from his pen, the one on Major Humphrey Atherton for instance, or that on Richard Mather. He may possibly also have been the author of the broadside elegy on Lydia Minot. At any rate, there is no Dorchester poet of the day (except perhaps Richard Mather for the first and third) who could seriously be considered as an alternate.

Among this first group of New Englanders there remain only three more of any importance: the accomplished scalawags, Thomas Morton of Merrymount and Sir Christopher Gardiner, the Knight of the Golden Melice, and then the arch-heretic, Samuel Gorton. Morton had tried to transplant waning Merry England to these shores, with maypole, dances, revelling, and the added fillips of selling guns to the Indians and baiting the Plymouth pietists. Sir Christopher had to be run out of town only once, but Thomas set a record of three forced exits, the last as an old man, though thereafter he was allowed to die peacefully in the new country which he loved so much in his own queer way.

After the second deportation Thomas Morton wrote his satirical exposé of the Puritan Utopia, the *New-English Canaan*, interspersing it with eight poems of varying length and quality. Best known is the Maypole Song: "Drinke and be merry, merry, merry boys." To cudgel the brains of the poor Plymouth fathers he affixed to the maypole the Sphynxian lines "Rise Oedipus, and if Thou canst unfould."

The last of the poems, "What ailes Pigmalion? Is It Lunacy" is also worth mentioning. They are fair examples of the light occasional verses of the day, competent, entertaining, but not at all remarkable. Sir Christopher Gardiner's verses, included in Morton's book, show almost none of his friend's talent for versifying.

Even more enfuriating to the Puritans than these two graceless scamps was Samuel Gorton (1592–1677), whose theological and political ideas make Roger Williams seem almost an orthodox Puritan by contrast. Whereas Williams throughout his life maintained cordial relations with the two Winthrops and other Puritan leaders, Gorton to all of them (except perhaps the younger Winthrop) was a creature utterly beyond the pale—just why, no student of intellectual history has as yet really tried to find out. His writings are not as unintelligible as we have been told they are, provided one understands something of his grounding in the transcendental mystical speculation of the century from Paracelsus to Boehme.

In the prefatory poem to his *Simplicities Defence against Seven-Headed Policy*, 1647, he embodied rather effectively (once one follows the symbolism) his main accusation, that the New England leaders were in effect setting up again what they claimed to loath in Papacy and Prelacy: a church supported coercively by the state, and therefore essentially unspiritual. Some of the best lines in it, deeply ironic in their setting, reflect the high hope with which he and the other radicals had heard the call from New England; they are reminiscent of Thomas Tillam's poem upon his first sight of New England in 1638. Gorton's assertion of freedom, with all its surcharged, broken line, has a noble dignity about it:

> Then walke through sea or land, by friends or foes
> Let prisons fast, hard irons thee, inclose,
> All take thy part, yea, plead thy cause for thee;
> The world vents its malice, in Christ's love thou art free.

III. The Younger Founders

The next age group of the founding fathers, that is of the men who were born around the turn of the century, is also largely composed of eminent early colonists who wrote verse only incidentally. None of the orthodox ministers of the group, however, reached even the moderate poetic height of John Cotton or John Wilson, though two others, a heretic and a layman, far surpassed any member of the preceding group, and another heretic, hitherto unknown, wrote one of the great poems of the period.

Typical of the ministers is the triumvirate of the Bay Psalmists, Thomas Welde, Richard Mather, and the still younger John Eliot. The painful accuracy with which the three rendered the original Hebrew Psalms into English produced rhythmic effects which even at that time aroused a certain holy risability. Poetry simply cannot be written by a committee; committee prose is bad enough. If one looks at their version of the 99th Psalm, for instance, one can safely say that few poems in the English language, until recently, have achieved the utter rhythmic and syntactic wreckage attained in it. In all fairness though, it must be added that in spite of their self-imposed restrictions the reverend versifiers do here and there attain to fairly reputable verse, as for instance in Psalms 103 and 107.

Thomas Shepard, as almost everyone knows, wrote a humorous quatrain of admonition to the three translators; it was first published in Cotton Mather's *Magnalia* and since then probably quoted more often than any other American verse of the century. But alas, the version we have known and cherished so long is a rather garbled one, apparently written down by Cotton Mather from memory, a very faulty memory of an old family tradition. A tiny crumbling scrap of paper in the handwriting of Increase Mather, the father, contains a prose account of the quatrain and then quotes it in what is undoubtedly a more original and authentic version:

> you Roxburough poets take this in Time
> see that you make very good Rythme
> And eeke of Dorchester when you the verses lengthen
> see that you them with the words of the text doe strengthen.

No further verse of the elder Thomas Shepard is known. Two other leaders of the church are also remembered for one poem each, the elder Samuel Stone for his elegy on Thomas Hooker and the elder John Norton for his elegy on John Cotton, neither poem of outstanding merit, though Norton's is well worth reading.

William Wetherell (1600–1684), pastor at Duxbury, was far less famed as a scholar than these three, but he was decidedly a better poet. The one elegy of his available at present, on Governor Josiah Winslow, ranks high among the elegies of his generation, and has a freshness and vigor which makes it hard for us to believe that he was eighty when he wrote it.

Of George Moxon (1602–1687), the first pastor of Springfield, Calamy says, apparently with reference to his days at Cambridge University, "He was so good a *Lyrick* Poet, that he could imitate *Horace* so exactly, as not to be distinguish'd without Difficulty." Nothing further seems to be known about these Horatian lyrics or about any verse which he may have written in New England.

Two other learned divines came over for only a brief stay and left poetic tokens of their visits. The one was Philip Vincent, first a pastor and then a far-travelled physician. He was at Heidelberg during the plague and seige, shortly thereafter came to New England, just in time to take part in the Pequot War, at the end of which he apparently took the first boat back to England and rushed to press with his *True Relation* of the war, early in 1638—our first example of breathtaking American journalism. To his little news book he prefixed a Latin song of thanksgiving for the New England victory. The other divine was Thomas Tillam, apparently a man of learning and vision, though New England history is completely silent about him, and the few facts ascertainable about his strange career had to be gathered from the most widely scattered sources. And yet, he wrote one of the finest poems about America in this whole century, "Uppon the first sight of New-England June 29 1638"; there is an inspired lyric quality about it that one finds all too rarely in this or any period. To judge from his later career, first as a Seventh Day Baptist and then as founder of his own communal religious sect (which he apparently took over to Heidelberg with him, under the protection of the liberal half-Stuart Elector), Tillam must, like Gorton, have become deeply disillusioned by what he found here, probably very quickly, for by the time he landed, the religious reins had already been tightly drawn with the conclusion of the Antinomian controversy.

Tillam was apparently on friendly terms with Samuel Hutchinson, the young brother-in-law of Anne Hutchinson, who managed to remain in Boston, a respected merchant, by channeling his religious-speculative tendencies into the Book of Revelations, the free and happy hunting ground of early Massachusetts, where the most respected divines could and did roam with utter exuberance, without fear of prosecution for heresy. When Samuel Hutchinson published his millenarian *Declaration of a Future Glorious Estate* in London in 1667, he included quotations from Thomas Tillam's similar work and also two sets of verses signed T. T. on the same subject—not forgetting to include verses of his own.

The finest poet among the heretics, however, was Roger Williams (c. 1603–1683). His thirty-three poems, all included in his *Key into the Language of America*, have suffered a strange fate at the hands of the literary historians. Kettell with an odd perversity quoted one of the weakest of the poems, Duyckinck did better with four fairly acceptable specimens, Moses Coit Tyler, though alert to the fine prose of the book, was almost completely deaf to the true beauty of its lyrics, and that deafness has since become a critical heritage. There have always been a few individuals, however, who have discovered these poems for themselves and have cherished them among their treasured literary experiences. If at least six of the poems had received the place in American anthologies that they deserve (and in school books too, for the poems are most readable), they would by now have become a vital part of our literary heritage.

There remains to be considered the solitary layman among the poets of this group, Edward Johnson (1598–1672), whose literary fame has suffered an even stranger fate than Roger Williams' at the hands of the nineteenth-century critics. But that critical divagation is such an involved affair that a review of it must be left to another time. Thrice blessed, therefore, is the reader who comes to Johnson's *Wonder-Working Providence of Christ's Saviour in New England* directly, freshly, and naïvely. Not knowing that Johnson is supposed to be crude, unlettered, and parochial, he will be thrilled at his mastery of style and composition, his magnificent command of prose rhythm, his amazing sense of the truly epic: the elevation of a set of local events into the universal under the span of a great unifying idea. Johnson succeeded where most of the epic writers since the Renaissance have failed: instead of mechanically taking over the conventional trappings of the art epic, he had the sure feeling of the artist for the essential behind the trappings and found his own valid and appropriate forms for embodying this essence.

This "unlettered ship-carpenter" must have known Virgil well—and in the original, perhaps also Homer; for he not only had a thorough understanding of epic principles, he was also perhaps the first writer in English to make a successful transfer of the Homeric dactylic rhythm to our language. In some passages his prose actually could be rewritten as line after line of perfect or nearly perfect dactylic hexameter, though perhaps even more frequently his rhythms group themselves into heptameter lines. Take the very first paragraph, for instance, an incomparable proem:

> When England began to decline in Religion, like luke-warme Laodicea . . . Christ creates a New England to muster up the first of his Forces in; Whose low condition, little number, and remotenesse of place made these adversaries triumph, despising this day of small things, but in this hight of their pride the Lord Christ brought sudden, and unexpected destruction upon them.

Let a brief passage from the eighth chapter illustrate its use in narrative:

> The summer after the blazing Starre (whose motion in the Heavens was from East to West, poynting out to the sons of men the progress of the glorious Gospell of Christ, the glorious King of his Churches) . . . as the ancient Indians report, there befell a great mortality among them, the greatest that ever the memory of Father to Sonne tooke notice of, chiefly desolating those places, where the English afterwards planted.

The magnificent fifteenth chapter, on the universal significance of the New England experiment, is also typical of his elevated style. Entirely different, in a strictly prose rhythm, is chapter thirty-six, describing the journey to and settlement of the first inland town, Concord. Literarily it is masterful; indeed, it is the first classical narrative of the American overland trek westward toward the setting sun.

Another surprising discovery that the unbiased reader will make is that Johnson, with all his high seriousness, has a charming sense of humor, and knows how to enliven his narrative with many a salty dash of satire and a splendidly human realism. Of course, the Victorian sentimentalist, with his emotional attachment to the heretics, would not appreciate Johnson's clever handling of them. The Anne Hutchinson and Robert Child episodes, for instance, he describes with finished satire, and in one of his wittiest passages he disposes of the opponents of education and a learned ministry. Most delightfully humorous and delicately ironical, however, is the autobiographical chapter forty-three which tells of his mental crisis upon his return to New England in 1636 during the Antinomian troubles.

Intellectually, too, the work is no mere reflection but a complete synthesis of the New England mind; it presents with the utmost candor the motivating forces and the psychological bent which led to the founding of New England, giving just place to the transcendental, apocalyptic, millenarian, utopian tendencies which were so strong in many of the leaders (Cotton, Hooker, Davenport, Chauncy, the younger Winthrop, etc.), though modern historians, embarrassed at these phenomena and not knowing quite what to do with them, have generally passed over them in silence.

The actual verse, sixty-seven longer or shorter passages of it scattered through the narrative, is more conventional than his prose, and is generally cast into the iambic pentameter or heptameter which he favored. Much of it, especially his many tributes to the spiritual and secular leaders of New England, is inhibited and all too often tortured in line by awkward inversions and surfeit of meaning, though a few of the tributes, such as those on Francis Higginson, John Eliot, Thomas Hooker, Roger Harlackenden, Thomas Shepard, and Peter Bulkeley, have much to recommend them, both in expression and characterization. However, the finest poem in the book is his great lamentation at the human weaknesses and shortcomings of New England's inhabitants, which are threatening to bring to ruin the great design and destiny of the new Zion in the Wilderness:

> From silent night, true Register of moans,
> From saddest soul consum'd in deepest sin
> From heart quite rent with sighs and heavy groans,
> My wailing muse her woful work begins.

In the poetic finale of the book he again envisions the founding of New England as one decisive step in the spread of the gospel in all its purity throughout the world, the final preparation for the last things:

> Thy workes are not in Israels Land confined,
> From East to West thy wondrous works are known
> To Nations all thou hast thy grace assigned,
> Thy spirits breathings through the World are blown.

The elegiac tone which becomes ever stronger toward the end of the book doubtless springs from the apprehension which he shared with William Bradford and many another New England leader that the great idea of New England would, after all, end in failure and frustration due to the decline of the initial high idealism and the trend toward materialism. The sunny good humor and the brilliant flashes of wit and satire of the earlier sections have almost disappeared, and a saddened, disillusioned, yet noble Edward Johnson is the image the reader carries away with him.

Earlier in life, when he set his first known poem at the head of the Woburn records for 1640, his whimsical, twinkly-eyed good humor predominated. Here Johnson represents the newly founded town as a squalling infant that causes its seven father nurses so much trouble that four of the seven desert it. Johnson rocks the baby while the other two make dresses for it (i.e. build houses).

> Its Rare to see how this poore Towne did rise
> By weakest means, too weak in great ones eys.

> And sure it is that mettells cleere exstraction
> Had never share in this Poor Towns erextion . . .
> If ever she mongst ladys have a station
> Say twas from Parentes, not har education.

—Then typically for Johnson, the poem concludes with earnest humorlessness.

On the basis of this Woburn poem and many a strikingly parallel passage in the *Wonder-Working Providence*, I have come to the conclusion that Johnson also wrote an intermediate work of true epic talent, the *Good News from New England*, printed 1648, though perhaps the first and better part was written years earlier. This is the second work with that title, and is not to be confused with Edward Winslow's *Good Newes* of 1624. It has nothing to do with Plymouth Colony or the voyage of the *Mayflower*, as Otis has stated and others have inferred. The embarkation, voyage, and landing which are so vividly described in verse are clearly those of the Winthrop fleet, and the progress of settlement described is that of Massachusetts Bay.

The introduction briefly suggests the growth of the idea of America up to the time of the inception of New England and the beginning of the Great Migration. Then follows a humorous description of the mixed motives of some who joined, in contrast to the unswerving, unselfish ideal of the main body and its leaders. The devil, foreseeing a major defeat, introduces hypocrites and heretics among the number. There is a lively description of the hustle and bustle at Southampton, the humorous incidents as well as the sorrow and tears of departure. Precious good fun is the description of the arrival of a young exquisite who offers himself as a leader of the new movement.

The poem continues with a description of the storm, which tosses about the little boat and its passengers, the hardships of the voyages, the birth of children, the seasickness, and the diseases bred in the confined quarters. In the brief narration of the ocean voyage there occurs that magnificent couplet describing the Sunday services on board during the storm (cf. Winthrop's diary for May 2):

> At ships mast doth Christs Pastors preach, while waves like
> Prelats proud,
> Would fling them from their pulpits place as not by them allow'd.

The exhilarating passage on the entrance into Massachusetts Bay comes next, then the marshalling of towns in the (approximate) order of their founding, a passage which has the epic sonority of Homer's catalog of ships, then a description of the country and the four seasons in it, which contains such sensitively apt lines as these on winter (a new kind of season for the emigrants from rainy, mist-shrouded England):

> Sharpe, sudden, yet with lightsome looks doth winters cold come in,
> With thicke, large Coat doth cloath the earth, both soft, smooth,
> white and trim.

The next part evokes the morning freshness of the land, and satirizes both the overreaching land hunger of the new arrivals and the sharp dealing of the old planters toward the eager, naïve, new immigrants.

This is the end of the main poetic section of the work. There follow prose passages on the civil and ecclesiastical organization of the new country with verses attached which are no longer at the high poetic level of the first part, lack its epic resonance, and also much of its humor, though they are far from uninteresting.

In place of the general high seriousness of the *Wonder-Working Providence* interspersed with passages of humor and satire, there is in the first part of *Good News* a general tone of good humor with an underlying tone of high seriousness—the same elements with a shift of emphasis. For reasons of space it is impossible to present here even a selection of the many and striking parallels to be found between Johnson's known works and the *Good News*. However, the relation of the *Wonder-Working Providence* to the *Good News* is never that of derivative to source, though it is distinctly that of a large, serious, fully developed work to an earlier, swift, spirited sketch. Johnson rarely quotes himself; like a good story teller he never tells a story the same way twice: now he narrates tersely, now expansively, always with new adornments of phrase, but always with the same strong personality behind it all. Sometimes the earlier version is the more trenchant, sometimes the later. However, I must add in conclusion that I shall not be too grievously disappointed if someone were to bring to light material evidence proving that another poet wrote the *Good News;* that would simply mean that we had two early New England writers of outstanding epic talents instead of merely one.

Another poem, "This lonesome lake," which has been attributed to Johnson under rather suspicious circumstances, has been examined in detail in the bibliography. Finally, there is an anonymous, and almost certainly authentic poem, a humorous ballad, which came down by word of mouth through the eighteenth century and was recorded almost at the last possible moment from the lips of an old lady (with the loss of four forgotten lines). It is the so-called "Our Forefathers' Song," full of high spirits, good humor, and a touch of gay satire. The conclusion is characteristically Johnsonian with its abrupt change from satiric humor to utter seriousness. In any case, it was written by a man with much the same temperament and outlook as the author of the *Good News*, there are also striking verbal resemblances, but whether Edward Johnson was the author or not, it is the earliest of our folk ballads and one of the very best.

IV. The Young Immigrants of the Founding Years

One of the largest age groups is made up of those who were in their late teens or early twenties when New England was founded. One strange phenomenon about them, in a century of high mortality, was their longevity; only one died at 50, another at 60, eight more in their 70's, and the majority in their 80's or 90's. Living thus to the end of the century, or even a few years into the eighteenth century, they became for later descendants the living embodiments of the founding years and ideals. Indeed, several of them waited till old age to take pen in hand and versify the sad contrast between the founding ideals and the steadily developing materialism of fifty or sixty years later. All of them came to America at an impressionable age, though their works make it clear that they did not become as thoroughly Americanized as did some of the next, less long-lived group, many of whom came over as children and never really knew Europe. Quite a number of the group were young college graduates of Cambridge or Oxford, and when they came over, they took up their pastoral and teaching duties alongside the older men, and have generally not been distinguished from them.

However, one of the most remarkable characteristics of this group and the next is the large number of verse writers who were laymen without the benefits of a college education. Though only one of them in this group, and one in the following, reached the high intellectual and literary level of Edward Johnson, they do in the aggregate bear witness to the fact that the New England people were living on a level far above the merely economic and genealogical.

John Fiske (1608–1677), the well known pastor of Salem, Wenham, and Chelmsford, physician and schoolteacher, has remained completely unknown till now as a poet. He would continue to remain unknown, or at least held in low esteem, if his verse were judged simply by romatic or modern standards, for measured against such anachronistic criteria, his verse at first seems very dull and unpoetic. It was quite some time after I had transcribed the poems from his manuscript that it dawned on me that his poetic will and technique were something quite unknown to the present, and therefore at first incomprehensible. However, once the basic understanding of his poetic intent was achieved, it suddenly became clear that here was a true master of a remarkable technique: this man composed his poems in somewhat the way that Buxtehude and Bach composed their music.

His method of procedure, like John Wilson's, is to derive an appropriate anagram from the name of the person to be celebrated, take this anagram as the basic theme and develop his poem contrapuntally about it. Even more than Wilson, however, he is the purist and master of this forgotten technique. For a person coming fresh from romantic poetry, this does not seem poetic at all, but dull, monotonous and repetitious, just as a person acquainted only with melodic music often can derive no pleasure from the old contrapuntal music.

There is another impediment to our understanding: the associations that the idea of anagram-making calls up in us, as at best a game of mental dexterity, at worst a futile puerility; and critics are fond of pointing to the anagram as one of the surest indications of the low state of Puritan poetry. Fiske's use of the anagram, however, as an integral thematic part of the poem, is a very different matter from its use later in the century where it has degenerated to the status of the acrostic, a merely external visual device of no intrinsic poetic importance. Did not Bach do something similar to Fiske, when, using the letters of his name as his musical theme (according to the German designations of the scale), he developed it into a glorious fugue? And the feats of other composers were even more remarkable, when they wrote compositions which could be turned upside down and played through as equally fine pieces in this position. Though no one nowadays would say that such technical virtuosity is proof positive of low artistic taste, many such composers suffered a long period of neglect before they were again revived and much longer before they were again generally understood. The fact is that both in poetry and in music there have always been melodic artists who could make an immediate and general appeal; in consequence they were always understood, always enjoyed an audience, and became the critical measuring sticks against which the other type of artist was set and found wanting. In the field of music this critical fallacy has been corrected, perhaps over-corrected; in the field of poetry there is a notable critical lag. One may safely infer that John Fiske is following an old European poetic tradition, to which students of literature have for the most part remained insensitive.

Perhaps Fiske's purest example of anagrammatic change ringing is his elegy on John Cotton, whom he anagrammatized as "O, Honie knott." This is for the purpose a really felicitous anagram, bringing out as it does the two salient features of Cotton's character: his personal charm and his subtle intelligence. Once the artistic principle is understood, it is a pure joy to follow these motifs through the poem in all their intricate interweaving and variation and development. In the course of the poem Fiske offers an illuminating epigram on Baroque aesthetics:

> The knott sometimes seems a deformity
> It's a mistake, tho such be light set by
> The knott it is the Joynt, the strength of parts
> the bodies-beauty . . . .

The poem has all the asperities and intricacies of its period and technique; it is not an easy poem to read, its virtuosities and subtleties will not readily be appreciated to the full, and one can hardly predict an immediate fame for it or its author. The brief poem which follows, addressed to John Cotton's widow and children, though intricate, is free from all asperity and is one of the gentlest and most graceful of Fiske's poems.

Fiske's next long elegy, on Samuel Sharp, ruling elder of the Salem church, employs a much simpler technique: instead of the subtle interweaving of motifs, developed and associated with similar and contrasting motifs, there is first a couplet which sets the anagrammatic theme, then five stanzas which develop the first part of the theme, then after two transitional stanzas, five more which develop the second theme and bring the whole to a conclusion.

Again on a higher poetic level is the third elegy, on Nathaniel Rogers, anagram "He in a large Rest. No." Though at first sight the anagram seems less felicitous than that on Cotton, its elements are nicely woven into the texture of the poem in a figure even more intricate than that of the Cotton poem, and fully as pleasing. Quotation from such a poem, which is a single, integral, continuous composition, is almost impossible; and any attempt to find isolated "fine lines" would simply be an indication that one misunderstood its artistic purpose.

Last and most picturesque of Fiske's elegies is the one about the near-centennarian Anne Griffin in 1655. The anagram which he derives is "In Fanne Rig," and his intricate combinations of the images of the threshing fan winnowing the wheat and of the well-rigged ship setting sail with its cargo of grain make it perhaps the most colorful and interesting of his poems, though it is less sternly perfect than that on Cotton.

A remarkable earlier example of this technique on a small scale is the poem which a nameless author sent to Governor Thomas Dudley in 1645. It is one of the most carefully wrought poems of the period, an aesthetic delight—if one does not allow modern objections as to its contents to obtrude. Its reception did not mean a nasty shock to Thomas Dudley, but a deep delight, and he probably cherished it during the eight years that still remained to him.

Thomas Dudley
ah! old, must dye

A deaths head on your hand you neede not weare
a dying hand you on your shoulders beare
you need not one to minde you, you must dye
you in your name may spell mortalitye
younge men may dye, but old men these dye must
t'will not be long before you turne to dust.
before you turne to dust! ah! must; old! dye!
what shall younge doe, when old in dust doe lye?
when old in dust lye, what N. England doe?
when old in dust doe lye, it's best dye too.

In technique this poem is closest to the consolatory verses addressed to John Cotton's widow and children, and it may very well have been written by John Fiske. At present we have poems of his from only a few years, 1652–1655, and it may be that further verse of his will come to light.

The other learned divines of this age group produced no comparable poetry. Henry Dunster and Richard Lyon revised the Bay Psalm Book and added versifications of the other "Hymns and Spiritual Songs" of the Old and New Testament, giving this popular book the form which it was to have for nearly a century. Dunster probably did the philological work and Lyon the versification. Giles Firmin, pastor and physician, left verses in Zerobabel Endecott's little medical book, and John Higginson in his old age sent off

Cotton Mather's *Magnalia* with a metrical blessing. Edward Bulkeley, the eldest son of Peter, does indeed show a practiced hand at verse in his two elegies on Samuel Stone and Jonathan Mitchel, though neither poem attains any high distinction. Abraham Pierson's elegy on Governor Theophilus Eaton is perhaps the most awkward and inept of the elegies, with all its obvious sincerity, whereas another Connecticut poet, John Bishop, wrote a fine brief Latin tribute to Richard Mather.

Two schoolmasters, Elijah Corlet and Ezekiel Cheever, both university educated, achieved some contemporaneous fame as Latin poets. Corlet wrote one of the finest of the early Latin elegies, upon the death of Thomas Hooker, and another, many years later, on the death of John Hull. Cheever's verse is enveloped in mystery; the manuscript volume of Latin poems at the Boston Athenaeum contains nothing by him except his signature; the poems are of earlier date, probably all European. All that we know is that Cotton Mather in his epitaph on Cheever refers to the latter's ability as a poet and teacher of verse. There is an unpublished elegy on John Winthrop the Younger at the Massachusetts Historical Society, which is signed E.C., but since it may be a calligraphic copy, it is impossible to say whether the author was Ezekiel Cheever, Elijah Corlet, or someone else with those initials.

John Josselyn, the naturalist, who spent some years at Scarborough, Maine, did show originality as a writer of verse, not only in the well known poem on an Indian beauty, but particularly in the lines on the sea storm in his *Account of Two Voyages*. The inspiration is more likely Virgilian than Anglo-Saxon, but the rhythmic and alliterative pattern is most unclassical, and refreshingly original:

And the bitter storm augments; the wild winds wage
War from all parts; and joyn with the Seas rage.
The sad clouds sink in showers; you would have thought,
That high-swoln seas even unto Heaven had wrought;
And Heaven to Seas descended: no star shown;
Blind night in darkness, tempests, and her own
Dread terrours lost; yet this dire lightning turns
To more fear'd light; the Sea with lightning Burns
The Pilot knew not what to chuse or fly,
Art stood amaz'd in Ambiguity.

The other laymen of this age group, all of them apparently without university education, are on the whole more interesting and important than the learned divines; they give body to the group, and without them John Fiske would stand almost alone amid a thin sprinkling of mediocrity. It is true, on the other hand, that only one among them, Anne Bradstreet, attains to real poetic stature, though several others are decidedly interesting.

Anne Bradstreet, daughter of Governor Thomas Dudley and wife of Governor Simon Bradstreet, was perhaps the first woman poet of Puritan New England, also the best one, though several later ones are well worth noting. In sad contrast to her beautifully balanced and essentially happy personality is that of Anne Yale Hopkins, the wife of Governor Edward Hopkins of Connecticut, whose literary career was cut short by insanity in the early 1640's. After the tragedy John Winthrop referred to her as "a godly young woman, and of special parts . . . and had written many books."

One characteristic that impresses the reader ever anew is the perennial charm and modest whimsicality of Anne Bradstreet's verse; she is a genuine poet, even though not a great one. The best known of her poems and most often reprinted, in selection, is her "Contemplations"; a few others have also appeared in modern anthologies. Even the poems that are generally left unread, her long and elaborate four-part poems on the Elements, the Humours, the Ages of Man, and the Seasons, contain some passages of merit, though her longest and most elaborate work "The four Monarchyes" has the least to commend it, being little more than a rhymed chronology according to the old Orosian pattern.

Of decided merit and interest is her "Dialogue between Old England and New," 1642, when old England was in the throes of civil war. Just as the section on "Old Age" in the "Four Ages of Man" is obviously a versification of personal reminiscences and political attitudes of her father (a possibility which has hitherto not been suggested), so this poem clearly contains the typical New England attitude toward the English civil war, most interestingly in the closing section, where the Cromwellian revolution is seen as the expansion of the New England experiment, eventually tending toward the reformation of the whole world.

The poems on Philip Sidney and Queen Elizabeth also reflect the interests of her father's generation forty or fifty years earlier, though the latter poem is also a defense of the intellectual calibre of woman. Likewise her references to nature pertain more to the English countryside which she had left so early, than to the New England countryside which she must have known so well. Her poems on the seasons, especially the one on autumn, are almost completely un-American, and show none of the sharp awareness of the newness and difference that we saw in the *Good News*. Her poem "In honour of Du Bartas" indicates the source (via Sylvester) of many of the duller and less personal sections of her work.

More personal and of better quality again is her affectionate tribute to her father upon his death in 1653, a noble and warm defense of a stern and gentle man. The brief concluding epitaph is one of the finest and surest word portraits of the period. Two of her most charmingly whimsical poems are her deprecatory address to her book when it came back from England in print (1650) and the one about her eight children (1658). The extravagant title, *The Tenth Muse*, must certainly have embarrassed her deeply modest soul, though typically she makes the good-humored best of it:

> At thy return my blushing was not small,
> My rambling brat (in print) should mother call.

Her poem on her other offspring is as charming and genuine a personal poem as one could hope to find:

> I had eight birds hatcht in one nest,
> Four Cocks there were, and Hens the rest.

Perhaps the most deeply touching and beautiful lines in her book were addressed to her husband "Before the Birth of one of her Children," when she feared she would not survive the ordeal:

> How soon, my Dear, death may my steps attend,
> How soon't may be thy Lot to lose thy friend,
> We both are ignorant, yet love bids me
> These farewell lines to recommend to thee,
> That when that knot's unty'd that made us one,
> I may seem thine, who in effect am none. . . .
> And when thou feel'st no grief, as I no harms,
> Yet love thy dead, who long lay in thine arms.

Several of the other poems addressed to her husband are well known and have appeared in anthologies. The burning of her house in 1666 was the occasion of another deeply felt poem containing three of her finest stanzas. A fitting close to her life and verse came in her last poem, the only one preserved in her handwriting, "As weary pilgrim, now at rest."

Her sister, Mercy Woodbridge, wrote at least one poem, an epistle addressed to Anne on the subject of her volume, but the last person who mentioned having seen the manuscript was Samuel Kettell in 1829. Mercy's husband, John Woodbridge, was probably chiefly responsible for the publication of Anne's poems; he added one of the prefatory poems, and was perhaps instrumental in securing the other prefatory poems from Nathaniel Ward, from his younger brother, Benjamin Woodbridge, and from others (probably English Puritans) not yet identified.

There was many a man of affairs in the New England colonies, particularly from this age group, who felt the urge to express his thoughts and sentiments in rhyme, though often not till late in life when he saw the old order passing. There was Anthony Somerby, who like the ancient Percival Lowell had been a merchant in Bristol and had come over to settle in Newbury, where he functioned as schoolmaster for a brief period, and as town clerk for most of his life. About the 1640's he wrote one of the longest efforts in verse of seventeenth-century New England, a synopsis of Bible history. The arrangement of stanzas is alphabetical, that is, each new stanza begins with the next letter of the alphabet, going from A to U, this going on for about eighty rounds of his twenty-letter alphabet in the surviving fragment. One can only hope that he did not use it during his short period of school teaching, for the pupils would have been thoroughly confused by his bland disregard of chronology and by his "method" of crowding three or four miscellaneous items into one stanza.

One remarkable feature of the work is its use of alliteration (along with rhyme) as a consistent poetical device. This poem and the short one of Jocelyn quoted above are perhaps the latest survivals by a century or more of this mainstay of old Germanic poetry. Let two examples suffice here, since others can be found in the excerpts included in the appended anthology:

> Good david from his kingdom driven
> was greatly greived in mind
> for his great sin against the lord
> and could small comfort find.

and the vocalic:

> Observe how waters do asswage
> on arrarat rests the arke
> the dove and ravens sending forth
> and noe's outgoing marke.

We can be sure that Somerby was oblivious to the humor of one stanza in which he casts unwitting aspersions upon the looks of Noah's wife:

> Lo maryages for beauty made
> which doth gods wrath procure
> and fearfull flod to drowne the world
> but noa is safe and sure.

John Dane, brother of the Reverend Francis Dane, settled as a chirurgeon at nearby Ipswich. Toward the end of his life, in 1682, he left his poetic testament for his children in the form of an autobiography, with the typical emphasis on God's providences toward him, adding also various religious meditations and advice to his children in verse.

Not far away in Salem Village, Samuel Fuller, planter and founder of the second iron works in the Bay Colony, also meditated upon the strange ways of God's providence, how he had come over as a young man simply out of curiosity, but remained because of the new way of life opened up to him by Shepard's preaching—the whole composure of small worth as verse, but valuable for its insight into the average active New England mind.

Roger Clap had come to New England as an inspired Puritan youth of twenty-one, and throughout his long and useful life he remained true to his early inspiration and ideals. The three elegies of his that have been preserved have little of the literary quality of his prose autobiography, but once again the contents compensate for their rather awkward form.

Thomas Tileston, another solid citizen of Dorchester, seems to have refrained from verse until the tragic death of his brilliant young relative by marriage, John Foster, in 1681. Literarily his poem is inferior to the other elegy on Foster by the younger man, John Capen, but it does show, what was so typical of the Bay Colony, the high admiration for learning among the leading townsmen of the day and the rather remarkable amount of reading and studying which they managed to do in their spare time. Some of his verse is not at all bad, and his anagram on John Foster, "I shone forth," is one of the most appropriate of the century. For the two Foster elegies, as for so many an early New England poem, the available versions are obviously faulty, and no effort has been made to establish a reliable text.

One of the most restless of the early New England pioneers, ever on the move, was Benjamin Bosworth, who finally settled down in Boston to spend his last years at ease under a clever old-age security plan which he had devised for himself and his wife. There in 1693, in the eighty-first year of his life he wrote two poems, "Signs of Apostacy Lamented," and "A Caution to prevent Scandal." They were published in a four-page leaflet, and since the first poem comes out strongly against periwigs, also Samuel Sewall's pet abomination, we may suspect that the latter may have committed it to print, for he was very fond of issuing little leaflets of verse, his own and others.

There is an anonymous poet of the Boston region, presumably from this age group, who wrote about one hundred folio pages of verse during the late 1660's and 1670's. The manuscript turned up in Lewiston, Maine, about 1859, and may have later been taken to Louisiana by its owner,

Dr. J. P. Fessenden. If the manuscript has permanently disappeared, it would be a great loss, for to judge from the one published poem, an elegy on Zechariah Symmes, 1670, the author was a poet of colorful and original expression. His spelling, especially of Latin derivatives, shows that he was another largely self-educated layman. He must have been one of the well-known men of his day, for such a striking personality could not have remained in obscurity. I have an inadequately substantiated theory that the author may have been Joshua Scottow. Scottow's preserved prose works indicate that he had a remarkable gift of expression and a great love of poetry, for he frequently quoted from the English poets, directly and indirectly. His properties in Maine, where his only son and heir established his residence, may account for the fact that the manuscript turned up there. Whether his or not, the manuscript is worth searching for; in addition to the usual elegies, some of them on interesting personalities for whom adequate biographical material is lacking, there are several religious-philosophical poems and one poem "upon the prevalency of the Indians at Sudbury" from the beginnings of King Philip's War in 1675.

King Philip's War also stimulated a pioneer and Indian missionary on far-off Nantucket island to his only known effort in verse. Peter Folger in *A Looking Glasse for the Times* declared in downright, rough-hewn Quaker language that the terrible Indian war of 1675 and '76 was God's visitation upon New England for the persecution of Baptists and Quakers contrary to the laws of Christian charity. The poem has attained a fame hardly in keeping with its slight literary merit, though the personality that is revealed in it will always remain interesting. One reason for the prominence of the poem is that the author happened to become the grandfather of Benjamin Franklin; another reason is that the far better poems on King Philip's War remained unknown, or virtually so, for a much longer time. Despite this prominence, the bibliographical and textual work on the poem has remained wretched.

To conclude this age group, there remain two of the leaders of Plymouth Colony, neither of them college man, but both possessed of an education above that of most of the laymen we have been discussing. Nathaniel Morton, the secretary and the author of *New Englands Memoriall*, 1669, which preserved so much of the early verse, wrote his tributes in verse to his uncle William Bradford and his aunt Alice Bradford. They are simple, sincere elegies, smoothly written, but undistinguished. Morton may possibly have been the author of the verses on Ralph Partridge and William Paddy preserved in his *Memoriall*.

Governor Thomas Hinckley displayed rather more individuality in the three elegies of his that have been preserved, and if the reader has the fortitude to read through their entire length, he will find much to reward him. Hinckley's tribute to Thomas Walley, his beloved pastor at Barnstable, is particularly commendable for its expression as well as its sentiment. It is one of the numerous lost broadsides only recently discovered in a manuscript copy. In the latter part of the poem he quotes a couplet from Urian Oakes' elegy on the younger Thomas Shepard. Hinckley's elegy on Governor Josiah Winslow also has several good passages, especially toward the end. However, the verses on his wife, who died when he was eighty-three, are his most uneven, containing long stretches of the commonplace, with occasional passages of heartfelt and expressive verse.

Looking back over this age group, one must admit that it is perhaps the most consistently mediocre of all the seventeenth-century groups, with only John Fiske, Anne Bradstreet, and perhaps the anonymous poet producing a body of works on a higher level. It is, in a sense, a transition group, consisting as it does of people who left England too soon to remain distinctly English, and yet coming to America too late to become thoroughly American (Morton alone being here excepted). And yet, paradoxically, this was the only group which chose overwhelmingly to remain in America, Giles Firmin offering the one slight exception, whereas the groups immediately before and after them contain unusually large numbers of those who returned to England. This very factor of their transitional nature, together with their surprisingly consistent longevity, made them important instruments in preserving the founding ideas and ideals for the generations rising round about them.

V. The Immigrant Children and Later Comers

The fifth group, born in the 1620's and early 30's, is far less homogeneous, and thus perhaps more interesting than the previous one. Many of them came over as children and really had only the dimmest recollection of England as a homeland, though a number of these, the first fruits of intellectual New England, returned to the land of their birth and assumed important positions in the Cromwellian Commonwealth alongside their elders who had felt the call to return and expand God's Republic on the New England pattern. At the Restoration and later some of them came back, and along with them came a number of English Puritans who had grown up in the Commonwealth and for whom New England was now spiritually more like home than Old England. In this group we already have one native born writer of verse, in the next group most of the poets are native born, and in the groups after that nearly all are natives.

Benjamin Woodbridge, the first graduate of Harvard, promptly went to England, continued his distinguished scholarly career, and became one of the prominent theologians of the Commonwealth. With all this, both of his known poems reflect his American background. There were first his graceful verses prefixed to Anne Bradstreet's volume, and then, of greater importance, his memorial poem to John Cotton, almost certainy not written at Cotton's death in 1652 but upon Woodbridge's return to America, and printed at Cambridge about 1666 or '67. The elegy deserves study as one of the outstanding examples of its kind, and it was much admired in its day.

James Ward, the son of Nathaniel, also enjoyed a distinguished scholarly career, at Oxford. His two preserved poems are completely English: one in an Oxford anthology of 1654 in praise of Oliver Cromwell, another in a similar collection of 1660 celebrating the restoration of the monarchy.

Another early Harvard graduate who left New England was Edmund Weld, son of the first Thomas. The last part of his brief life was spent as pastor at Inniskean, Ireland, and shortly before he died at the age of thirty-seven, he wrote a poetic "Dialogue between Death, the Soul, the Body, the World, and Jesus Christ," the manuscript of which was soon sent to New England and finally printed in 1814. Though at first sight it seems to be in dramatic form, it has none of the internal attributes of drama, the various parts of the dialogue being simply set pieces.

One further brief meteor on the New England scene was George Starkey from the island of Barbados. He did not take to divinity at Harvard as his reverend father and friends had hoped, but apparently came under the influence of Robert Child, the younger John Winthrop, and the other alchemist physicians of New England. In consequence he chose the Paracelsian career for his own, becoming a combination of physician, chemist, alchemist, and mystic, like his honored mentors. However, he let his youthful imagination roam more extravagantly through these broad fields of speculation and soon claimed to be the possessor of great universal secrets entrusted to him by the mysterious adept, Eirenaeus Philalethes of New England. He assumed this as his pen name and wrote works under his real name and under his pseudonym. In one work he followed the lead of the great early English alchemists, George Ripley and Thomas Norton, writing his *Marrow of Alchemy* entirely in verse, rather able verse on the whole. He died during the great plague of London at the age of thirty-seven.

A much more quiet and less brilliant career was the destiny of the second John Wilson, son of the great Boston divine, and himself pastor of Medfield through many years. His daughter Elizabeth married the third Thomas Weld, pastor of Dunstable, who preserved in his remarkable commonplace book "A poeticall Epistle sent from my Father Wilson to my Wife after her shoulder bone was set, composed on Lords day evening." It is no poetic masterpiece, but is full of the warmth and affection of Puritan home life at its best. Only one stanza of another poem of Wilson's seems to have survived.

A group of men closely connected with Harvard now engages our attention. Jonathan Mitchell, the successor of Thomas Shepard at Cambridge in place and esteem, was widely lamented in elegies at his untimely death at the age of forty-four. His elegy on President Dunster, who had turned Baptist, is a noble monument to the catholicity of the Puritan spirit at its best; unfortunately, only a few stanzas of it have come down to our time. The elegy on John Wilson, signed J. M. and till now generally attributed to Joshua Moody, was more likely written by Jonathan Mitchell, to judge from its similarities in form and style to the Dunster elegy and its dissimilarity to the verses newly identified as Moody's. Naturally, in keeping with the subject, the middle portion of the poem is devoted to memorializing Wilson as the *malleus haereticorum* which he was, though his personal charm, simplicity, integrity, and deep kindliness first come in for their mede of praise. Perhaps Mitchell's last verses are those prefixed to Michael Wigglesworth's *Day of Doom*.

Only through the recent discovery of a partial copy by Samuel Sewall are we able to identify the mutilated broadside elegy on the younger John Reiner as the work of Joshua Moody, and to reconstruct a fairly complete copy of it. The strength of imagination displayed in it must make us regret that we have no other long poems of Moody's, though again its Baroque tension would for many a modern reader be lacking in appeal. Moody's most original achievements in verse, however, still adorn two tombstones on the old Watertown graveyard, those of Thomas and Lydia Bailey, brother and wife of the Reverend John Bailey. They are perhaps the only examples of conscious free verse in English in seventeenth-century New England. The first on Thomas is designed as a series of balancing epithets in two columns, the second on Lydia, the more remarkable of the two, employs the opposite technique of a series of contrasting epithets (reading across, instead of down each column):

Good betimes	Best at last
Lived by faith	Died in grace
Went off singing	Left us weeping.

Three graduates and successive presidents of Harvard have each left us one example of their verse. Leonard Hoar appended to the first college catalog (a broadside) some noble Latin lines on the founding of New England and Harvard. Urian Oakes, after the death of his friend, the younger Thomas Shepard, wrote an elegy which has long been famous as one of the best of the early New England elegies. John Rogers is remembered for the gracious tribute which he wrote to Anne Bradstreet upon her poems. It came to be included in the second edition of her works and is certainly the best of the prefatory poems, a charming echo of old Hellas in Puritan New England.

One of the greatest of Puritan educators, Charles Morton, the teacher of Daniel De Foe and many another outstanding personality, was invited to come over from England to bring Harvard out of its languishing state, though because of a conflict of interests he had to content himself with the vice-presidency and the pastorate of Charlestown. His two poems at first glance seem to be merely short Biblical epics: *Some Meditations on . . . Exodus*, and *The Ark, its Loss and Recovery*. But even a first hasty reading of them reveals that the author's interest was contemporaneous rather than archeological. He makes it quite plain that under the guise of the Exodus from Egypt he is really recounting the exodus of the Puritans from Old to New England. In *The Ark* (of the Covenant) it is equally plain that he is recounting the religious degeneracy of England and the departure of God from among them, followed by the religious reformation under Cromwell. This sort of poetical double talk, though it has many precedents, can perhaps be traced back most clearly to the works of a German (from Brandenburg) active in the literary life of Elizabethan England, Jacob von Falckenburghk. A copy of his poems is still preserved among the Mather books at the Massachusetts Historical Society and may have come to Increase or Cotton from Charles Morton. Slightly later examples of this same technique are, of course, Dryden's *Absalom and Achitophel* and our own Richard Steere's *The Daniel Catcher*. Morton's verse is vigorous and sustained on a relatively high level, though it never reaches any exalted heights of poetic imagination.

The long-lived institution of the Cambridge almanac was begun by a tutor at Harvard, Samuel Danforth, with his almanacs from 1647 to 1649 (several of earlier date have disappeared). He likewise introduced the custom of filling the blank spaces with verse. The long poem in the 1648 almanac, "Awake yee westerne Nymphs," certainly has as high a poetic quality as any of the almanac verse of the century, carrying through, successfully and wittily as it does, the image of New England as a flourishing young tree, with Justice at its roots and Liberty in its top, and Peace, Unity, Truth, Plenty for its chief fruit. Some of the references are cryptic, the one on "the mighty cow," for instance, having been interpreted in two different ways, both of them probably wrong. The verses under each month of the 1647 almanac and the long poem of the 1649 almanac are on a decidedly lower level as poetry, but they show the same love of cryptic symbolic reference to New England affairs, often with a humorous touch; the last is particularly full of references to the early history of the settlement.

One almanac poem which has been preserved in manuscript, "Resplendent studs of heaven's frame," possibly belongs to one of the lost almanacs of the 1650's. Its author is unknown, for its present attribution is manifestly incorrect.

Of the college-educated poets, the most famous though hardly the greatest poet of this age group, was Michael Wigglesworth (1631–1705). With all the fame he has enjoyed, our knowledge of him and his works is still most imperfect. On his two chief published works there has been good bibliographical work done as to the recording of editions, but none at all as to the extensive variations among the different editions. With one exception, the rest of his work still lies neglected, some of it presumably still unpublished.

The poetic best seller of the late seventeenth and early eighteenth century was his *Day of Doom*, which went through many and varied editions here and in England. The poem has been subjected to much abuse and ridicule by anachronistic critics who have deplored the fact that its fundamental premises were not those of the more comfortable nineteenth-century theology.

The most amazing phenomenon that Wigglesworth shows throughout his poetic career is the range of his literary expression from the most utterly shallow and diffuse drivel to truly concentrated and impressive verse. The first poem in *The Day of Doom*, "To the Christian Reader," is in stanza after stanza little more than weak prose put into trivial rhyme, though the nobility of mind and suffering of body, which come to such inadequate expression in it, still somehow succeed in being deeply moving. The "Prayer unto Christ" is just as bad poetically, but then with the very first stanza of "The Day of Doom" proper there is a sudden tightening of the slack poetic reins as the author in a few swift, sure lines brings the reader into the atmosphere of the last night before the judgment. Then the verse loses tension once more until, from the fifth and sixth stanzas onward, it again becomes wholly adequate in relating the awful suddenness of the breaking of the last day and the paralysing fear of sinners awakening from their last sleep.

Thus the poem continues alternating between strength and weakness, though there is certainly enough good verse in it to keep it a worthy object of study in early American literature. The poems that follow the main section also contain many fine passages. It is truly commendable how the author manages to keep the 500 odd lines of "A Postscript to the Reader" at such a decent level of poetic adequacy; and the "Vanity of Vanities" which concludes the volume represents no falling off.

Perhaps Wigglesworth's masterpiece is a poem which remained in manuscript until 1871: "God's Controversy with

New England. Written in the Year of the great drought, Anno 1662." Here again he manages to sustain his imaginative intensity at a relatively high level. The inspiration for it obviously came to a large extent from Edward Johnson's *Wonder-Working Providence;* this, however, is literary influence in the best sense of the word, and Wigglesworth gave a worthy treatement to a noble subject.

He called his collection of religious lyrics *Meat out of the Eater*, because (like the *Day of Doom*) they came out of a long period of illness and agony when he was too weak to serve his Malden congregation from the pulpit, and therefore turned to writing to help fulfill his pastoral duties. Here again, just as his fine gallant soul shone forth through a poor sickly body, so in his lyrics the sincere and noble spirit is generally clothed in inadequate dress. There are here and there groups of lines, or even whole poems, which attain poetic quality, but the general average is rather lower than in his other two large works. None of his almost unknown smaller works are particularly noteworthy.

Two pastors somewhat apart from the university group were Samuel Arnold and John James. A sharply satiric poem was written, apparently by young Ben Tompson, when Arnold, originally a fisherman, was ordained at Marshfield by a blacksmith and a farmer, but Arnold was highly respected among his colleagues and, though partly self-educated, he was a solid theologian. Just before his death he wrote his "last Farewell to the World" which was published with the elegy on him by Ichabod Wiswall.

John James was eccentric and rather unstable, though sufficiently learned to secure for himself an honorary M.A. from Harvard. His elegies on Gershom Bulkeley and Governor John Haynes have been known for some time. Another elegy of his, on Noadiah Russell, was also published, and recently a group of his poems has turned up, written with characteristic eccentricity on the margins of a large-paper edition of William Drummond's poems of 1616, which later belonged to Fitz-Greene Halleck. Almost an unerring means of identifying James' verse is the alchemical symbolism which he introduces, though Tompson and others also make occasional use of alchemical figures. Probably the finest of his preserved poems is his shortest, "Of John Bunyans Life"; only occasional passages in his other longer poems approach it in power and pregnancy.

One other Connecticut man of this group deserving mention is the wealthy New Haven merchant, Samuel Bache. All that we have of him is a fourteen-line excerpt from his elegy on John Wilson, this of rather high quality in the concentrated, intellectualizing manner of mid-Baroque verse.

The laymen are all interesting, and one of them, John Saffin, attained to greatness in a few of his poems. Amusing and of small importance is Peter Easton of Newport. He was an inveterate scribbler in the almanacs he owned, and once or twice managed to write some spirited lines. He evolved the following sententious lines, for instance, after several preliminary efforts:

> When Rich man their Riches doe not so much respect
> and wise men their wisdom doe seeme for to doubt
> when men in great authority have great Defect
> then peace wilbe found from out of a rout
>
> for when rich men on riches doe seem for to doate
> and wise men of their wisdome to convenient are
> when men in great authority by all are counted noate
> then everything seemes the begining of warr.

The verses have an authentic American twang about them in their failure to be impressed by the stuffed shirts of this earth.

One man from southern New England who showed a real talent for verse was a farmer of Little Compton, Massachusetts (now Rhode Island), Samuel Bailey, though he left us only one brief satiric poem. A young Harvard smart-aleck was the occasion of it: John Richardson who adorned the second last page of his almanac for 1670 with a poem, "The Country-Mans Apocrypha," filled with mock meteorological predictions, and such punning quips as:

> Hunger will so prevail for many years,
> Rather than famish, some will Roast their Ears

—a corny joke dating from Samuel Danforth's almanac verse for August, 1647, though for the students it continued to be excruciatingly funny for the rest of the century. Bailey, who apparently had great faith and some talent in meteorological forecasting, took the verses as a personal insult and proceded to roast the green Harvard corn in the oven of his seething wrath. His choice of words is magnificently apt, and the poem culminates in the devastatingly bucolic verdict:

> These are grave sophisters, that are in schools
> So wise they think their aged fathers, fools
> That plough and cart; and such they are indeed
> Or else they would not work so hard, to breed
> Their boys to flout them; but I cannot stay
> Foddering of asses thus; I must away
> And give my sheep their breakfast, who, I fear,
> Wait at the stack, while I write verses here.

Just across the line from Rhode Island lived a prosperous weaver, Philip Walker. Like Folger, Clap, Dane, Tileston, Samuel Bailey, Gookin, Scottow, and many another early planter he bears witness to the surprising spread of intellectual interests, far beyond the circles of the university educated, deep into the New England populace. Only in rare cases as in Johnson, Saffin, and the great leaders of the Plymouth Colony, do these men attain high intellectual and literary stature; the rest of them, however, offer us most important historic evidence of the homogeneity of New England culture and the high spiritual level of the leaders among the people.

Walker came over to New England as a boy, soon settled in Rehoboth and became one of the most influential of its townsmen and church members. The Reverend Samuel Newman and his son Noah no doubt played a great part in the forming of his mind, and perhaps many of the books he read came from their library. Like other men of his kind, he took his pen in hand only when something urgently needed to be said, and stopped writing when it had been said. So far as we know, he is the author of only one work, and when we reflect that it was only the strangest chance which brought it, and several others of its kind, down to our time, we cannot help wondering how many similar works were lost in the course of the centuries.

The event that called forth his effort in verse was King Philip's war, 1675–1676, which he experienced at close hand: the burning of his and his neighbors' houses, the anxious period of waiting in the garrison house of his pastor, Noah Newman, and most particularly the tragic ambush in which the gallant Captain Pierce and most of his small band were killed. Like Folger, and indeed like most of the thoughtful New Englanders of the day, he set the whole trend of his thought toward fathoming the mystery of Divine Providence which had brought this sudden, awful reversal of fate upon a happy and peaceful land.

The long poem, "Captan Perse and his coragios Company," is not so much a narrative of the events as it is an analysis of the whole situation and a call upon New England to unite in self-defense. It gives evidence throughout of a strong mind, considerable power of expression, quite some knowledge of ancient and modern history, and the most uninhibited spelling of an unorthographic century. Walker spelled the way he talked or the way he felt, so that the poem is a veritable repository of orthographic individualism and of peculiarities of dialect which were perhaps already tending toward the development of a New England idiom. In the way he spelled such simple words as "do," "go," and "who," one can see what a good ear Walker had for the sliding-trombone effects of the language: "whoea," "goea," and "dooea." The Indians are, of course, "varments," "tent" no doubt represents the way he pronounced "it ain't," whereas he elegantly spelled the boundless main "otion" on the analogy of "notion"—a good example of the "hyper-correct" forms in which the less educated indulge. He reached his verbal triumphs, however, in the spelling of proper names such as Alexander and Xerxes; the former became "Elikssander," and Xerxes was unsurpassably rendered as "Zurksses." Walker displayed considerable originality in the use of words; for instance he used the old word for buccaneer, "marooner," in the sense of "Indian hunters or cow killers" (his own marginal definition), and made "grovers" mean "hunters in the woods."

Generally his stanzas are forthright and downright, in spirit though not in form somewhat resembling Peter Folger's. In the first hortatory part he analyses the causes of Captain Pierce's disaster and advises on ways and means to defeat the foe, particularly by the use of the friendly Indians, "Imploy a wily Roag—to cach a thefe." After a prose passage, the high point of which is a letter from Emperor Satan to his good friend, the Powwah, there follow twelve of Walker's most colorful stanzas, on the founding of New England, entitled "The First smile of god in this land." He compresses most of his classical imagery into the first stanza, in the second he indulges in a scientific explanation of vapors, by the third he is his old self again:

So has owr Light From Sixtenehundrd twenty
Throu gods permitanc shind gloriosly and plenty.

He tells of the idealistic motives that led to the founding of New England, and attributes the present miseries to a fall from grace and to forgetfulness of the great mission of the founding fathers. Perhaps also, he fears, there may be some secret sin festering away in the commonwealth, and he proposes that a diligent search be made for it, so that it may be removed before God quite destroys them. He suggests pride, hypocrisy, avarice, and also suggests intolerance toward the neighboring New Englanders who have left the orthodox Congregational way:

Lett us not slight owr felow neibours then
that doea desent from us in Aprihention
who cary singuler Like honest men
Seem not to make like us so great declention

If thay in som things Ear we Er in others
The proudist hartts the wildest hart Im schure
Lett pratting pharisis deny ther brothers
Tent what we say but what god ses is pure

This liberality is in welcome contrast to Walker's attitude toward the Indians, an attitude which was to become the traditional American one of admitting to only one kind of good Indian. He mentions several Indian atrocities, and describes their treacherous fighting methods which would defy the military skill of the greatest generals in history. The poem is manifestly the work of a naturally gifted but untrained amateur, with the defects and the surprising originality likely to result from such a combination.

Two other men from Plymouth colony, likewise not college graduates, but on a much higher intellectual plane than Walker, are of importance in this group. The one, Josiah Winslow (1629–1680), was the first native-born governor and general of New England, with the reputation also of being the most accomplished gentleman and most magnificent host of the colony. We can add here that he was also, to our present knowledge, the first native-born writer of verse, being thirteen years older than Benjamin Tompson, who has long enjoyed that frankly meaningless rank but is actually about in eighth place.

Winslow's only known poem is his elegy on William Bradford. Considering the social reputation of the author, one might expect some high Baroque flourishes in the poem, but these are almost totally absent, the whole poem being held to a tone of noble and appropriate simplicity. There is nothing very great about it, it has a certain awkwardness, but it is also hard to imagine a more fitting tribute to the sterling worth, simplicity, gentleness, and luminous clarity of the old governor.

The other man, John Saffin (1632–1710), also of high fortune and office, was not so outstanding in these as was Winslow, though in poetic talent he far surpassed him. Indeed, one might venture to say that when the best of his verse becomes known to literary historians, his name will have a place high in the second rank of early New England poets, with two poems at least which were unsurpassed in their time. As with John Fiske and several other important early poets, American literary history is completely silent about Saffin, and it will therefore be necessary to examine his life and work in somewhat greater detail.

Saffin came over to Plymouth Colony as a boy of about twelve, apparently under the guardianship of Edward Winslow, Josiah's father, to judge from his mother's letter of 1654. His writings show that his classical education was not neglected, though he never went to college. When he was twenty-two, he went on a mercantile venture to Virginia, evidently very successful. Just before his departure he fell deeply in love with Martha, daughter of the Honorable Thomas Willett, of Plymouth. He married her after his return, in 1658, and soon settled with her in Boston as an important merchant and public official, being at various time deputy, judge, and councillor.

Unfortunately, the only phase of his life with which historians are generally acquainted is the legal complication about his slave Adam, and all the sympathies have naturally been on the opposing side with Samuel Sewall, whose *Selling of Joseph* was called forth by the controversy, apparently the second American anti-slavery tract, following the Germantown manifesto of Franz Daniel Pastorious and his group. Sewall was deeply prejudiced against Saffin from the start, because the latter dressed fashionably and wore a powdered wig, this being to Sewall the visible outward symbol of a child of the devil. It has not been noted that the following biting epigram of Sewall's was directed against Saffin at the height of the controversy in 1703:

> Superanuated Squier, wigg'd and powder'd with pretence,
> Much beguiles the just Assembly by his lying Impudence.
> None being by, his bold sworn Attorneys push it on with might and main
> By which means poor simple Adam sinks to slavery again.

Governor Dudley too thought him superannuated, and would not allow him to sit in the council to which he had been duly elected, though his writings from this time show not a trace of senility, but on the contrary a remarkable clarity and vigor of thought.

His courtship of Martha Willett called forth some of the most charming love poetry of early New England, and it must be confessed, he never again attained to the lyric quality and only twice or thrice to the poetic stature of these early poems. Charming and amusing is the first poem "A Dialogue between John and Martha or Exonus and Plimothenia" (referring to their native towns). Truly and tenderly poetic is the letter in verse (the beginning seems to be missing) telling her of his departure from her while she was asleep. Upon his return, as his ship entered the bay and headed for home, he was inspired to his finest lyric effort, one of the best of early America, a poem of the most artful simplicity and quiet perfection:

> Sayle gentle Pinnace Zepherus doth not faile
> with prosperous gales, Saile Gentle Pinnace Sayle
> Proud Neptune Stoops, and freely Condescends
> For's foremer Roughness, now to make amends;
> Thetis with her green Mantle sweetly Glides
> With smileing Dimples Singing by our Sides
> Sayle Gentle Pinnace Zepherus does not faile
> With Prosperous gales, Sayle Gentle Pinnace Sayle.

In the pure love lyric he never again attained this height—nor perhaps did any other American during the century.

A year or so after he and Martha were married, he had to be away from home for some time, and he made his absence the occasion of another delightful poetic epistle to her, this the perfect counterpart of Anne Bradstreet's poems to her absent husband. It is a moving tribute to their love and happiness in each other, though there is also in the lines full of paternal pride and affection toward his first-born an ominous note of concern, all too premonitory, of his fate in losing his spouse and all eight of his children.

Meanwhile, however, in the twenty years of their life together in Boston, Saffin contributed variously to the occasional verse of the day, not only the inevitable elegies upon departed relatives, friends, and famous personages, but also the social verse on gay occasions, betrothals, marriages, Valentine's Day, almost the only such which has come down to us. Then there were such products as his philosophical lines "To his Dear Friend W. T." delineating Lady Virtue, and his prefatory verses in William Hubbard's *Narrative of the Troubles with the Indians*, (the latter, signed J.S., having always been attributed to John Sherman or to Jeremiah Shepard).

His elegiac verse is typical of its day, rather better than average in his verses on John Wilson, Jonathan Mitchell, Charles Chauncy, Thomas Willett, and Governor John Leverett, and somewhat later, truly distinguished in the verses on Josiah Winslow and John Hull. A strange fate has overhung Saffin's poetic fame: of the five broadside elegies by him certainly printed at the time, and two others possibly printed, not one has come down to us in even a single copy; of the other sets of verses published in his life-time, one remained anonymous, and the other two, signed with his initials, have been attributed to other men; all bibliographies have remained totally silent about him. Had his commonplace book not had a happier fate, we should not even know that he had written a line of verse.

In 1678 tragedy broke in upon John Saffin, when the smallpox epidemic took away in swift succession his son Simon, a lad of twelve highly gifted as an artist, his son John, who stood at the head of his class at Harvard, and then his beloved wife Martha. Saffin's elegy on his son Simon is one of the most winsome portraits of a Puritan childhood, though when the second and the third death came, he was too choked with grief for verse, and could produce nothing but perfunctory epitaphs. Grindall Rawson wrote the elegy for his departed college friend, and Saffin's real poetic tribute to his wife did not come till twenty-five years later, in one of the finest poems of his old age, his "Revived Elegiac Lamentation," an idealized picture of the Puritan woman at her finest; gentle, strong, intelligent, pious, active in good works, a good manager, a good mother and teacher of her children.

In the years after his wife's death he wrote not only the fine elegies on Josiah Winslow, John Hull, and Thomas Danforth, or such occasionalia as his warning lines on the solar eclipse of 1681/2, unimportant literarily, but also his most finished philosophical poem, and a number of interesting formal satires or "characters"; "on a proud upstart," "of a Pernicious Backbiter," "of a Proud man," and the contrasting piece "of a meek Spirited Peace Maker." His philosophical poem "Consideratus Considerandus" treats the age-old theme of the vanity of all earthly things, excepting only virtue, with no great intellectual originality (as who can?), but in some of the most consistently excellent verse of his time and place. In fact, it is so good that one might at first suspect it of being copied from an English source, like the Wotton poem which follows on the next page; however, the last line with its American Indian allusion, together with other internal evidence, clearly indicates that it is American and Saffin's.

Saffin always showed himself courageous in defending his rights. When he was unseated from the council by Joseph Dudley, he sent the governor a strong poetic epistle, pointing out his rights and the governor's trespass beyond the bounds of his authority. He passed on to the young governor Apollo's advice to Phaeton, and no doubt privately expected that the governor's guidance of the chariot of state would turn out as disastrously. With beautiful symbolic irony Fate played into Saffin's hands, for the following winter, in January, 1704/5, when Dudley was taking his wife and daughters for a sleigh ride on the frozen Charles River, "the ice suddenly broke, and all the horses falling into the River the two hindermost Horses were Drowned, and His Excellency and His, hardly Escaped but were Wonderfully preserved Laus Deo." Saffin naturally took full advantage of this cooperative and illustrative act of Divine Providence in a second epistle, interpreting the event for the governor, a fine piece of early New England patriotism with a sharp reminder to the Anglicized governor of his Puritan origins.

In the year between the two epistles, in 1704, he wrote his loving tribute to his first wife, which was briefly characterized above, and also his "Thankfull Memoriall," reviewing all the reigns and interregnums of England during his life, from Charles I to Queen Anne—the whole composition definitely below his poetic average. Much better again is his elegy on Sarah Leverett, the widow of the governor, at her death later that year; here again he shows his skill at portraiture, and with personal warmth and affection he draws the picture of an elder matron in the Puritan Zion, a companion piece to the picture of the wife of his youth.

His last two important poetic compositions came during July, 1708, and the following winter. The first was an epistle to Benjamin Colman on his book, *The Government and Improvement of Mirth.* Saffin heartily endorsed its enlightened Puritanism which presents "The severall Sorts of Merriment." Colman in reply sent him his elegy on Samuel Willard, *A Poem on Elijahs Translation*, which in its turn called forth from Saffin an interesting bit of literary criticism, in which he commended Colman for his ingenious stabilizing device of writing explicitly about Elijah and only tacitly and implicitly about Willard (perhaps following Charles Morton in this). He commended the poem's sublimity, its "Towering Phansey," its "vesture suitable to the nature and Eminence of the Theme you Insist upon: which Doth Adorne Poetry: Viz To be Elligant, Emphaticall, Metaphoricall, and Historicall: Running in a smooth Channell thô all Subjects cannot Wear the same, or like Vesture or bear the same Straine, or Stile."

From this criticism, as from the earlier formal satires of Saffin and his "Consideratus Considerandus" we can perceive that we are already encountering late Baroque attitudes toward poetry, John Saffin being the only one of his age group who succeeded in his later years in making the transition to the later style, which properly belongs to the next generations.

And lastly there is Saffin's "New England Lamented," 1708/9. The first part describes graphically the economic depression, the stagnation in trade which then overhung New England: many men lately broken, the ships of others lying at the wharves, the farmers unable to sell their produce or pay their taxes, and yet "Our Pomp & Gallantry in this poor Land" never ran so high. In the second part, after a passing glance at the stupid commanders who cheat their soldiers of victory, he turns his satiric barbs against the vain, ignorant judges and the unscrupulous, greedy lawyers who between them pervert the cause of justice. In the third part he preaches his pre-Anti-Saloon League lecture, chiding New England for licensing "So many Bowsing Dens" simply for the revenue and regardless of the human misery they engender; "So we must live by the Evills of the times."

To the very last Saffin did not lose his satiric bite and his aptness of phrase. Though he wrote much that is trivial, derivative, and of small literary value, he also wrote a respectable body of verse of high literary excellence. He wrote the century's most musical love lyric, one of its best philosophical poems, several good or even excellent elegies, and the only considerable body of society verse which has survived from this period.

The whole age group shows a decided advance over the previous one in general quality, independence, and sureness of poetic touch. The previous group had little of outstanding quality beyond the works of John Fiske and Anne Bradstreet, whereas this group has Saffin, Wigglesworth, and Oakes among its outstanding members, and has among its large body of lesser writers a definitely higher level of literary achievement, for several of them have each a poem or two of real merit to their credit. The next group represents the culmination of this period of our early verse, with no less than four poets of the highest relative rank, after which the inevitable decline sets in with the two concluding groups.

VI. The First Native-Born Group

In the preceding age group most of the writers had come to New England as children, one of them even was native born, and essentially there is no difference between them and the native born who now follow, so far as the adjustment of most of them to their environment is concerned. There is this major difference, however, that the previous group did grow up among men whose ties to England were still strong, and they entered upon early manhood when the Puritan dream came to realization upon the then greater stage of England in the Cromwellian Revolution; thus many of them were drawn back to the country of which they had only vague childhood memories. In the present group, on the other hand, only one important writer, John Crowne, and he really not an indigenous product, was drawn back to play his not inconsiderable part upon the stage—of the Restoration. His departure was more than compensated for by the arrival of two other young men on these shores, Richard Steere and Edward Taylor, who, with the native born Ichabod Wiswall and Benjamin Tompson, were to become the leaders of this most important group.

One conspicuous feature about the group, especially in its minor members, is the appearance in a younger generation of old familiar names, when the second Peter Bulkeley, Thomas Shepard, John Cotton, and Samuel Stone make their greater or lesser contributions alongside Samuel Bradstreet, Samuel Cheever, and the Chauncy brothers. Indeed, there are only a few new names among the minor writers. Another significant feature of this age group is that the poetry of the common man, which occupies such a large place in the two preceding groups, at this point disappears almost completely. From now on for the rest of the period the verse is almost entirely the product of college graduates or their equals in formal education, and the verse of the common people is submerged below the literary level into almost complete anonymity, though not a few of the collegians do cater to the tastes of the populace. We can, therefore, adopt a different method of procedure for this rather homogeneous group, first glancing at the works of the minor writers, and then examining the four or five more outstanding men at greater length.

The second Thomas Shepard was brought over to New England in the year of his birth, 1635, and died at an even earlier age than had his father. In his two preserved elegies, on John Norton and on John Wilson, he exhibits a ductility and mastery of verse almost approaching that of Urian Oakes in his elegy on the younger Thomas Shepard himself. In strong contrast to him is the younger Samuel Stone, perhaps the most unfortunate and unstable of all the scions of the great spiritual founders of New England; he wrote his one preserved elegy, a mediocre one, on Governor Leet, just a few months before the night when, after making the rounds of the Hartford taverns, he staggered homeward, fell into the river, and was drowned.

Increase Mather, unlike his father and his son, wrote almost no verse, the one outstanding exception being the Latin couplet which he sent to young John Foster who was close to death. The Chauncy brothers, however, continued their father's inclination toward small sets of occasional verses, the eldest, Isaac, adding a juvenile couplet to his father's "Novae Angliae Lamentatio," Nathaniel and Israel contributing their share of collegiate almanac verse, and Elnathan making the only noteworthy contributions of the four in his elegies on his college mate, Silvanus Waldern, and on President Henry Dunster.

Samuel Bradstreet did not dishonor his distinguished mother by the verses in his almanac for 1657. The verses developed the conventional almanac theme of Apollo wooing Tellus, the earth goddess, and were among the better collegiate efforts of the day. Samuel Cheever's almanac verse is also quite passable; in his two almanacs of 1660 and 1661 he handled the same Tellurian theme with more originality and less clarity than had Bradstreet, sometimes even approaching the enigmatic strains of Danforth's verse; in the second the whole set of monthly verses is tied together in a wild narrative of allegorical intrigue. With much less obscure imagery and rather better poetry Daniel Russell took up the same theme of the change of the seasons in his almanac for 1671. Some of the verses, as those under April, June, July, and September are pleasingly done and rank high among almanac juvenalia.

Two Connecticut men, Wait Winthrop and Stephen Chester, stand somewhat apart from the Harvard group. Stephen Chester wrote an elegy on Wait's father, the governor of Connecticut, which, though good, is hardly comparable to either of the two Tompson elegies on John Winthrop the Younger. It is significant that by this time the old art of anagrammatic poetry was no longer understood, for though Chester duly placed an anagram at the head of his elegy, he only introduced it into the first line of the poem and made no use of it as thematic material. The anagram by now has become just as unintegral and merely visual a part of the verse as the acrostic.

To Wait Winthrop is generally attributed the sturdy ballad on the Swamp Fight during King Philip's War, the earliest preserved ballad on a New England event. There is nothing conspicuously poetical about it, but in its simple narrative style it catches the true popular note. Neither his father nor his grandfather, the two great governors, are known to have written any verse, though his son John turned out to be as ready a versifier as ancestral Adam Winthrop had been. If Wait Winthrop really wrote the ballad, it seems rather strange that there is not the slightest reference to it in the letter from his friend, Stephen Chester, which contains so much about the latter's broadside elegy written about the same time.

Of the two broadside elegies by the younger John Cotton, of Plymouth, which are known to have appeared, only the one on John Alden seems to have survived. It is a decent, pedestrian performance, rising to poetry perhaps only in the last four lines. It is overshadowed by another broadside elegy on the ancient John Alden, printed anonymously, but in all probability coming from the able pen of Ichabod Wiswall, Alden's pastor at Duxbury.

Ichabod Wiswall (1627–1700), noted in his time as a scholar, particularly for his attainments in astronomy, has also been long known as the writer of a poem on the comet of 1680, published a few years later in London. This poem takes the common seventeenth-century line of interpretation that a comet is a warning sign from God of dire events to come. The verse is able and spirited, easily holding the reader's attention. His words extending his warning to sailors particularly show his talent in popular poetry:

> You nimble Lads, who Neptune ride,
> And dreadless through fierce Ocean slide,
> Reef it awhile: All hands aloft!
> Mind well your Helm; for you'l have oft
> Salt breeming Waves, which will not burn,
> Yet must become your dismal Urn.

Wiswall's elegy on the Reverend Samuel Arnold, of Marshfield, is a fitting tribute to a man who, like the apostles, had started out as a simple fisherman and by his great soul and fine intelligence had developed into one of the most highly respected pastors of the commonwealth.

The elegy on John Alden, probably by Wiswall, will certainly take an honored place among the elegies of the century for its complete appropriateness to its subject, a serenely powerful evocation of the spirit of a modest, upright personality who in his long span of nearly ninety years had come to stand as a symbol of New England virtue and love of country,

> That love that made him say, 'Tis good being here,
> Its good, yea better than to be else-where.

—a conviction which has become a New England tradition.

Young John Crowne was the son of a remarkable father, Colonel William Crowne, of Nova Scotia, Mendon, and Boston, who like many another early New Englander, came over after extensive travels (or residence) on the Continent. Though the father became a New Englander, the son remained in America only long enough to enjoy a bit more than three years at Harvard College, returning to England late in 1660. His novel *Pandion and Amphigenia* was, to judge from the introduction, written at this time, though not printed till five years later. And indeed, it bears some internal evidence of its Harvardian origin, for in the last, longest, and perhaps best of the poems scattered through the volume, "Sweet day, so calm, so cool, so bright" there is the favorite theme of the Harvard muse: the wooing of Tellus by Apollo, though on a decidedly higher poetic level. Perhaps Crowne had looked forward to preparing the next Cambridge almanac. If these poems were really written at Harvard before his return to England, they are certainly the best collegiate verse of the century.

The rest of his work in lyric and dramatic poetry is really outside the scope of this study and belongs to English literature. Only in his first drama, *Juliana, or the Princess of Poland*, is there a song, a charming one, with an American theme, about "The fair new golden world," asleep like a maiden till surprised and ravished by the Spaniard. Though his novel is very poor, and his dramas rather minor products of the Restoration, he did have an occasional but true gift for song, one or two of his lyrics having even enjoyed the honor of being set to music by Henry Purcell. There is never again, however, a reference to America; in his best comedy, *Sir Courtly Nice*, there is a pleasantly exotic song between an Indian man and woman, but alas, they are from India, and not from the Penobscot region he knew from a summer's holiday.

Peter Bulkeley the Younger (1643–1691) is on about the same poetic level as Ichabod Wiswall, that is, rather above the common average, though hardly in the top rank of poets. This Peter is the youngest son and namesake of the founder of Concord, and is often confused with his prominent nephew of the same name who was two years older than he. The year after his graduation from Harvard in 1662 he removed to Fairfield, Connecticut, with his widowed mother and remained there as a physician and merchant for the rest of his short life. Only last year his medical, theological, and poetical manuscripts came to light.

His verse is far more consistently good than his father's, though it must be added that he rarely achieved that pregnancy of phrase which characterizes a few of his father's best lines. All but one of his poems are religious, most of them carried safely past the cliffs of dogmatic theology by a lyric pietism. His first poem is perhaps his best, an eloquent restatement of the old theme, the transitoriness and vanity of this life:

Like to the Grasse thats Green too day
Or like the flower inth month of May
Or like the smoake, that cends on high
hereto O man I thee discrie
The flower thats fresh too day, too morrow dys
The Grasse Cutt down, and so it lys
The lofty smoake by blast of wind,
is so disperst you Cant it find,
They wither, fade, consume away
no time, nor art, Can make them stay . . .
Thou Canst not Clip, the wings of time
but it may Clip thee, in thy prime.

The poem is sustained at this level through more than two hundred lines. Most of the images are traditional, the ideas conventional, and yet in some strange way, through the ductility and grace of his verse, through a fine rhetorical and even dramatic talent, he is able to hold the reader's attention and interest to the end, even past lines that by themselves would seem flat. The poem is reminiscent of Michael Wigglesworth at his best.

The next poem "Of the Trinity and the Unity of the Godhead" lapses from poetic grace into a theological exposition of that mystery; it is mercifully brief. The third poem is somewhat better again, with the more amenable theme of God's unbounded love for man, as is also the one following on "The dignity and Transcendant Excellency of Jesus Christ." His longest poem, "A Loving Conference had with Christ and the deceast soule," in the form of a dialogue, contains some eloquent passages and is an interesting exposition of the moderate Puritan's concept of the processes of grace and salvation. It thus furnishes an interesting parallel to Edward Taylor's "Gods Determinations," though in poetic quality it is hardly comparable. The two short concluding poems, "The humanity of Christ" and "O Death where is Thy Sting," are also uneven poems, with a few good passages, especially in the latter. Bulkeley wrote one secular set of verses, apparently intended as a prefatory poem to a popular medical treatise. It seems to have been written toward the end of his life, for he calls it his "last farewell" and refers to his impending death.

Though Bulkeley is almost as uneven in his verse as is Wigglesworth (he is never quite as weak or flat as Wigglesworth can be), he did at least once write a poem of sustained quality, and all his poems together are a worthy document of a gentle and deeply pious Puritan mind.

Benjamin Tompson (1642–1714) was talented, witty, facile, and perhaps a bit unstable and erratic, to judge from his verse and the few facts we know about his life. Though trained for the ministry, he never occupied a pulpit. He began well as master of the Boston Latin School, was displaced by Ezekiel Cheever, and stepped down to the Charlestown school; then he remained unemployed until he was able to make arrangements with his home town of Braintree, where he taught school for the rest of his life, except for a brief period at Roxbury. To judge from a passage in Cotton Mather's unpublished diary for 1712, all was not well then with his old schoolmaster's religion, and this may help explain his lifelong failure to secure preferment. Popular and charming he no doubt was, able too as a schoolmaster, and always eager to stand well with the men in power, but his volatility and cleverness probably rendered him somewhat suspect to the more solid and unimaginative citizens of the province. He seems to have been both facile in writing his verse and careless about preserving it, for unpublished poems of his have been turning up regularly in the most widely dispersed localities.

At a very early age (if the verses be his) he displayed his gift for satire in the poem on the ordination of the fisherman-pastor Samuel Arnold, which was performed by a farmer and a blacksmith. His poem on the death of his father, William Tompson, 1666, already shows a practised hand at verse and is one of the liveliest and most readable of elegies, as well as an apt characterization of a noble and unfortunate man. The elegy which he wrote for his predecessor in the Boston Latin School, Robert Woodmancy, in 1667 (and then with true New England economy used over again forty-one years later at the death of his successor, Ezekiel Cheever), stands as the high point of his achievement as a punster and demonstrates that the New Englanders could have as much fun at a funeral as the Irish of a later day.

Tompson's longest and most popular poetic effort was called forth by King Philip's War and appropriately entitled *New Englands Crisis.* The Prologue offers us the wittiest and most charming picture of early New England since the *Good News* and the "Forefathers' Song." It is an incomparable mixture of praise for the "good old days" of the founders and gay persiflage at everything from the whistling leather breeches of the men to the pudding growing cold under a long-drawn-out Grace—ending in a solemn warning to New England to take stock of its sad divagations during the brief half century since its founding.

The title poem, the longest in the little collection, carries on in the same mixed manner. Rollicking is his satirization of King Philip's throne and court, and his royal address beginning with the perennial lines:

> My friends, our Fathers were not half so wise
> As we our selves who see with younger eyes.

From this he quickly goes over to the grim description of savage warfare, culminating in his exciting description of the winter swamp fight, the subject of Wait Winthrop's ballad.

In "Marlburyes Fate" he describes an imaginary painting of an Indian raid, which if it had actually been executed on canvas would rank as one of our most lurid primitives. In "Seaconk Plain Engagement" he narrates the ambush of Captain Pierce and his small band, with which Philip Walker had begun his poem. The final piece "On a Fortification At Boston begun by Women" is once more jolly good fun and worthy to be included in an anthology of Puritan humor, which, by the way, is not so rare as the printed evidence would make us believe, for the two great Puritan New England joke books still remain unpublished.

The first two parts of *New England Crisis* (up to "A Supplement") had previously been sent to London where they were issued as *Sad and Deplorable Newes from New England;* the rest of the little volume soon also appeared in London under the title *New-Englands Tears*, with several additions. "Sudburies Fate" is a highly-figured but tense narrative of the Indian stratagem which led to another tragic ambush. In the piece on the death of Miantonimo (the younger) we have a vivid, realistic portrayal of an Indian encampment; the conclusion of it is a satiric account of the upsetting of the boat in which the apostle Eliot, with Gookin, Danforth, and Stoughton, had set out on an errand of mercy to visit the Christian Indians who were interned on an island in Boston Harbor. Here Tompson voices the ugly prejudice of the general populace which a few enlightened leaders had to combat.

The most notable addition in *New-Englands Tears* is one of the two elegies which Tompson wrote on the death of John Winthrop the Younger, the most enlightened and universal mind of early New England. It is an excellent example of late Baroque, gorgeously and appropriately composed in a setting of alchemical figures, integral in composition, and adequate in its representation of a remarkable personality.

Tompson, being a physician like Winthrop, and also apparently of the Paracelsian school, showed himself extremely well versed in the philosophic concepts of the school and, what is more, could make readable verse out of them. The other elegy on Winthrop, printed as a broadside, contains a passage descriptive of the ideal alchemical physician, in contrast to the pretentious conventional one, a passage almost literally translated from Paracelsus:

> The lavish Garb of silks, Rich Plush and Rings
> Physitians Livery, at his feet he flings.
> One hand the Bellows hold, by t'other Coals
> Disposes he to hatch the health of Souls. . . .

With all its interesting content and several fine passages, this elegy is nevertheless not as well-wrought a poem as the other.

His other elegies, on distinguished New Englanders, have at least a passage or two each of typical Tompsonian opulence, the best probably being those on Peter Hobart, John Leverett, Samuel Whiting, and Edmund Davie. Simple and touching are his lines on the death of Rebecca Sewall, the little granddaughter of Samuel Sewall. Tompson had the good taste not to ornament the elegies on members of his family with Baroque flourishes; though striking images and fine passages occur in them, they are on the whole on a simple domestic level. Perhaps the one on his elder brother Samuel is the best, though the one on Samuel's wife, Sarah (still unpublished), is also commendable.

Among his later secular poems, the one on William Hubbard's *Narrative of the Troubles with the Indians* again puts all his allusive virtuosity on display. Indeed, a most interesting secular New England library could be listed from the direct and indirect allusions scattered through Tompson's verse. He was far from being narrow and provincial, and his verse reflects in a striking manner the breadth of his reading in the European literatures. But the traditions of American literature also were being established in this early period, as his poem to Lord Bellamont shows. In the pageantry during this nobleman's reception as governor, Tompson, clad as the Simple Cobbler of Aggawam, stepped out of his shop to greet him with a charming, witty set of verses. One of the best passages in the poem is clearly taken over from Edward Johnson's humorous description of the Indian's reaction to the first European ship that entered Massachusetts Bay. Even as late as 1760, when the new school of English poetry had long since conquered America, these verses still charmed the circle of Ebenezer Parkman and Mather Byles.

Richard Steere (1643–1721) is almost unknown to New England biography and literary history, and yet when his works become better known, he will certainly take his place among the best poets of the period. He was a citizen of London who came to New England possibly in the 1670's but more probably not till 1682; we do know definitely that he made a trip to England in the winter of 1683/4 and returned to Boston the following summer. He settled in New London, Connecticut, as a merchant, defended the rights of the Rogerenes to their manner of religious observances, and as a result removed to Southold, Long Island, where he died.

It has not previously been noted that in 1682, while he was apparently still residing in England, he published a narrative poem, *The History of the Babylonish Cabal.* In the dedicatory preface to the Earl of Shaftesbury he indicates by a satiric allusion that he has written the poem in reply to John Dryden's *Absalom and Achitophel*, a satire against that Whig nobleman. When later that year the Earl of Shaftesbury proved himself more of a traitorous Achitophel than a faithful Daniel and fled to Holland, Richard Steere no doubt found it advisable to put the Atlantic between himsel and current English political events. Though Steere's narrative verse flows along pleasantly enough, the poem contains only a few distinguished passages and occasional striking lines which give promise of better works to come.

The terrible storm at sea which battered and nearly sank the ship on which he travelled back to London a year or so later inspired his best narrative poem, *A Monumental Memorial of Marine Mercy*, which was published in 1684 upon his return to Boston. The narrative is as fresh and direct as a sea breeze, swiftly carrying the reader along to the coast of England where the storm arose, which tossed the little ship "like a ball in sport, From wave to wave in Neptunes Tennis Court." The sighting of an Indiaman in distress, the wrecking and washing away of their own boat's superstructure, the meeting with a foundering Virginia ship, the partially successful rescue, the agony of almost making safe port and being driven out again, and the final landing after a full month of storm—all this is told in such tense, exciting language that one is almost oblivious to the occasional awkwardness of the verse. It is an emphatically realistic narrative built up with a nice selection of vivid detail of which a modern novelist might well be proud. Steere appended a little poem addressed to a boy born during the return voyage, again with an exhilarating description of the aspect of sea and sky on the occasion.

Years later, in 1713, he issued the last known volume of his poems in Boston, reissuing his first poem and entitling the volume after it, *The Daniel Catcher*. The other political poem included, "Antichrist Display'd," was apparently written about 1688 at the accession of William and Mary after the "Glorious Revolution." The finest of Steere's longer poems is in blank verse, "Earth Felicities, Heavens Allowances," a philosophic poem upon the rightful enjoyment of all the beauty and benefits that God's good Earth has to offer man. This is not so anti-Puritan a theme as conventional opinion might lead us to believe, for Benjamin Colman issued a treatise on a similar theme in 1707, and Edward Taylor revels in the same kind of imagery drawn from all the senses, though in his case sublimated to spiritual ends. Steere's lines on the pleasures of the senses are particularly felicitous and show the late Baroque aesthetics in full flower. Just a few lines on the pleasures of the ear:

> Sweet Musicks pleasant and harmonious Sounds;
> The chirping notes of winged Choresters,
> And Purling Murmurs of the Gliding brooks,
> Modulate Accents of a well Tun'd voice,
> Joyn'd with the Sweet Allurements of the Lute . . .
> Pleasing discourses, Histories and Novals,
> Am'rous Converse, when Innocent and clean,
> All give a Charming Sweetness to the Muse.

Contentment, temperance, and restraint are virtues simply because they are necessary for the full enjoyment of the earth's felicities:

> However Superstitious Stoicks, may
> Refuse those blessings which are freely giv'n:
> As if not making use of Earthly good,
> Were to obtain Heav'ns Glory in Exchange . . . .
>
> But for a man to know the highest joys
> This world affords, and yet without offence;
> To live therein, and as a Master use them,
> In all Respects, and yet without abuse . . .
> This Man subjects to one, Commands the other,
> Owns God his Master, makes the World his Slave.

Here is another side of the New England mind which has been long and unjustly neglected, for it is as characteristic of the New Englanders of the day, particularly in the prosperous mercantile towns, as is the other-worldly, transcendental attitude. We have already noticed something comparable in John Saffin; even though he is more impressed than Steere with the vanity of all earthly things, he frankly enjoys the good things of this life in so far as they accord with virtue. "Earth Felicities," like Saffin's "Consideratus Considerandus" is a fine example of the early American philosophical poem, written with skill and good taste, demonstrating that in this field, where we might least expect it, the New England poets could stand independently and successfully beside their English contemporaries.

Quite different is Steere's Christmas poem in lyric stanzas on the embassy of the angels to the shepherds. Though it will never rank among the great poems on Christ's Nativity, it is probably the first written in New England, a strange combination of the naïve, the winsome, and the cosmically imaginative. Steere's lyric masterpiece and one of the greatest poems of early New England is "On a Sea-Storm nigh the Coast." We have already seen some evidence of Steere's realism, objectivity, keen awareness of characteristic detail, closeness to nature, and particular affinity for the sea. All of these, together with his strong rhythmic talent and aptness of phrase, unite here in a nearly perfect poem of its kind, divinely objective with not a trace of moral reflection, a pure impression of a phenomenon of nature.

Among the first-rate poets of early New England, Steere is perhaps for the modern reader the most approachable and engaging. Only John Saffin and Benjamin Lynde perhaps share this immediacy of appeal with him, occasionally, too, Roger Williams. Near the other end of the scale of approachability, though even greater than he, is Edward Taylor, the culminating figure of this age group, whose works, like those of John Fiske, require close and sympathetic study before their full beauty and import are revealed to the reader.

The history of Edward Taylor's poetic fame is even stranger than Steere's, and just as typical of the sluggishness with which the study of our colonial literature has been pursued. Attention was first called to his poetry in several publications from 1879 onward, particularly in the second volume of Sibley's *Harvard Graduates*, 1881, where the poems are adjudged "not of a very high order, though some have considerable merit," and a rather full bibliographical description of them is appended. Nothing further was done about them for more than a half-century, when they were finally rediscovered, and the best of them published in 1939.

Edward Taylor came over to New England in July, 1668, as a young man of about twenty-five.[1] He entered Harvard with classmates generally about nine years younger than he, including Samuel Sewall his roommate, two other poets, William Adams and the younger John Norton, and the college wit, Thomas Welde III. Soon after graduation in 1671 he went as minister to the frontier town of Westfield, held the little community together through King Philip's War, and remained there till his death.

Taylor's extensive poetic work falls into four parts: the elegies and other occasional poems in the traditional New England manner (together with two strange works, on Pope Joan and on the giant fossil bones found near Albany), his splendid lyrical-theological cycle "Gods Determinations," his two hundred-odd "Sacramental Meditations," and a set of eight poems in various lyric stanzas.

Most of Taylor's elegies, especially those of his early years, are inclined to be somewhat labored, awkward, and overextended, though scattered through them there are

[1] The date of Taylor's birth is unknown. His contemporaneous tombstone states that he died "1729 in the 87 year of his age," which would make 1642 or 1643 the year of his birth; but the obituary in the *Boston News-Letter* has "the 85th year of his age," which would give 1644 or 1645. His recent biographer and editor, Thomas H. Johnson, considers the latter date the more likely one. Cf. *The New England Quarterly*, vol. 10, esp. p. 294, note 10.

frequent fine phrases, lines, or even passages which presage his future poetic excellence. His acrostic epistle to his two brothers and his sister, perhaps his earliest preserved effort in verse, has apparently not been examined or mentioned since 1892; the elegy on Richard Mather has probably been lost. His first preserved elegy on Zachariah Simms, is mediocre and diffuse in imagery. His second, on Francis Willoughby, is far better, particularly in the middle portion with its ornate but unified imagery, though the reader is vexed rather than enraptured by the elaborate acrostic pattern which has no integral relation to the poem but merely disturbs the reading of it; his elegy on Charles Chauncy employs the same quadruple acrosticon but with less poetic distinction. The elegy on John Allen is perhaps closest to his later verse in its use of an odd, complex, though consistent set of images and in its bizarre yet strangely appropriate choice of word and phrase. Linguistically Taylor is one of the most original and creative of American poets, and his peculiar genius is apparent even at this early age.

His last declamation at college, in praise of the English language, was an even more elaborate piece of philological punning than Benjamin Tompson's elegy on Robert Woodmancy, which preceded it by four years and may have influenced it. It is one of Taylor's gayest and wittiest pieces and displays not only the typical collegiate humor but also some of the more subtle strains which appear occasionally even in his later religious poetry.

His "Valentine" to Elizabeth Fitch, in which the verse is fitted with incredible ingenuity into and around the figures of dove, triangle, ring, and heart, is most notable for the fact that the verse is rather good in spite of the external artifice imposed upon it. His second poem to his beloved is carried by the imagery of weaving, of which he was later to make such distinguished poetic use. Taylor's love poetry never approaches the charm and perfection of John Saffin's, though his elegy on the death of his wife, especially part three, an idealized but true portrait of the Puritan woman at her finest, is remarkably like Saffin's "Revived Elegiac Lamentation," more complex and detailed, and perhaps less perfect poetically. The last couplet seems to indicate that Wigglesworth's *Day of Doom* was one of his wife's favorite books.

Among Taylor's later elegies the long one on Samuel Hooker, son of the famous Thomas, is particularly noteworthy for its second part, one of the most vivid, detailed, realistic portraits of an early Puritan divine. Taylor went far beyond realism to the spade-calling naturalism of which his epoch was capable, in his account of the career of Pope Joan. For sharp, pornographic satire it has no preserved equal in the verse of Puritan New England.

But Taylor's talent for realism as such is only a minor note in his whole poetic work; his genius lies in his remarkable ability to infuse abstract concepts, even theological dogmas, with the pulsating breath of life. In contrast to the few great poets who share this talent with him (Lucretius, Schiller, Shelley, and others) Taylor does not generally provide a poetic incarnation on the same exalted level which the ideas occupy. His means of achieving this materialization is his rich store of images drawn from every phase of daily and Sunday life; he rather prefers than scorns to use the most homely or plebeian image to embody the most exalted idea, and will even use an occasional vulgarism if it suits his purpose. He may thus be said to domesticate these ideas, to make them familiar and comfortable furnishings for a New England country parsonage. It would be a sad mistake to place Taylor among the great metaphysical poets; he does not have their eagle's flight nor ocean's surge, but on his own quieter, more domestic level he is genuine and of unquestioned quality. We must turn to Richard Steere or to John Saffin for a New England poet who wrote on the much more distinguished and aristocratic level of European tradition; Taylor's way, however, was to become the more truly American way, as we can see it in Emerson's metaphysical bucket of potatoes on the back porch.

Taylor employs his treasure of images in a typically late Baroque manner: lavishly but purposefully and consequentially, in an ordered, well-disposed intricacy. Late Baroque poetry is not as integral as the best of the high Baroque. Whereas it is almost impossible to excerpt or quote from Fiske's poems without doing violence to their central purpose, Taylor is eminently quotable, and conversely, some of his poems would be distinctly improved by the omission of an occasional stanza or couplet. In spirit and method he is astonishingly like the German pietist poets of his day (I speak here of parallels, not of influences), and the common source for both is probably the mystical literature of the later Middle Ages.

Taylor's senses were extraordinarily acute, and his verse is replete with images of touch, smell, and taste, as well as of sight and hearing. He was apparently of a very passionate and sensuous nature, but, as with the older mystics, this was dominated by his intense religious yearning and sublimated to symbolic expression in the service of God. This in contrast to Steere who had the same extraordinary sensibilities, but was convinced that God intended them to be expressed, with moderation, in an earthly manner.

Taylor's largest and greatest work, "Gods Determinations," takes up the forbidding theme of the process of man's conversion and salvation according to the Covenant theology, and handles it with sovereign mastery of the means necessary to bring it to poetic life: a well marshalled array of images, a variety of lyric forms, with passages of epic progress and dramatic tension—all combining to achieve the almost impossible, a fine poem upon this scholastic theme.

A good example of the variety of imagery in even a small passage occurs in "Christ's Reply" to the soul frightened by the devil:

> And if he run an inch too fur,
> I'le Check his Chain, and rate the Cur.
> My Chick, keep close to mee.
> The Poles shall sooner kiss and greet,
> And Paralells shall sooner meet,
> Than thou shall harmed bee.

Or the soul chiding the body:

> My Muddy Tent, why hast thou done so ill
> To Court and kiss my Soule, yet kissing kill?
> Why didst thou Whyning, egg her thus away,
> Thy sensuall Appetite to satisfy?
> Art thou so safe and firm a Cabinet,
> As though thou soaking lie in nasty wet,
> And in all filthy Puddles: yet the thin
> Can ne're drench through to stain the Pearle within?

The whole work ends with three lyrics that have much of the sweet, naïve winsomeness of the late Middle Ages about them: the charming poem on the flower garden of the Church with its culminating refrain, the lyric on divine music, and the engagingly quaint, child-like last poem on the singing saints riding to Glory in Christ's Coach. This is a pleasing and just ending, for the tone of the whole cycle is one of luminous piety rather than of magnificent faith; the mighty eloquence of a Luther or a Milton is entirely lacking, though the perennial divine beauty of a Herbert or a Spee is there.

The "Sacramental Meditations" written throughout the course of his pastoral life are most varied in content and quality, but they are all written in the same six-line stanza.

The very first on the boundlessness of God's love is finer than the younger Peter Bulkeley's on the same theme. Indeed, the first, the fourth, and many another of the "Meditations" are superb examples of the ecstatic lyric of self-surrender to divine love in the tradition of the Medieval mystics, for this theme is almost as much the unifying element in the "Meditations" as the Covenant theology is in "Gods Determinations." He finds ever new images in which to express this attitude: a guest at God's table, a metal to be coined in God's mint, an earthen vessel to receive God's wine, a branch to be grafted on God's tree.

> Hence make me, Lord, thy Golden Trumpet Choice,
> And trumpet thou thyselfe upon the same
> Thy heart enravishing Hymns with Sweetest Voice.
> When thou thy Trumpet soundst, thy tunes will flame.

He is ever seeking for new images to express God's other attributes and his relations to mankind. To mention only one more of the "Meditations" from among the many worthy of our attention, the fifty-sixth of the second series is rather outstanding for its consistently high level, its unified composition, and its preference for images from the "great world" of Taylor's learning rather than from the "little world" of his familiar experience. It is masterful the way he marshals all the glories of nature and art, and finds them but inadequate symbols for expressing the glories of Christ.

There remain the poems in lyric measures: "An Address to the Soul Occasioned by a Rain" with its strange imagery and lovely rhythm, "Upon a Spider Catching a Fly" and "Upon a Wasp Chilled with Cold," acutely realistic observation in the service of doctrine, "Huswifery" (in two versions) and "The Ebb and Flow," his most perfect expressions of self-surrender to the creative power of divine love, "Upon Wedlock and Death of Children," a moving expression of complete submission to God's will in his domestic sorrows, and strangest of all "Upon the Sweeping Flood," an enigmatic symbolization of personal passion.

In determining Taylor's place in early American poetry one needs to exercise caution in both directions: though his particular type of verse can become a bit wearisome in its repetitiousness and exaltation, and though he does lapse frequently from poetic grace, he did write a remarkably large body of verse of high quality and can never be dismissed as an unimportant poet. On the other hand, to call him the best poet, or the only good poet, before Freneau is perhaps going too far. He does indeed stand head and shoulders above the old familiar group of poets that have stalked through our literary histories for so long. But whether he will maintain his complete superiority when we have come to know all that can be known, not only about the New England poets, but also about those of the Middle and Southern colonies, that only time can tell.

With the age group of Tompson, Steere, and Taylor, seventeenth-century New England verse reaches its culmination. The earlier groups as well as the ones that follow also have their important figures, and in several cases have a richer group of interesting minor writers, but in none of the others is there quite this concentration of great poets born within a year or two of one another nor quite as large a body of first rate verse. Though much of the mature work of this and the two following groups falls in the next century, they are still seventeenth century in spirit and not primarily transition groups to the new eighteenth-century English manner; the real transition figure is the even younger Benjamin Colman who did not start writing verse until the very last years of the century and continued active almost to the middle of the eighteenth.

VII. The Second Native-Born Group

With this second native-born group, as with the first, we can begin with the minor writers, passing them in quick review and then examine the work of the few important writers in greater detail. The almanac makers need detain us only briefly. John Richardson's impudent "Country-Mans Apocrypha" in his *Almanack* for 1670 has already come to our notice in connection with farmer Samuel Bailey's vigorous answer to it; its references to folk dress, customs, and beliefs give it added interest. John Foster in his series of almanacs does once or twice write charming sets of seasonal verses, particularly in his *Almanack* for 1676 where the course of the year is paralleled with the course of man's life. In the quatrain for January there is a reminiscence of Thomas Dudley's verses on his old age. Under June of his 1679 almanac he describes with humorous indirection how the students are torn between swimming in the Charles River and cramming for examinations. The other almanac verse of this group is of small interest.

Two other young men are also remembered only for their college verses: Joseph Browne who in 1667 wrote a brief elegy on the death of Katherine Chauncy, President Chauncy's wife, and, far more important, Francis Drake who wrote an elegy on the death of Jonathan Mitchell in 1668. Cotton Mather recounts how this young man, who was living at Mitchell's house, was so deeply impressed by the dying words spoken to him that he was impelled to write the elegy. It is a learned and ornamental effort in the elaborate elegiac tradition, with a number of fine lines and striking images, as for instance after the listing of the sorrowful forces motivating his verse:

> These are my Muses; These inspire the Sails
> Of Fancy with their Sighs instead of Gales.

About the further career of this promising young writer we know nothing, except that he went to England with an Indian student from Harvard.

Even more mysterious is Philip Pain whose *Daily Meditations* were published in 1668 and again in 1670, attesting to their popularity at the time. All that we know about him is what the title page tells us, that he had lately suffered shipwreck and was drowned. We also know from various passages and from the postscript that he must have been young at the time of writing, possibly about eighteen or twenty, and the preserved verses cover only sixteen days, from July 19 to August 3, 1666. As with so many a New England poet of the day, the verse of George Herbert was an important influence. The single theme running through all the sixty-four meditations is the contemplation of mutability and mortality from all its aspects. In spite of a resulting monotony and repetitiousness, very little of the verse is really bad, and a few of the stanzas, for instance Meditations four, ten, twenty-nine, fifty-six, and sixty-two, are well done and worthy of a more mature poet. It is interesting that several of the couplets appended to each page of daily meditations seem to anticipate the famous American child's prayer, "Now I lay me down to sleep," which first made its appearance in mid-eighteenth-century editions of the *New England Primer*.

Thomas Bailey also left only a slim volume of juvenalia, in manuscript, and William Adams and the younger Daniel Gookin wrote, so far as we know, only two youthful elegies each. Adams wrote one on his college friend Seth Flint and another, in Latin, on Urian Oakes. Gookin also wrote an elegy on Urian Oakes and somewhat later one on the mintmaster John Hull. All four are characterized by smoothness, competence, and mediocrity, though Gookin's on Oakes has some saving merits.

In this generally ephemeral and short-lived age group there are, however, two writers who in their single preserved efforts have attained the authentic ring and firm tension of real poetry. Deodat Lawson, whose origins and end in England are not fully known, was pastor at North Scituate when he wrote his elegy on the shipwreck of Captain Anthony Collamore. Stanzas three to six of this "Threnodia" are among the finest ballad verse of early New England, a swift, straight narrative of the little fleet sailing forth from Scituate harbor for Boston upon a clear December day which was soon blotted out by a blinding snowstorm.

> Some Boats with Sailes Expanded led the way,
> Out of the Harbour; and did fairly glide;
> Thus one by one stood out into the Bay,
> With Wind at East North East and Flowing Tide.
> The Captain in the Rere did Hoise up Saile,
> And hasted after with a Steddy Gale.

Unfortunately, the other twenty-three stanzas do not carry out the promise of these four, but become lost in weak narrative, lament, and eulogy.

By contrast, the elegy which the younger John Norton wrote on the death of Anne Bradstreet has none of the originality of Lawson at his best, but is, on the other hand, sustained at a high poetic level throughout. It is completely in the classical tradition, with the nine Muses in mourning for the death of their sister, and with comparisons of the latter's poetry to the best of the ancients'. Even the hyperbole is inoffensive, and the description of earth's darkening and the sun's eclipse in mourning somehow seems just and fitting for the occasion.

The third Thomas Welde, pastor of Dunstable, might have ranked with Norton as a master of the elegy, if his verses on the death of Samuel Danforth had been preserved, for the eight lines which Cotton Mather quoted from it have that intensity and immediacy of expression which all too rarely raises the elegy of the period to the status of poetry. Welde's commonplace book is one of the most unusual of the period, containing as it does a collection of humorous anecdotes of early New England. Most of the witty epigrams in verse, occurring later in the volume, seem to be of English origin, though a few of them may turn out to be by Welde.

The only two writers of this group who left any considerable body of verse are Nicholas Noyes and Samuel Sewall. It is very difficult to write about Nicholas Noyes, for his poetic fame is still enshrouded in the pall which Moses Coit Tyler cast over him. Quite recently Tyler's verdict was again quoted with approval that Noyes was "the most gifted and brilliant master ever produced in America, of the most execrable form of poetry to which the English language was ever degraded." Another critical dictum of Tyler's on Noyes should, however, give us pause: "even in his old age, he continued to write the sort of poetry that, in his youth, had been the fashion, both in England and in America—the degenerate euphuism of Donne, of Wither, of Quarles, of George Herbert. To this appalling type of poetry, Nicholas Noyes faithfully adhered, even to the end of his days, unseduced by the rhythmical heresies, the classic innovations, of John Dryden and Alexander Pope." After sixty-five years there are perhaps few people left who would care to maintain that John Donne is utterly beyond the poetic pale, or that Dryden and Pope have been an unmixed blessing to English poetry, rendering their predecessors forever unpalatable to refined poetic taste; and yet these old Victorian standards are still maintained in the criticism of early American literature. The irony is that Noyes was not the most gifted and brilliant master of the style which Tyler found so execrable, for Edward Taylor and several others far outdid him in every feature that Tyler loathed. It is a blessing that they have remained unknown until recently, for Tyler would surely have turned purple in the presence of "Gods Determinations" and "John Kotton: O, Honie knott." As in the case of Edward Johnson (where Tyler's divagation was even worse, since he allowed his prejudices to involve him in errors of fact), we shall simply have to disregard traditional judgments and look at the verse itself. This is not so easy, for Noyes' verse is widely scattered in rare publications, and only about half of it has ever before been bibliographically listed.

Most of his early poems seem to have been lost; indeed a full two-thirds of his preserved verse dates from beyond the turn of the century. We do know, however, that he enjoyed fame as a versifier from his early years onward. His college friend Nehemiah Hobart sent to him for criticism verses on the "dreadful fire at Boston" (probably lost), "because I knowe you retain that poetical genius, for which you were so remarkable, when a student at Camebridge." His only preserved piece of collegiate verse was appended to Josiah Flint's *Almanack* for 1666, "A short Discourse about 66." A large part of the intellectual world of the day was stirred with anticipation about the coming of the prophetically ominous year 1666 ("the mark of the beast," etc.). His attitude is the cautiously skeptical one (shared by many another interested New Englander) that even though the Papacy might not fall nor the Millenium begin in that year, yet the succession of years was tending inevitably toward that goal.

> The Lord a Furnace is preparing ready
> To Cast the Heavens and Earth anew, and speedy.

Though the theme is rather far from our present interests, and the allusions at first seem obscure, it is at once clear that both theme and verse are competently handled.

The next group of Noyes' preserved verse consists of prefatory poems for his friends' works, one for William Hubbard and two for Cotton Mather. The rather charmingly naïve one for Mather's *Christianus per Ignem* is memorable for the comparison of Mather's range of thought to a swarm of bees:

> The thoughts are like a swarm of Bees,
> That fly both when and where they please;
> Those little folks both work and play
> About a thousand flow'rs a day,
> Yet in their lawless range contrive
> To bring in Honey to their Hive.

—a bit of friendly fun about a useful weakness of Mather's. The poem on the *Magnalia* is especially interesting for its exposition of the New England attitude toward learning and history. By way of contrast he first dwells upon the Indians whose origins and history are covered over in black oblivion, and on the "light-within-enthusiasts, who let fly Against our pen and ink divinity," and then he paints the opposite picture of a people with consciousness of origin and continuity of tradition kept alive by such historians as Mather. The concluding sections contain illuminating comments on Mather's interweaving wit and learning, profit and delight into a single texture.

> Dearly it loves art, air, and eloquence,
> And hates confinement, save to truth and sense.

—an excellent summation of the anti-classical attitude.

His next poem was also addressed to Cotton Mather, though on a sad occasion, the death of Abigail Mather, his beloved wife, after a long illness. The poem is characterized by simplicity and dignity; naturally it is in the late Baroque style with the turns, flourishes, and striking images proper to that manner, though these are employed sparingly and with far more restraint than we have noticed, for instance, in Edward Taylor.

Upon Mather's endeavors to raise the spiritual (and material) welfare of the negro slaves of the province, Noyes wrote a brief commendatory poem, giving utterance to the Christian principle of equality before God:

> The pious Master & the pious Slave
> The Liberty of Sons of God shall have.
> But these are riddles unto Mammons fooles,
> That use their Slaves as if they had no Soules.

This is hardly great verse, but it is the dawn of a great tradition.

The poem which Noyes sent to his friend James Bailey to console him in his agonized suffering from "the stone," the scholar's disease, has long been a stone of offence in the path of the genteel critic. It hardly deserves the space that has traditionally been devoted to it; it is a light, whimsical effort much appreciated in its day, and doubtless achieved its main purpose of entertaining its recipient and diverting him from his suffering. If one takes it in the spirit in which it was intended, there is much about it that is admirable: a warm glow of friendship, a well blended mixture of fun and seriousness, a confident intimacy that allows jokes about serious things between friends. Greatness the poem certainly does not have. Noyes was, indeed, something of an eccentric, but both in life and verse his eccentricity seems on the whole to have taken a whimsical and lovable turn, and he was long remembered in anecdote for such things as his extemporaneous rhymes on the patchwork quilt being made by one of his parishoners.

When John Higginson, the last of the patriarchs of New England, died in 1708, after having witnessed the whole development of the Bay Colony from its founding at Salem and after having preached for seventy-two years, it was fitting that his colleague Noyes should write the tribute on his passing, and Noyes did so in a long and interesting elegy.

After reflections on the blessings of the old pastor's presence and the sad presages of his departure, he launches upon a long description of Higginson's life and career with a candor and detail equal to that of Taylor on Samuel Hooker, and with boldly characterizing strokes that make the old gentleman's appearance and character unforgettable. He describes the last months of his life, when the dusk that was falling upon him was often pierced by the flashes of his old spirit:

> So lights Expiring blink about;
> Are sometimes in, and sometimes out;
> Yet ne're the Candle discommend,
> That burns So clear from End to End.

His little elegy on the death of Mary Gerrish, the daughter of Samuel Sewall, is a simple and moving lament that impartial death should take off one so young and so beautiful just as her life as a wife and mother was coming to fulfilment.

Another elaborate elegy is that on the death of the young pastor Joseph Green who had brought peace, unity, and complete Christian charity back again to Salem Village, which had been torn and lacerated by the tragedy of the witchcraft trials. To Noyes it must have seemed that he could not find a more appropriate theme for his composition than the two parts of Joseph Green's name, significant (without being anagrammatized) of the blessing and security he had brought to that imperilled community and of the flourishing state in which he had left it. All this is implicit in the poem and clear to its admirers at the time; without it we should continue to misunderstand it as gravely as it has been in the past. In composition it is masterly, one of the few of the later elegies, indeed, to excell in this respect, and it is fascinating to follow the sequence of Noyes' thought and imagery. In the one digression of the poem, feeling that in delineating such a wonderful character as Green's it is necessary to insist that his verse is free from all hyperbole, the author adds an interesting bit of literary criticism:

> By over-praising of the Dead
> Nor they, nor we are Bettered.
> Poetick Raptures Scandalize,
> And pass with most for learned Lies . . .
> Such high Flights seem Design'd to raise
> The *Poets*, not the *Person's* praise.

Noyes' last elegy, still unpublished, laments the passing of a number of prominent men, of Sewall's wife and other members of that family in rapid succession, and finally of his young and promising colleague, George Curwin. A few weeks later Noyes himself was dead.

The sum of his work can hardly entitle him to a place among the great or near-great of New England poets, but his verse does have a vitality and originality which keep it far above dull mediocrity and should insure for him a modest place on the slopes of the Puritan Parnassus, once the prejudices against him are forgotten.

His friend, Samuel Sewall, likewise a mildly eccentric and generally lovable character, took the greatest delight throughout his life in the making of little sets of verses, both Latin and English, on any sort of an occasion or idea. These couplets, quatrains, and little poems he would then revise with loving care, leaving them in several versions and at times in two languages, quite guilelessly bequeathing upon the present writer a bibliographical nightmare. To top it all, he was fond of issuing his (and his friends') verses in little printed leaflets, occasionally in several variant editions: an eight and twelve-line version, a three and a six-stanza version. The labor of bringing all this into some order was one of almost unrequited love, for most of the verse is only the trivial toying of a great mind. It is likely that he was brief rather because he was poetically short-winded than because he was nobly self-restrained. But with all the trivia removed, a few pieces remain, simple, terse, adequate, deserving a respectable place among our minor verse.

His earliest preserved set of verses, composed on a trip to Cape Cod in 1676, is in its lovable intimacy with nature one of his best:

> The Humble Springs of stately Sandwich Beach
> To all Inferiours may observance teach,
> They (without Complement) do all concur,
> Praying the Sea, Accept our Duty, Sir,
> He mild severe, I've (now) no need: and when—
> As you are come: go back and come agen.

Characteristically he could not resist publishing it in a much revised version forty-seven years later in the *Boston News-Letter*. His earliest little broadside was written on the death of his aunt Mehitable Holt, his next on his mother-in-law Judith Hull, the first simple and dignified the second infelicitously elaborate. His lines for a sundial again show him at his best:

> Keep in God's way; keep pace with evry hour
> Hurt none; do all the Good that's in your Power.
> Hours can't look back at all; theyl stay for none
> Tread sure, keep up with them, and All's your own.

When Samuel Willard after a long illness returned to church again on Thanksgiving Day, 1700, Sewall issued another of his little broadsides, a fitting gesture, but of no consequence as verse. Far better are his verses on the beginning of the new century, recited by the bell-men at dawn on New Year's Day, 1700/1. They are a prayer to God for the fulfilment of the millenarian prophecies which occupied so much of Sewall's attention. The first stanzas on the future of New England are particularly fine, among the best that he ever wrote. He frequently exchanged verses with the school teacher, Richard Henchman, and one of the results of this exchange was a splendid ode by Henchman expanding the theme of Sewall's New Year's verses. There seems indeed to have been a lively interchange of verses in Boston at the time, in which Henchman, Hobart, Mather, and others participated. Sewall also distributed the printed poetic leaflets of the time rather freely, generally remembering to enclose a number of them when he wrote to his friend, Edward Taylor. Whether he sent a piece of his daughter's wedding cake to the captain of a British man-of-war anchored in the harbor, or a book to the visiting Spanish governor of Carthagena, the inevitable Latin verses always accompanied the gift.

Two of Sewall's epitaphs were certainly out of the ordinary: the one on Tom Child the Painter who "had often painted Death, But never to the life, before," and the one on New England celibacy, upon the death of Nicholas Noyes. His couplet on his wife's death has a classic terseness and restraint about it:

> What signify these Locks, and Bolts, and Bars?
> My Treasures gone, and with it all my Fears.

His longest poem, thirty-six lines, was written "Upon the drying up that Ancient River, the River Merrymak," here again, as in his New Year's broadside, with reference to the fulfilment of the Scriptural prophecies (the drying up of the Euphrates). These are among his most delightful verses, in tone and spirit like his earliest on the springs at Sandwich, though far more developed, a charming example of the Puritan's affection for his New England countryside. This concluded Sewall's poetic endeavors, except for further Latin occasionalia and an elegy on the death of his grandson in 1727.

This age group is perhaps the most generally unproductive and mediocre of seventeenth-century New England; many of the authors were short-lived and are remembered for only a poem or two. Lawson, Pain, Drake, and Norton indeed showed promise, but only Noyes and Sewall lived to produce a considerable body of verse which has come down to us. The next, and last, group is again a fuller and more productive one, with three important writers and several others of decided interest.

VIII. The Third Native-Born Group

In this last age group which came to literary expression during the seventeenth century, we again have a number of writers who are known for only a poem or two. The long line of collegiate almanac poets, which began with the first Samuel Danforth in 1647, now came to an end with the second Samuel Danforth, his son, in 1686, the few succeeding Cambridge almanacs being verseless. The younger Samuel's poem, "Ad Librum," is one line longer than his father's longest, but alas, it shows little of the elder's poetry and none of his good fun; the last couplet, however, offers a fitting epitaph to an old institution:

> Oh Eighty Six; Thou'rt quickly come about!
> This Sheet that brought thee in shall lay thee out.

A few years earlier William Brattle in his 1682 almanac had tried to carry on the old seasonal word-play, with some success for May and July, though other of the monthly verses show that the old vein had been exhausted. Many years later, when pastor of Taunton, Samuel Danforth made yet another effort in verse, on the death of Major Thomas Leonard. It is completly pedestrian, without a spark of poetry, a faithful recital of the career of a virtuous self-made man, with the appropriate reflections.

Three other students did rather better in carrying on old traditions, in the elegy. Eleazar, an Indian, wrote some very respectable Latin and Greek verses on the death of Thomas Thacher in 1678. His elegy is very well composed, with proper restraint, good taste, and a well ordered sequence of images and ideas. The second elegy is an elaborate youthful performance, on the death of Governor John Leverett, by L.O., presumably the son of Urian Oakes, Lawrence, who like Eleazar died a few months later. It is an ornate production, first picturing Leverett's death under the classical picture of the sun god setting and leaving the darkened world to the lesser luminaries. The elegy continues with the depiction of his character and virtues as a man, a soldier, and a statesman. With all its stately splendor, however, the poem is diffuse and poorly composed, with few memorable lines and little sustention of interest. By contrast, Grindall Rawson's elegy on his deceased college friend, John Saffin, Jr., has life, movement, and sequence; it also has its elaborate figures, well adapted to their purpose, and what remains memorable is the heartfelt expression of sorrow for a brilliant and dear friend. Some twenty years later Rawson wrote a small set of complimentary verses for Mather's *Magnalia.*

When the gifted craftsman and mathematician, John Foster, died in 1681, two commemorative poems were written, one by old Thomas Tileston, the other by young Joseph Capen. The latter is the more eloquent, and in spite of a few lapses in taste and verse, it is decidedly readable and interesting, contrasting Foster's wasted consumptive body with his ardent soul which sought increasing knowledge and skill to the last, and beyond to its final perfect attainment. In the conclusion he elaborates Benjamin Woodbridge's image of John Cotton as a book which will appear in a new edition without errata, and gives it the form from which Benjamin Franklin, no doubt, derived his famous self-epitaph.

Perhaps the earliest preserved example of blank verse in New England (probably preceding the writing of Steere's "Earth Felicities" by some years) was Nehemiah Walter's elegy on the old schoolmaster Elijah Corlet, in 1687. In the first section Walter, as he explains, chose blank verse as "The most becoming of this Tragick scene." After an intricately figured expression of his poetic inadequacy for the task, he procedes to delineate Corlet's skill as a teacher and his remarkable learning in the Greek and Latin tongues. Even Urian Oakes submitted his Latin orations to Corlet for approval; had Athens and Rome survived, Demosthenes and Cicero would have disputed to which city he pertained. After Walter has Corlet safely straddling the two cities like the Colossus, he transports him to heaven in Elijah's chariot. The poem is not quite that bad, but with all its single virtues it does show something of the decline of the elegiac tradition into pretentious mannerisms.

Edward Tompson's touch is plainer and surer on the whole, though he has only a modest share of the talents of his uncle Benjamin. His elegy on Seaborn Cotton, 1686, does carry to an extreme the Baroque device of *vers rapporté:*

> He drew & drove, woo'd, warn'd with all his might
> Mens souls, by love, by fear, by force, by Fright.

But generally this device is not carried through consistently and the succession of epithets is not perfectly matched, as it was with the old New England masters of the style. His verse, however, is smooth and the succession of images congruous, in contrast to the inflated and scrambled images of Walter. His other elegy, on the death of his father, is heartfelt and truly fine, as good a picture of the ideal Puritan layman as one could hope to find. There are echoes throughout the poem of earlier New England elegies, a phenomenon frequent in these last age groups, but the poem as a whole is firm and consistent in texture, and the inclination toward parallelisms here results in some really effective passages.

One of the most movingly awkward and inept elegies since Abraham Pierson's on Theophilus Eaton was the one that Edward Payson wrote on the death of his elder colleague at Rowley, Samuel Phillips, in 1696. It is a long five-part composition obviously the work of an amateur who under the stress of deep emotion labored valiantly to put his grief into rhyme. But in the fifth part, "Mr. Phillips Buried," the miracle happens: a brief passage of naïve and perfect folk poetry. When the old pastor finds his resting place near two of his predecessors, one of them says to him:

> Come Brother Phillips, come to Bed,
> Here's room enough, lay down thy head.
> Thou held'st out long, it's time give out,
> Come rest with us, here is no rout.
> Let's fall to sleep, and silent be,
> A little while; I, thou, and he.
> Thus these three Saints in silence lie,
> Scarce whisper aught to him that's by.
> These Triumvirs got into their old Mother,
> Lye very still, and sweetly sleep together.

Three men are remembered poetically only for their connection with the central figure of this age group, Cotton Mather. His short-lived, precocious brother, Nathaniel, left a hymn which is far more commendable for its piety than for its poetry. Nathaniel's friend, Robert Hale, left a finely wrought short elegy on him. He later wrote a congratulatory poem for one of Cotton Mather's tracts. Timothy Woodbridge contributed one of the prefatory poems to the *Magnalia*, emphasising the benefits of this history of origins in keeping New England mindful of the one right way.

The phenomenon Cotton Mather is such a vast and paradoxical one that we are only just beginning to comprehend it. In his youth Mather must have been rather unbearable, and some of his worst conceit and conceits came out in his early poems, but even here his underlying virtues began to appear. As his experience and humanity increased with the passage of trying years, his character and works gradually became freed from the dross and a truly good and great man emerged who was able to put some of his finest self into verse.

In 1682, at the age of twenty-one, he published his first poem, a pamphlet of sixteen pages on the death of Urian Oakes. Like Lawrence Oakes' elegy on Governor Leverett, the poem rides along on a high poetic horse, and yet at first never quite seems to get anywhere. Once he has labored through the proem, however, the verse comes to life; the section on Oakes' career, highly ornamented and allusive though it is, reads very well, and the section on Oakes' return to America is almost inspired. Later in the eulogy there are some good lines, though when speaking of Oakes' great soul in a little body, he cannot refrain from the couplet:

> How many Angels on a Needle's point
> Can stand, is thought, perhaps, a needless point.

The concluding prayer to God for constant replenishment of New England's losses is noble and fitting.

Three years later he issued his second long poetic effort, an elegy on Nathaniel Collins, this time with its multifarious allusions heavily annotated. Some of the notes are merely pretentious, others referring to his literary models are significant in showing us how far beyond the well known English poets we must go in our study of the sources of Puritan verse. Occasionally the notes also refer to direct obervations incorporated into the poem, as for instance, in his discovery through his microscope of hundreds of little organisms swimming about in a drop of water. In the introduction Mather calls upon the Heavenly Muse to inspire him, "Showr On a bereaved Clod of Earth a pow'r to yield a spire of grass," and is shocked at the thought that Collins should be dead "without A Paper winding sheet to lay him out." In a less mannered and more effective passage he tells how he came upon a noble lady (the Church of Middletown) mourning her loss in the wilderness; it is she who speaks the elegy, though not without lapses into the character of the young pedant. The poem is packed with allusions and lightened with occasional startling images, as when the sallies of Collins' youthful humor are described as "Facetious Snowballs" or when the author speaks of the coming of more calamities "than can be wrap'd in a pale Comets Hair."

The eulogy dwells on Collins' urbanity, his piety, his earthly learning and his higher wisdom in the trivium and quadrivium of heaven, his temperance, his patience, and other virtues—much of it a mosaic of quotations and allusions, yet making a good design as a whole. The verse technique is at times almost incredibly bad, with its halting rhythms and jarring inversions, and then suddenly there are a few limpid lines or stanzas, some of the best coming toward the end where the shade of Collins speaks, and in the conclusion where the poet offers a prayer for New England. As poetry the elegy is a failure, but characteristically for Mather the contents are so varied and interesting that it could profitably be studied in greater detail.

Mather's very brief elegy on Shubael Dummer, victim of the Indian attack on York, Maine, is, by contrast, unpretentious and moving. The little prayers and hymns that he occasionally inserted in his diary and in various of his publications are also completely simple and sincere, and in a few cases they rise to true poetry. He wrote one of his most perfect and beautiful little poems upon the death of his dearly beloved wife Abigail in 1702; it is a simple and delicately sensitive farewell to the wife of his youth, as fine a poem as Mather ever wrote.

Throughout his life he devoted himself to writing religious verse for children, trying to ease the burden of the vast amount of religious knowledge which the Puritan child was expected to acquire. He put the Lord's Prayer into verse, the Ten Commandments, even "A Little Body of Divinity" in fifty-four lines, and a treatise on Conversion of slightly greater length. His "Scriptural Hymns for Children" are still preserved, but not a copy of his little volume of verse *Good Lessons for Children* has survived the intense reading habits of the little Puritans. The only man in New England who rivalled him as a writer for children was the journalist Banjamin Harris, to whom the *New-England Primer* is attributed, with its rhymed alphabet and its "Dialogue between Christ, Youth and the Devil." Harris was perhaps also author of a collection of Bible stories, *Divine Poems for Youths* (Boston, 1694).

Mather's mature ventures in the longer and more elaborate elegy are of decided interest and some poetic grace. As the bibliography shows, several elegies long attributed to him were actually written by other men; indeed his elegy on the death of seven young ministers, the one on Sarah Leverett, and the one on his old schoolmaster Ezekiel Cheever are the only ones, after his youthful efforts, which can definitely be attributed to him. The first of these, "On the Graves of my Young Brethren," contains some of his smoothest and clearest verse. By this time, 1706, he had read Dryden, indeed he cites him in the course of the poem, though negatively, and the effects of the new school of English verse are unmistakable. Steere and Saffin before him probably knew Dryden, and Sewall about the 1690's copied excerpts from Dryden's American drama, *The Indian Emperour*, into his commonplace book. On the other hand, Mather did not simply imitate, he accommodated these influences to the established American tradition. Furthermore, other than English influences are at least equally apparent; the neo-Latin poetry of the Continent was of immense importance to him and to his predecessors. In this poem there is even an indication of the influence of Persian poetry, whose beauties had been first adequately revealed to Europe by Adam Olearius and Paul Fleming after their expedition to Persia in 1633–39, with the account of which Mather was well acquainted. But even in poly-historical Mather the indigenous New England traditions probably remained strongest, and he never hesitated to use local images, as here:

> Churches, Weep on; & Wounded yield your Tears;
> Tears use to flow from hack't New-English Firrs.

The old punning tradition is still strong, often in juxtaposition to some of his most effective and colloquial lines; these young ministers were:

> Not Lads, whom for their Levity alone
> The Punning Tribe, De Tribu Levi, own.
> Not who to Pulpits hop Unfledg'd and there
> Talk twice a Week, and Preach not once a year.

The elegy on Ezekiel Cheever is completely in the New England manner, restrained in its word play in comparison to Tompson's on Woodmancy and Cheever, but quite as cheerful, lively, and witty, yet sincere and earnest in its tribute to a remarkable personality. The best lines perhaps are those which describe Cheever's youthful appearance at the age of ninety-four and his peaceful end:

> Death gently cut the Stalk, and kindly laid
> Him, where our God his Granary has made.

Fine too are the lines which the poet has Cheever speak to the tutors who come after him, advising to gentleness, the appeal to honor and reason, as the most effective principles of teaching. Mather's elegy on Sarah Leverett is inferior to Saffin's.

Two works of Mather's entirely in verse have failed to

survive, his *Songs of the Redeemed* and his *Poem of Consolations under Blindness*, but a third, his *Psalterium Americanum*, 1718, has survived as his largest volume of verse. Even earlier he had attempted to improve on some of the worst doggerel of the *Bay Psalm Book;* here he tried to displace it altogether, making a translation which preserved the old meters for the favorite hymn tunes but eliminated all rhyme. Over-ingeniously he printed the verses so that they could be sung both to the longer and shorter tunes, with the sad result that his translation is as unpoetical as the older one, though in a different way. It was a failure even in its own day.

Toward the end of his life he wrote one of his most heartfelt hymns "O glorious Christ of God; I live," and also a set of "Plain Songs of the Pious Husbandman," one or two of which come up to the standard which his admired friend Isaac Watts set in his pietistic hymns.

His most amazing production, "The Pidgeon Py," dates from the last year or so of his life. It is a gay, witty satire on the earliest published piece of Yale juvenalia, John Hubbard's bathetic *Monumental Gratitude*, 1727, a poem depicting the miraculous preservation of several students caught by a storm on Long Island Sound. One would not believe that Mather had written the satire, if it were not written in his own hand on the title page and blank leaf of the publication, with many cancellations and revisions. It sounds more like Mather Byles or one of the other Boston Wits. The punning epigrams on the title page set the tone:

> Soon as the Muse beheld these lines, She said,
> The Members are preserv'd: But ah, the Head!
>
> Poor Lads! the Storm has whirl'd your Brains around;
> And all the Sense is ship-wrack'd in the Sound.

The poem proper describes the making of the pigeon pie amid the hellish fury of the fired ovens, and then the equally noisy process of its consumption by the trenchermen gathered around it, all of it a parody of the description of the sea storm.

Even aside from this last poem, Mather is one of the most unpredictable of poets, with the most gorgeously ornate verse alongside some that is heavily labored and some that is chastely simple, with stretches of limping rhythms and awkward inversions and passages of lucid ductility. He is a poet of transition who can at times alternate masterfully between both poetic chairs and at other times fall miserably between them.

The other poet of this age group who maintained a steady poetic production throughout his life was John Danforth. Like his younger brother Samuel, he made his first poetic appearance in the Cambridge almanac (in 1679), but in a far more felicitous fashion. Some of the monthly verses are weak, but those for April, May, and September are as good as any of the almanac rhymes. Another of his youthful poems, "What if a day or a month or a year," already exhibits his love, which he shared with Taylor, for metrical variety. Most of the early New England poets clung to the simple iambic tetrameter or pentameter, and only a few ventured to experiment with different verse forms. The second stanza is characteristic both of his poetic potentialities and of certain technical weaknesses of his:

> The earths but the point of the world, & a man
> Is but a point of the earths compared center
> That then the point of that point be so vain
> is to triumph in a sylly points adventure
>   Fortune, honour, beauty, and youth
>   Are like shadows flying
>   Wanton pleasures, doting love,
>   Are like blossoms dying
>   Al our joyes are but toyes
>   Idle thought deceiving
>   None hath powr half an hour
>   Of his life and breathing.

This poem remained popular in broadside form deep into the eighteenth century.

Throughout his long ministry at Dorchester he wrote epitaphs for his parishoners, and also a number of elegies. The first of his epitaphs may be the one on his short-lived predecessor, Josiah Flint, a simple and adequate tribute, without any great poetic distinction. Perhaps the earliest epitaph to a New England school mistress is the one to Miriam Wood, 1706, who had started countless Dorchester children on the path of learning.

When in the neighboring town of Roxbury the venerable Indian apostle John Eliot died, a few years after the death of his wife, Danforth wrote two long and elaborate elegies upon them, the one on Anne Eliot in lyric stanzas. As is characteristic of much of John Danforth's verse, these poems on a first reading seem rather unpoetical and lacking in appeal, and it is only a second or third reading which will do full justice to their real merits, though some arid stretches will always remain. His versification, for instance, of John Eliot's advice on the best means for civilizing and Christianizing the Indians makes sound sense, indeed, but hardly good poetry.

The same lack of immediate appeal characterizes his "few Lines to fill up a Vacant Page," a personal lyric about a soul crisis, when he went astray in the "Regions of Discontent" and lost all sense of values earthly and divine. In this mood while he is steering his little craft on its darksome course, he espies the Lord coming toward him upon the waters and at first mistakes him for the Evil One, but at Christ's words, "Be not afraid,"

> . . . all my Discontents resil'd;
> The Ruffling Winds, and Waves were still'd;
> By what Time, Faith and Hope my Sailes could hoise,
> I got safe and firm Anch'rage in a trice,
> Within the very inmost Bays of blissfull Paradise.

He contributed a Latin epigram and a "Pindarick" to Mather's *Magnalia*, terse and apt. His longest venture in irregular "Pindaric" verse is his elegy on Samuel Willard, 1707, again with the obvious asperities and latent qualities characteristic of the poet. His elegy on Thomas Bromfield, the twelve-year old son of Edward Bromfield, is uneven but has some good passages. The same is true of his elegy on young Mary Gerrish, and of his long poem, "Love and Unity Encouraged, and Contention and Division Disswaded." His lost elegy on his uncle Jonathan Danforth, the famous surveyor, may have been one of his most vivid, to judge from the few lines of it that have been preserved:

> He rode the circuit, chain'd great towns and farms
> To good behavior; and by well marked stations,
> He fixed their bounds for many generations.
> His art ne'er fail'd him, though the loadstone failed,
> When oft by mines and streams it was assailed . . . .

A broadside elegy on his other well-known uncle, Thomas Danforth, has very recently come to light; it is one of his best.

Among his elegies on worthy matrons, Elizabeth Hutchinson, Maria Mather, Susanna Thacher, and Hannah Sewall, the last is perhaps the best known. Some of its most interesting lines describe her father, the mintmaster John Hull, and his prosperous, pious career:

> The Hull, soon Built upon, became an Argo;
> Deep fraighted with Terrene & Heav'nly Cargo:
> Immortal Vertue gave Immortal Name;
> Long Life, Power, Honour, Added to His Fame.
> Stretching his Course, Refresh'd with Prosperous Gales,
> Quitting New-England's Coasts, to Heav'n He Sails.

The passages on the daughter contain a good portrayal of a charming, graceful, serene, wise, and lovable personality, though the lines addressed to her bereaved husband, Samuel Sewall, are far less successful.

His elegy on Elizabeth Foxcroft also takes the biographical approach, telling of her parents, birth, baptism, regeneration, education, marriage, virtues, children, and all too early death. Again the middle portion descriptive of her character is the best. The elegy on Joseph Belcher of Dedham is well sustained throughout, though likewise not on a high level; there are a few strong characterizing passages such as this:

> A friend unto New England's first-best-ways;
> To th'constitution that the Scripture lays.

Danforth's last elegy, 1727, a double one on the death of his brother Samuel and his friend Peter Thacher, is one of his most vigorous and interesting. Their deaths followed closely upon one another, a few weeks after an earthquake, and after the news of the death of King George I had reached America. All this adds liveliness to the introduction, as well as background to his feeling that a period is now ending:

> The Council-Board, the Bench, the sacred Desk
> Long shone with Heroes, who are now at Rest.

The poem outlines the course of the two pastors' lives and characters which were so similar in their general usefulness and beneficence. Their pastoral work engaged both of them far beyond the demands of duty; both learned to preach to the Indians in their own language. One added to his usefulness in his community by his knowledge of medicine, the other by his knowledge of civil law; "They left a sacred Stamp where'er they trod."

> For Foresight, and good Forecast, few their Match;
> Were ever on their Guard, and on the Watch.
> Both Men and Things they studied well and knew;
> Their Bow they seldom at Adventure drew.
> In Councils frequent and in Travels oft,
> Success (like joyful Streamers) seen aloft.

One further little poem of Danforth's remains to be noted, "The Mercies Of the Year, Commemorated: A Song for Little Children in New-England. December 13th 1720," a charming poem, filled with the realized hopes and averted fears of New England: the government preserved, the Indians at peace, the contagion stopped, the pulpits well filled and new churches gathered, and a further respite given to sinner, the crops fair.

> Tho' ripening Heat came late, yet Frost held off,
> We Reap the Harvest, and have Bread enough.
> Provision's dear, Goods high, Bills low, Cash none;
> And yet the Suffering Tribe is not Undone.

Including these New Year's verses there are eleven of Danforth's broadsides which have survived, together with nine other poems of his in contemporaneous publications, just about a record for a period from which so much verse has been lost or is known only through later copies. Danforth was a faithful, pedestrian versifier who could be relied on to produce a good copy of verses whenever the occasion demanded it. The poems were always done with integrity and good taste, and though they often lacked spirit, there was generally a compensating fine passage or two. Blake, the Dorchester annalist, gives a good summation: "He was exceeding Charitable, & of a very peacefull temper. He took much pains to Eternize the Names of many of the good Christians of his own Flock; And yet the World is so ungratefull, that he has not a Line Written to preserve his memory."

Two of the ablest writers of this age group, Richard Henchman and Benjamin Lynde, are known for only a few of their productions. Henchman's splendid ode on the theme of Sewall's New Year's poem has already been mentioned. He also made an excellent translation of Nehemiah Hobart's Latin verses sent to Sewall "our Israel's Judge and Singer Sweet." In his letter to Sewall enclosing the translation he added some humorous doggerel on Nantasket versus Mount Sion. Henchman's only other known poem was addressed to Lady Phips upon the receipt of a large gift of silver from her; with all its single virtues it is hardly up to the level of his other two poems. The connection with the Phips family must have been a close and cordial one, for Richard's young brother, Daniel, wrote the elegy on the death of Sir William Phips. It is not only an astounding performance for a lad of seventeen, it is actually one of the most brilliant poems by any of the younger generation. Its strange external history is briefly outlined in the bibliography.

Most of Benjamin Lynde's verse remains unknown. Sewall mentioned two broadsides of his of which no trace can be found, some of his other poems still remain unpublished in private hands, and only his lines descriptive of Tompson's Island are at present available. This is one of the most readable and enjoyable descriptive poems of the period, very much in the Horatian manner, and yet a perfect evocation of the New England landscape around Boston Harbor. Many New Englanders of the first century, no doubt, came to love and understand their new country very well, but only a very few were able to put into verse the magic of its particular natural charms. If Lynde's other poems are as fine as this, we can only hope that they will soon see the light of day.

It is only fitting that we conclude this age group with the verses of a lady, Sarah Kemble Knight. She was in the habit of writing small sets of verses when the spirit moved her; the few preserved rhymes of hers are to be found in the journal of her overland trip from Boston to New York and return, in 1704. Swamp Yankees in their miserable hovels, a genteel family that had gone queer, topers keeping her awake at an inn, and the moonlight coming up over a darksome woods, all furnish themes for her verse. Her description of the imaginative city which the rising moon conjures up out of the wooded landscape before her is a remarkable combination of Romanticism a century too soon and of echoes of old nursery rhymes and folk books out of the deep past:

> Here stood a Lofty church—there is a steeple,
> And there the Grand Parade—O see the people!
> That Famouse Castle there, were I but nigh,
> To see the mote and Bridg and walls so high.

Upon her return she scratched another brief poem on a window pane of the Knight mansion, the strangest kind of manuscript in our literary annals.

This concludes the last age group of seventeenth-century New England, but one even younger man remains, Benjamin Colman, who, born like young Daniel Henchman in the 1670's, began his literary career before the end of the century. He wrote some graceful social verse during his stay in England, and a few years after his return he wrote the culminating piece in the long tradition of elegiac verse, *A Poem on Elijahs Translation, Occasion'd by the Death of the Reverend and Learned Mr. Samuel Willard*, 1707. In content and purpose it is still traditional; many of the elegies on deceased pastors had used the image of Elijah's chariot ride to heaven, and the falling of his mantle on Elisha, and here Colman, following the precedent of Charles Morton and Richard Steere, retold a Bible narrative with modern implications. However, in verse technique and syntax the poem belongs to the new English school, with its perfect smoothness, regularity, and clarity. Later when the works of Alexander Pope began their course of conquest through the English literary world, Colman became a warm admirer of his, and under his inspiration wrote his last poem, "The Transport. To Mr. Pope, on looking again into his Essay on Man." It is dated "Febr. 14. 1739. America."

With Colman's age group and those that follow we enter into a different literary atmosphere. The old tradition did of course live on, at a submerged level, but its remaining champions did not carry it beyond 1730. The last decade or two had already become alien times for the survivors who saw a new and temporarily dominant poetic art rising round about them.

A Selection of Newly Discovered Verse

Most ot the poems included are from previously unpublished manuscripts; the rest are from broadsides preserved only in manuscript copies. From lack of space more than two thirds of the material intended for this anthology had to be omitted. Philip Walker's "Captan Perse and his coragios Company" will be published separately in a later number of the *Proceedings.* The poems of the younger Peter Bulkeley of Fairfield, Connecticut, those of John James, John Danforth, and others will probably also be published later.

The necessary external information about these poems can be found below in the bibliography, a brief discussion and critical evaluation of them is included in the preceding survey. The introductory matter at the head of each poem offers whatever other background material and commentary seemed necessary. The original spelling, capitalization, and punctuation of the manuscripts have been retained, except that the typical manuscript abbreviations (superior letters, etc.) have been resolved according to the printing practice of those times.

115

Thomas Tillam

Both historically and literarily Tillam's poem upon the first sight of New England deserves to stand at the head of this anthology. 1638 was one of the great years of the migration. Winthrop in his diary for that year mentions that twenty ships came over during the summer with at least three thousand passengers, and also tells of the amazement in the English ports at the high religious idealism and enthusiasm, which finds such noble expression in this poem.

Uppon the first sight of New-England
June 29 1638

hayle holy-land wherin our holy lord
hath planted his most true and holy word
hayle happye people who have dispossest
your selves of friends, and meanes, to find some rest
for your poore wearied soules, opprest of late
for Jesus-sake, with Envye, spight, and hate
to yow that blessed promise truly's given
of sure reward, which you'l receve in heaven
methinks I heare the Lambe of God thus speake
Come my deare little flocke, who for my sake
have lefte your Country, dearest friends, and goods
and hazarded your lives o'th raginge floods
Posses this Country; free from all anoye
heare I'le bee with yow, heare yow shall Inioye
my sabbaths, sacraments, my minestrye
and ordinances in their puritye
but yet beware of Sathans wylye baites
hee lurkes amongs yow, Cunningly hee waites
to Catch yow from mee; live not then secure
but fight 'gainst sinne, and let your lives be pure
prepare to heare your sentence thus expressed
Come yee my servants of my father Blessed

Thomas Tillam

Charles Chauncy

While Charles Chauncy was still pastor in Scituate, the deaths of the great religious leader, Thomas Hooker, and of the great secular leader, John Winthrop, occurred within less than two years of each other. New England laments that she is now blind, bereft of her two guiding lights, the Moses and the Aaron, who brought her people to the promised land, the Zerubbabel and the Jesus (the High Priest Joshua) who brought them out of the Babylonian Captivity. Line seven derives from the first chapter of Ruth; lines nine and ten, inserted after the last couplet was written, add the Classical images of the repositories of evil: the box of Pandora, the Lernaean swamp, and the wooden horse. New England concludes with bitter irony that she can now truly be called independent, for there is nothing left on which her hope can depend. Young Isaac Chauncy, then seventeen, added a simple couplet.

Novae Angliae Lamentatio.

Heu! me nunc caecam, quis ducet filius orbam
luminibusque binis, quae mihi nuper erant.
Hookerum extinctum deflens Ecclesia vidit,
Winthropum Res nunc Publica lapsa videt.
Hic velut alter erat *Moses*, ille alter ut *Aaron*:
His *Zarubbabel*, *Jesus* ut ille fuit.
Non me *Naomi*, sed Nunc me dicite *Maram*,
nam dedit Omnipotens Pocula amara mihi.
Nam quae Pandorae Pixis, quae Lerna malorum;
quae nobis properat Durius alter Equus.
Verè independens iam nunc *Neo-Anglia* dicor,
non est spes Terris pendeat unde mea.

Charl. Chanc.

1649.

Abstulit una Dies, qualem nec multa tulerunt
secula, nec (vereor) secula multa dabunt.

Isaack Chanc.

JOHN WILSON I

Claudius Gilbert, pastor of Limerick, Ireland, was, like many another pastor during the Commonwealth, shocked and indignant when the first fanatic wave of Quakerism passed over him and his parish. In defense of the old religion he wrote *The Libertine School'd* (London, 1657), and sent a copy of the tract to his friend John Wilson. Wilson, himself a hammer of heresy, was delighted and wrote the following anagram and commendatory poem on the verso of the title page. Gilbert, Wilson, and other Puritans firmly believed that the Jesuits were behind the Quaker movement, using it to help spread chaos through the Protestant world.

Claudius Gilbert.
Anagram. Tis Braul I Cudgel.

[Tis Braul I Cudgel,] Ranters, Quakers Braul,
Divels, and Jesuites, Founders of them all.
Their Brauling Questions whosoever reades
may soone perceive, These are their proper heades.
What Better Cudgels, then Gods holy word,
(For Brauls so cursed,) and the Civil sword?
By God Ordained to suppresse such evils,
Which God Abhorreth as he doth the Devils.
Oh! Lett these blessed Cudgels knocke them downe.
Lett Sathan fall, that Christ may weare the Crowne.
Let Baal pleade for Baal; who are Christs,
Abhorr, oppose, Confound these Antichrists.
yea Lett the Lord confound them, who with spight
Against his Truth maliciously Fight.

I W.

John Fiske

The contrapunctual pattern of John Fiske's verse with its varied application has been discussed in the preceding survey. To the elegy on John Cotton he appended consolatory verses addressed to Cotton's widow and children and to his colleague John Wilson. This group is followed by shorter sets of verses, most of them addressed to friends and neighboring ministers, and by three elegies. The only one of the thematic anagrams which may require explanation is that of the last poem, on Anne Griffin, "In Fanne: Rig." The poem develops this double theme of the threshing fan of a Christian life which leaves the pure wheat of the saved soul, a cargo for the well-rigged, ever ready ship to transport at the appointed time to the destined port. On a first reading, certain passages in the poems may seem obscure; this is a natural accompaniment of Fiske's unusual poetic technique, and upon better acquaintance the seeming obscurities vanish. The several small Latin sections also offer some difficulties, for Fiske did not adhere strictly to classical usage, and at times even introduced a Mediaeval word such as "Conthoralis," meaning "wife."

Upon the much-to be lamented desease
of the Reverend Mr John Cotton
late Teacher to the church at Boston N. E.
who departed this Life 23 of 10. 52.

John { Cotton
Kotton after the old English writi'g

Anagr:
O, Honie knott

With Joy erst while, (when knotty doubts arose)
To Thee we calld, o Sir, the knott disclose:
But now o and alasse to thee to call
In vayne tis thou no Answer give or shall.
Could loud Shrickes, could crys recall thee back
From deaths estate we wold our eye ne're slack
O, this our greife it is, lament shall we
A Father in our Israel's cea'st to be
even hee that in the Church a pillar was
A gurdeon knot of sweetest graces as
He who set fast to Truths so clossly knitt

as loosen him could ne're the keenest witt
Hee who his Flesh together bound ful-fast
no knott more sure whilest his life did last
Hee who the knotts of Truth, of Mysteries
sacred, most cleerely did ope' fore our eyes
even hee who such a one, is ceas'd to bee
'twixt whose life, death, the most sweete harmony
Knotts we doe meet with many a cue daily
which crabbed anggry tough unpleasing bee
But we as in a honi-comb a knott
of Hony sweete, here had such sweetenes Gott
the knotts and knobbs that on the Trees doe grow
the bitterest excressences we know.

his soule Embalmd with grace
was fit to soare on high
and to receive its place
above the starry skie.
now grant O G[od that we]
may follow afte[r him]
surviving worlds ocean unto thee
our passage safe may swim.

A vine tree seene, a plant of Gods owne hand
In it this knott of sweetest parts did stand.
The knott in place sublime: most eminent
As, his, no Branch could challeng like extent
The knott sometimes seems a deformity
It's a mistake, tho such be light set by
The knott it is the Joynt, the strength of parts
the bodies-beauty, so this knott out-starts
What others in that place, they ought to bee
even such a knott exemplar'ly was hee
Knotts now adayes affrayd of are most men
of Hony if expose'd feare none would then
I guesse why knotty Learning downe does goe
'twould not, if as in him 'twere sweetned soe
Meeknes Humility forbearance too
this lovely knott to love the most did woe

In knotts what greate adoe to gayne the hearte
yee had it heere, he did it free impart
When knotty theames and paynes some meet with then
as knotty and uncouth their tongue and pen
so 'twas not heere, he caus'd us understand
and tast the sweetnes of the knott in hand.
When knotty querks and quiddities broacht were
by witt of man he sweetely Breathed there.
His charity his wisdom meeknes eke
left none that loved light, in knotts to seeke
Hee tho invincible thrô softnes did
the knottiest peeces calme and cleave amid
Such was hee of such use in these last dayes
Whose want bewayle, o, and alas alwaies
This knott so we have seen lien broknly
By knotts so breathlesse, so crookt, crackt, or fly
This knott thereof so surfetted we see
By hony surfetted we know som bee
The cause nor in the knott nor hony say
Thrô Temper bad, unskilfulnes this may
O knott of Hony most delightfull when
Thou livd'st, thi death a sad presage hath ben
Have Ben? yea is, and is, and is alas
For woe to us, so greate a Breach when was
Woe to that knotty pride hee ne're subdude
Woe they who doe his Truthes dispenct exclude
and woe to them that factions there contrive
woe them whose wayes unrighteous survive
Woe they that by him warning did not take
Woe to us all if mercy us forsake
A Mercy once New England thou hast had
(you Boston cheifly) in thi Cotton clad
Some 'gan to count't too meane a dresse and sought
Silk Velvetts Taffeties best could be bought
these last will soyle, if first doe soyle also
how can we think but Naked we shall goe
must silken witts, must velvet tongues be had
and shall playne preaching be accounted bad
I feare a famine, pinching times t'ensue

Time Such may have, slighted mercy to Rue
My wakened muse to rest, my moystned pen
mye eye, my hearte which powred out this have ben
cease try no more, for Hee hath gayn'd his prize
His heavenly mansion 'bove the starry skie
Returne thee home and wayle the evills there
Repent breake off thi sins Jehovah feare

O Jehovah feare: this will thi wisdom bee
And thou his waies of mercy yet maust see
Returne thou mee; And turned bie
Lord unto thee: even so shall I.

Jo: Fiske

* * *

In obitum Reverendissimi
Viri, eximae tum eruditionis tum pietatis
Domini Joannis Cottoni etc.
Joannes Cottonas
Anagr
Canon sis: Tot è uno?
Vitâ erat Exemplar, jam mortuus Ipse reliquit
Quot vix ex uno: Tot canonesque suos.
Englished

He a choyce paragon of his Time
(A burning shining Light)
His Life exemplar'ly did rsie
'bove many a Mortall wight
Thô death him seas'd yet hath he left
Canons so many heere
as scarce from any one to flow
doth yet to us appear.

J: F

* * *

Ad Matronam pientissimam spectatissimamque
Ipsius domini vixit Conthoralem dilectissimam
Sobolemque eique Charissimum.
John Cotton
1 Anagr
Thô onc', I not.
2 Anagr
I onc', thô not.

To 1st

Of me, Why doe you thus with dreary cryes
with sobbs, with Teares, with sighes with weeping eyes
Lament / your losse. In me / bewayle your lot?
Saying thô once I was; I now am not?
What I was once to you, and you, remind
You now will oft, and matter there youl' find
to aggravate that here, that breach is made
by Hand divine, with greife your selves to lade.

To 2d

But what thô I as now be not, who was
And what if I thus from you all doe passe
ner' to returne to this vayne world and state
that transitory is: mind it your Fate
And eeke remind that once I was, and blesse
that Hand that me you lent, yea and confesse
your portion greate that his rich grace in Mee
enricheth you, abids, tho cea'st I bee.

J: F

* * *

Reverendo viro Domino Joanni Wilsono
Ecclesiae Bostoniensis pastori fidelissimo
Fratri ac Amico plurimum observando
John Wilson
Anagr.
W'on Sion-hil.

When Jah so rare a Gem pleas'd to distrayne
as once thee Gave, what priviledge remaine?
That Blessed pearle enjoy'd w'on Sion-hil
Him thô translated hence, yet heere we still:

What doe we heere when such a one is gone!
What? heere's that Lamb, who may suffice alone
As then that presence of rich grace we had
He graunt it now, a double blessing adde.

Tuus συνκοινωνοπενθής
Tibique addictissimus

Wenh. 7. of 11th
52

Jo: Fiscus

* * *

Thomas Parkerus
Anagr.
Charus es, promat.

Omnibus es charus quibuscum vivere gaudes:
Demissus neci, gemitus de pectore promant.

* * *

Upon the decease of the Reverend
Mr Tho: Hooker &c
Thomas Hooker
Anagr.
A Rest; oh com'! oh

A Rest's at hand after thy weary dayes
After thy Tossings heere in wildernes:

A rest is it? oh com'! oh, no delayes
let bee! of this life end the wretchednes.

* * *

To his very good freind mr Snelling
phisitian
William Snelling
Anagr
All mine will sing

To sing some scruple much wishing the guise
Abolisht out th' assemblies now adayes
But I shall care, and hope to ground likewise
My charge so as All mine will sing, alwaies

Margaret Snelling
Anagr
In't rar' Angells—Gem.

William } Snelling
Margaret }

Anagr
Grant mee all: Sr, I am willing
al.
Sr, Grant mee all: I am willing

* * *

In obitum viri tum pietatis tum integritatis probate,
simul et senio confecti, et fidelitate tecti,
Domini Samuelis Sharpij
in Ecclesia Salemensi nuper inspectoris.
Carmen funebre.

Samuel Sharpias
Anagr.
pura samis; selah.

Impurum, quicquid Mundus desiderat Ipse
Tu Samuel Sharpi, sumere pura velis
Sumere pura velis, vixisti vivere puris
puris et vivis; summaque pura capis.
Selah.

Englished

The filthy Elfe, like to it selfe, in scorne what's pure hav[.....]
And more impure, ought to be sure, the more it straightly cra[ve....]
But thou whilest heere, didst choose what ere, of purity did tast
With purest thou, doest Live even now: and thy desire hast
The Just attend,
peace, is his end.
J F:

Upon the departure
of
the worthy aged useful servant of god Mr Sa: sharp
late ruling-Elder to the Church at Salem.
deceased the 72. y. of his age.
when he had borne office 26. yeeres in the church
upon the 3d. of 3d. mo. 1655.
Samuel Sharpe
Anagr.
Us! Ample-share.

Us) saies, whose is the losse: The Gayner Hee
Whom changd for ample-share of Blisse you see
Alias
Whil'st we Thee mind, Deere Sharpe, whose presence sweete
Erstwhile did us refresh, whose watchfull eye
holpe to prevent exorbitances greate
and to relax them [that] in snare did Lye

O us! our Losse! our Losse! how sad it is
this breach in fam'ly greate, in church, in Towne
who each bereft as of a Father Now
are forc't to wayle our heavenly-Fathers frowne

oh! who shall us! us! comfort, hope, helpe, give?
who shew shall what hath us of him depriv'd?
where may supply? how may the worke be done?
our safety peace, tell us, which way contriv'd

Looke here seeke there, sorrow doth us beset
us, God corrects in this a stroke so greate
our sin the cause, no cause we should forget
Mercy alone tis that we need entreate

The Losse is ours who survive, and who
unto this Brother did erst'while relate
The losse not his, of all whose toylesome care
and weary-warefare and his pilgrime state

Of all whose Teares, conflicts, and watchfull paynes
Suffering for christ, hard measure heere below

wants, weaknesses, Temptations, and what else
done, borne by him, or what he did bestow

What counsells, prayers, comforts, or reproofes
what censures, Tryalls, faithfulnes in these,
what diligence, what travel, meeknes, Zeale
He now of all, reapes the reward in blesse.

An Ample share he had indeed i'th' first
whilest heere he liv'd, and served all his dayes;
And in a good old age (with patience firme
his station kept) departs, no longer staies

An Ample-share in the Reward he has
which layd up is in Heaven, therefore none should
his Losse Lament; A Gayner Hee, and then
not greive, but Joy on his behalfe Love would

Love leave thy fruits, Love speake and act thy kind
to those of His which may him soonest want
Eye those Relicts which hee hath left behind
find they an Ample share in it, not scant:

The larger share they find in that they Love
the larger testimony thou shalt give
of thy Repentance for the Sin that strove
Thee, Thee of such a blessing to deprive

So much the more as thou a comfort art
the widdow orphane by such fruits unto:
so much the more Ample a share thou shalt
of blessing reape, even thou when hence thou goe.

J F.

* * *

Ezechiel Rogersius

Anagr

Reus zeli, hoc eriges.

Erigis ipse Reus zeli quodcunque conaris
In zelo, fertor, quisque reatus inest.

Upon the decease of the Reverend Learned
and faithful servant of Christ Mr Nathaniel Rogers
late pastor to the Church at Ipsw. in N. E.
interred the 5th of 5. 55°.

Nathaniel Rogers
anagr.
He in a larg Rest.
No.

Hark what saies Gods decree of Him deceast
that (He in a larg Rest) be henceforth plac't.
Yet see we not Mans will to crosse't is prest
And with a (No) resisting it's disgrac't

Alias

The Dove no Rest which found in all the earth
yet in the Arke her Rest she had: so This
our Brother Deere in this world Rest none found
His Dove-like spirit in its Arke now is.

The Sabbath is a Day of Rest all know
How many Sabbaths did He heere enjoy
The feeling-sweets of that Sabbath I trow
which now to him a Rest most sweet is aye

This weary pilgrime glad of shady-Tree
(Under the which heere oft a Rest he made
That Tree of Life, his Right, his food, his Cure
still heere.) now Rests for aye under its shade.

In this worlds wildernes no Rest He found
But heavenly Canaans Rest his hope it was
His weary Travells now dispatcht hath He
and by our Josua that Rest He has.

Who will; who dare to say, He none of them
for whom prepared was that Rest of old
did not his Faith, His piety declare
to Him it appertayn'd, even manifold.

When Death arests: the Godly rest in dust
even then In grave there Flesh shall Rest in Hope
There Soule to Rest in Abrams bosome must
Death unto Him this dore of Rest doth ope.'

The wicked all there Rest have heere below
No Rest for them when hence they goe: but Now
Even Each the Lords (when these there vengeance have)
after there Troubles heere; sweet Rest shall know.

God hath decreed a Rest, a large Rest, to
such as are His, for whom procured tis
By Christ, whom thereto fills his Spirits worke.
All this in Him: therefore in Rest He is

He sought this rest, whilest heere, exemplarly,
He instrumentally many thereto
hath brought by His incessant labours heere
and therefore He in Rest himselfe also.

If such, as to this Rest many shall turne,
shall shine as starrs in Firmament most bright!
then He is now in Rest, yea His excells
if so in it degrees allow we might

yee His Relates therefore o're Him that mourne
with quietnes and cheerefulnes submitt
wrong Him you should if you your (No) could have
Mind Gods decree, strive not to undoe it.

Mourne over your selves, your Losse looke to make up
in Him who full supplies hath yet in store
B'take ye to Him in faith and holines
And you will never leave forevermore

Willing He would have ben for your sakes
heere to have stayd, your perfect rest to build
God it accepts from Him, His will it is
He should no longer from his Rest be heild

If our Losse and suffering tis; as tis
a most sad stroke to us of Gods keene hand
a providence awakening, a just squorge
a Losse irreparable as things stand

It tis even so, yet mark a Fathers hand
Our good Hee seekes, our Rest this way ith' end
Hee would promoote, and off our sinfull Rests
Hee us would take, and mercy Hee entend

Our Sins they are that then Him hastned hence
such sins as which His Restles-Labours all,
His prayers, Teares, sighes, grones, nor Councells grave
nor ought He did, could to Amendment call

Such Sins as which of Rest would us bereave
Such as from us like Blessings may withhold
Such Sins as whereto we in Rest did cleave
Such as This stroke alone may shake the hold

If God place Him in Rest, Restlesse that we
become a while, till's Favour we Regayne
A Happy losse it may so prove and bee
which else a sad presage of woe, and payne

Thy (No) into a yea, turne silently
thy sorrowe turne thy sin upon; and say
What of this crosse improvment make should I
that be with Him once in that Rest I may

Once in that Rest I may, if follow Him
in that way He hath taught and walkt long while
'mongst us: if led by the same Spirit I bee
and watchfull be against satans-each wile

Sure Time it is Each should think of there Rest:
Tis God that it provids, for it prepares
Hee tenders it, prepar'd for it that we
And yet to give a (No) by sin, who feares?

Is't good Him to Resist? will this bring Rest?
or shall all Men find Rest i'th' end, I trow
not so, nor so, as this our Freind deceast
in His Life time still strove to make us know

The way of Rest but One, this way He found
this way He preach't, by Christ, by Grace alone
by such a holy Righteous Life as Hee
hath led the way, and now to Rest is gone

Mind we the name of this our Dearest Freind
Mind we the Truth He taught Evinceingly
Mind what Experiences He had: and Now
That Onely way of all true Rest doe Try.

J F

Upon the decease of Mris Anne Griffin
(the wife of Mr Richard Griffin late Ruling Elder
to the Church in Concord) departing this life
upon 23 of 10. 55 being about 96 yeers of Age
Anne Griffin
Anagr
In Fanne: Rig.

Canst thinke the Cargoe wherewith ship is fraught
pure wheate should bee, and shee unrig'd? And why
should't once be thought, the Soule which Grace hath caught,
and stor'd its ship therewith, unrig'd should Lye.

Whil'st wheate in Fanne, the ship in Rigging is
the Tackling fitt and fastned to there use
When Season is, that it set forth, amisse
that nought there bee, to gayne the haven it chuse

Like to the wheate, Thy wheate appeare that't may
as twere in Fanne; thou now at last hast ben
Even such a Fanne, none like to it they say
Thou knew'st before; in yeeres nigh ten times ten

O're all Thy changes Chelmesford Granary
must be where Fanne caus'd Thee Repose to have
Yet still the Fanne, thy portion there doth Lye
Thy seas nor calme, tho Thou heere Rest didst crave

Yea that thy ship, (wherein thy soule Imbarkt)
had heere as in a hoped safe Port, cast
Her Anchor, found fresh feares in eares were har[kt]
Heere no abode, up, Rig, to flight make hast.

Time calls, be Gone, hoyse yards, out, get the home
longer abroad tis not for Thee to bee
Deathes Summons tells thee when wilbe Thy Dome
and Thou an End of weary dayes shalt see.

See! now Thou seest, Thou feels't, Thou find'st thy Re[st]
the sweetest Rest, the surest Anchorage
in such a haven, in Earth as not exprest
where Rockes endanger not nor Billowes Rage

We who surevive, hence double duty ken
Her change, her Gayne to Count: her blest to Judg[e]
We must the Fanning heere expect till done
Hye Time, when once in Fanne, thinke hence to Trudg[e]

When once Afflictions doe thee seaze, thinke then
Death will ere long approach, to thy long home
Thee hence to fetch: to Rest prepar'd who ben
who Tyrant-like to unprepared come.

J F.

But more, in Fanne of tryalls seest a saint
Yea one whose aged yeers the Deeps might know
think't time for us to Rig, for us acquaint
will God with Tryalls such, And lay us Low

Yea lay us Low, and humble us Hee will
or first or Last ere that he us will rayse
and follow us with waves and billowes still
Ere that for aye him we in Glory prayse.

J F.

What thou heere soughtst pray'd for, hop'd for, desir'd
which heere is not our portion to Enjoy
that there Thou hast more fully then requir'd
or understood could bee whilst sin annoy

Anthony Somerby

Only a few selections from Somerby's rhymed synopsis of the Holy Bible are printed here, from Genesis and from the Book of Ruth. Somerby's frequent use of the alliterative technique has been discussed above.

The Holy Bible in Verse

Genesis

At first Jehovah with his word
did make heaven earth and light
the firmament the moone and stars
the glistering sun so bright
By him the earth was fruitful made
and every creature good
he maketh man like to himselfe
and doth appoint his food
Creation ended god then rests
and sabboth day ordaines
plants eden and the fruite forbids
for feare of endles paines
Dust of the ground was man made of
of rib out of his side
the woman: adam nameth all
wedlocke is sanctifide
Eve by the serpent is deceived
they fall most shamefully
god them arraignes, doth serpent curse
and putteth enmity
foule serpent twixt and womans seed
mans punishments set downe
their first cloathing, thir casting out
the lord at them did frowne
Given are to Adam here two sons
Abell by name and Cain
their trade and their religion see
and godly abell slaine
Here cain is curst first citty built
two wives dot[h] lamech take
here seth and henoch both were borne
to god men prayers make

In his likenes male and female
god did at first create
then adam in his owne liknes
his third son seth begate
Know here the pedigree age and deth
of patriarchs related
from Adam to the dayes of noe
how henoch was translated
Lo maryages for beauty made
which doth gods wrath procure
and fearfull flod to drowne the world
but noa is safe and sure
Marke all the order of the arke
the fashion and the frame
all that the lord did bid him doe
Just noe performed the same
Noe with his family: and paires
repaire into the arke
the floods, do flow, god shuts them in
o then his judgments marke
Observe how waters do asswage
on arrarat rests the arke
the dove and ravens sending forth
and noes outgoing marke
Preparing then an alter he
doth praise and god adore
god doth accept his sacrifice
will curse the earth no more
Quite fred from feare god blesseth noe
mans feares the[n] meats the bow
which signifyes gods covenant
by noa the world doth grow
Read how noe doth a vineyard plant
in tent he drunken lyes
he curseth cham, for Japhet prayes
he blesseth shem and dyes
Se here of noe and of his sons
the mighty generations
nimrod first monarke he begins
dividing of the nations

The world one languag had at first
    confusion babell rent
    marke shem and terahs progeny
    to haran terah went
Up abram and thy country leave
    I will preserve thy life
    dearth makes him fly feare maks him faine
    and say shees not my wife
A plague on pharo and his house
    the lord did send that day
    for abrams wife: the king reproves
    but sends all safe away
Both lot and he richly returne
    but discord parts them both
    lots lot is sinfull sodoms sinks
    to heaven abram goeth
Conquered are five kings by foure
    abraham rescues lot
    melchisedeck receiveth title
    spoyles abram taketh not
Devine blessings are promised
    which he beleves most true
    but first his seeds must servants be
    and then their foe subdue
Even by his faith hees Justified
    god promiseth againe
    and by a signe confirmes the land
    wherin he shold remaine
For Issue Sara gives her maide
    She Sara doth disdaine
    afflicted then she runs away
    is bid returne againe
Greiveing full sore the angell chers
    saith shees conceived with child
    who must be called Ismaell
    a feirce man and a wilde
Here god renewes thir covenant
    their names are changed they blest
    abraham here is circumcised
    with Ismaell and the rest

In loveing sort good abraham
three angels entertaines
at gods strang promiss Sara laughs
and is checkd for her paines
Knowing that abraham his wold teach
the lord doth here declare
the fall of sodom abram prayes
for ten Just men to spare
Lot doth two angels entertaine
the sodomits struck blind
lots sons do mocke he Zoar craves
wher he doth safty find
Make hast saith th angell save thy life
marke sodoms fiery slaughters
lots wife a pillar of salt is made
he drunke defiles his daughters
Now abraham denyes his wife
shee taken by the king
the lord reproves him in a dream
[and] Sara for that same thing
Of him both man and wifes reproved
he Sara doth restore
the king then and his house are heald
when abraham prayed therefore
Passing great joy good Sara hath
for Isaac newly borne
he is circumcised, wild Ismaell
at him doth scoffe and scorne
Quite out of doore hagar and hee
are cast and sit forlorne
twixt abraham and abimelech
a league of peace is sworne
Read here how abraham tempted is
his Isac deare to kill
his faith and how he ready is
to execute gods will
Stayd is his hand by gods angell
the ram for him is slaine
the place is named; marke nahors race
and abraham blest againe

The mournings marke which abram makes
for death of Sara old
machpelah bought to bury in
which Ephron to him sold
Unt' Abraham here his servant swears
he prayes a signe doth crave
rebecca meets fulfils the signe
and Jewels doth receive
And when she shews her kindred dear
she home doth him invite
hees entertained he blesseth god
and message doth recite
Both laban then and bethuell
his message well approves
rebecca gives consent to goe
Isaac her meets and loves
Children are borne to abraham
is goods devided bee
his age his death his buriall
and Ismaels petigree
Declared is his age and death
rebecca barren lives
but Isaac prayes and she conceives
two children in her strives
Esau and Jacob being borne
their difference moses tels
the birthright Esau to Jacob
for meat prophanely sels
Forced by a famine Isaac is
to gerar for to goe
his wife he to the king denyes
hees blamed for doing so
God both instructs and blesseth him
in wealth he growes and thrives
he digeth wels: the king compacts
observe here Esaus wives
He sends his son for venison
by mother Jacobs taught
and of his father then is blest
while Esau ven'son sought

Isaac doth feare and tremble much
when esau venson brings
too late yet by his earnestnes
hees blest with earthly things
Kindled full sore is esaus wrath
against his brother deare
his mother disappoints his rage
and bids him fly for feare
Lo Isac blesseth Jacob first
and sends him then away
to padan aram for a wife
with laban their to stay
Marke esaus wife and Jacobs ladder
he stone of bethell takes
and sets it up annoints with oyle
a vow to god he makes
Now Jacob comes to harans well
doth Rahell kisse and weepe
laban doth entertaine him well
hees set to keep his sheepe
Of him for seaven years service hee
for wife doth rahell crave
but laban full deceitfully
in her stead leah gave
Patiently for rahell he
againe will seaven years serve
shees barren but leah conceives
foure patriarchs observe
Quite out of hart for barrennesse
here rahell gives her mayde
so leah who her husband buyes
good Jacob here is stayd
Rahell conceives and Joseph bears
Jacob would bee released
by pollicy of Jacobs rods
his flocks are much increased
Secretly and upon mislike
the lord commanding so
Jacob departing with his wives
doth from that country goe

Then rahell steales her fathers gods
her father follows after
complaineing of the wrong sustained
both by his son and daughter
Upon the Idols rahell sits
therby the same to hide
Jacob complaines they covenant both
in freindship to abide
At mach'min Jacob angels sees
to esau he doth send
whom he doth feare: he prayes to god
that he would him defend
By servants he a present sends
by prayer he assaults
and with an angell wrastleth
prevailes and after haults
Coming together both do kisse
weepe, esaw gifts do take
doth use him kindly home returnes
and doth kind offers make
Departing he to succoth comes
at shalem buyes a feild
of hamors children where he doth
to god an alter build
Entiseing shechem doth defloure
good Jacobs gading daughter
they yeld to circumsicion
then comes a fearfull slaughter
For simeon and levi both
when people where full sore
doe kill them all their citty spoyle
and Jacob greives therfore
God sendeth Jacob to bethell
his house he purifyes
from Idols all an alter builds
and then nurse deb'ra dyes
Hees blest of god called Israell
in travell rahell dyes
the sons of Jacob, Isaacs death
ruben with bilhah lyes

Into the country from Jacob
esaw to goe intends
with wives and sons: mules are first found
what dukes from him desends
Kind Joseph deadly hated is
for two dreames which he had
and for complaints of brothers made
they were exceding mad
Let us this dreamer slay say they
when father had him sent
to visit them: to murder him
they all save, reuben meant
Maliciously to Ismaelits
they then good Joseph sell
potipher buyes him; bloody coate
sore greives old Israell
Now Juda doth three sons beget
called shela, onan, er
observe here onans filthy fact
er taks to wif thamar
Of Juda she conceives two sons
Zara and phares by name
he wisht her burnt; she sends her pledg
he cleares her to his shame
Potipher Joseph doth advance
his mistris tempts to sinne
he flat denyes, she falsly lyes
and shameles doth begin
Quite voyde of grace him to accuse
that she her selfe might clear
she is beleved he cast in ward
but god is with him there
Read how the butler and baker
By pharo: imprisoned are
how Joseph hath the charge of them
how dreames expounded were
Sad butler be not trobled
thou hapy man shalbee
have me in mind: o baker marke
the gallowes grones for thee

Thus were ther dreames interpreted
and thus they came to passe
the butler Joseph quite forgate
and most unthankfull was
Unto the king was Joseph brought
his fearfull dreames to tell
the butler had him told that hee
therin did farre exell.
All wisards faileing in their skill
them Joseph doth expound
and gives the king most grave advice
and counsell wise and sound.
By pharo: Joseph is advanced
two sons begetteth he
mannasseh and ephraim by name
great dearth begins to be
Corne for to buy in egipt land
his ten sons Jacob sent
for spyes they were imprisoned
and by their brother shent
Do this sayth Joseph and you shall
at liberty be set
your brother Ben: you told me of
go all save one and fet
Even then they have remorse [in this]
and say one to another
god plagues us justly for our sin
in selling of our brother
For pledge is Simeon kept in ward
with corne they home do goe
tell all to Jacob who will stay
his Ben: he loves him so
Go buy some food, good Jacob saith
the sons they durst not goe
except he would send benjamin
for Joseph charged so
He very loath yet sends his son
they presents bring to'th'court
Joseph confers his brother cals
and feasts in wondrous sort

Joseph to stay his brethren five
comands that coyne with corne
shold both in their sacks mouth be put
with them backe to be borne
Know that in sacke of yongest son
was Josephs cup convayd
which found, they feare their fathers pledg:
for Ben: wold now be stayd
Loe now doth Joseph make himselfe
knowne to his brethren deare
them comforts in gods providence
and bids them not to feare
My father Jacob fetch quoth he
and bid him come to me
for him and his I will provide
in goshen dwell shall he
Now when the king of this did heare
he is full well content
and bids all needfull furniture
for Journy shold be sent
Oh how they kis and weepe for Joy
he bids them all agree
when Jacob heares this joyfull news
a joyfull man is hee
Passing great comfort from the lord
he at beersheba finds
thence he and his to egipt goe
with all things to their minds
Quietly all this number goe
Joseph doth Jacob meet
[and] tels his brethren what to say
when Pharo shall them greete
Reporting that his freinds were come
five brethren he presents
with his father before the king
who gives them their contents
See here how Joseph gets the coyne
the cattell and the land
all that the egiptians did possese
into king pharos hand

The preists land was not bought nor sold
old Jacobs age is here
to bury him with forefathers
he maketh Joseph sweare
Unto his father being sicke
he comes and sons doth bring
old Jacob lifteth up himself
to give them his blessing
Allmighty god appeard quoth he
to me in canan land
and sayd I will the multiply
and make thy seed as sand
Behold manasa and ephraim
as his owne sons he takes
of mothers grave of their returns
old Jacob mention makes
Calling his sons in blessing them
he doth particularize
he chargeth were to bury him
and then forthwith he dyes
Death haveing Jacobs dayes dissolvd
here read good Josephs praise
who weepes and bids he shold be balmd
the mourne full forty dayes
Exceeding willing pharo is
that Josephs house shold go
to bury Jacob as he sware
with many elders moe
Forgiveness Josephs brethren crave
he grants them their request
he will maintaine both them and theirs
in quiet peace and rest
Great age he lived and of his sons
he saw three generations
he makes them sweare his bones to bear
and foretells their translations

Ruth

A famine drove Elimelech
his native country fro
his wife naomi; and his two sons
doth likwise with him go
Bethlem Juda they went from
in moab led their lives
the father dyed, the sons then tooke
two moabits for wives
Chilion and mahlon were their names
who haveing wedlocke tride
they did not long injoy the same
but shortly after dyed
Daughters in law by naomi
were wild at any hand
that they shold not turne home with her
but stay in moab land
Exceeding constant good ruth is
and cleaves with all her hart
to naomi; orpha forsakes
and did from them departe
Full gladly are they both received
when they to bethlem came
the bethlemits rejoyced in her
she was of such good fame
Gracious ruth gleanes barly store
in Boaz barly feilds
he taketh knowledge of her then
and grace and favor yelds
He bad her gleane with his maidens
and at meale times to eate
she caryed store of barly home
for hers and mothers meate
Instructed first by naomi
she lyes at boaz feete
her kinsman he doth say he is
and doth her well intreat
Kindly six measures of barly
he gave to her that day

she brought it home to naomi
and told what he did say
Lo boaz then next kinsman cals
into the judgment place
to him before the elders grave
he doth relate the case
Makeing an offer unto him
which he doth flat refuse
he buyes the land takes ruth to wife
and kindly doth her use
Note that of her was obed borne
Jesse his father deare
who to king david father was
read phares ofspring here

Thomas Hinckley

The Reverend Thomas Walley (1618–1679) was a victim of the second great persecution of non-conformists in England, beginning in 1662. He came over the following year and was very soon ordained minister of Barnstable, a town racked with schism and dissention ever since its last settled minister, John Lothrop, had died ten years previously. Such was the persuasive charm of Walley's personality that the bitter, spreading quarrels of a decade were allayed in a short time, and he was loved and blessed of all in the town, except, as Hinckley indicates, the Quakers. Governor Thomas Hinckley was Walley's most prominent parishoner, and here wrote a noble tribute to his pastor. His quotation from Urian Oakes' elegy on the younger Thomas Shepard comes from the second stanza.

Mr. Thomas Walley, The Reverend
Pastor of the Church of Christ at Barnstable
Who on the Lords day, being the 14 of March
1677/8. He Died entring into 62 year of his age.

The Lord who holds the starrs in 's own right hand,
Did send one shining bright into our Land
From 's pleasant country, friends and People dear,
To follow him, he knewn't for what, nor where,
Who steer'd his course so steadily of 's grace,
At his own cost, unto this worthless place,
Wheir not's own gain, but trouble did expect,
Yet nought mov'd him his Lords work to neglect.
Was WALLEY sent to the, O Barnestable!
When thy condition was most miserable;
Through thy Divisions hadst lost all thy glory,
And of thy wounds went: lamentable story,
Like gangrene that infected other parts
Of th' Colony to th' grief of many hearts.
Spreading into our Churches, Courts and Towns
The pois'nous influence of those fretting wounds:
And though thou hadst Physitians farr and near,
Yet left uncur'd and froward didst appear,
Even then did God his soveraign grace extend
When thou unwilling seemdst thy cure t attend;

And his Own of a thousand to thee brought
Before he was by most of the out sought;
And ere thou wast aware he got within
The heart of one and all for thee to win:
And God by him hath hear created peace,
And made those ten years alterc[a]tions cease
Which threatned ruine to more then this place,
But for the Lords all healing matchless grace.
God's work alone; for who but he could bend
And bow our distant Spirits to attend,
To close in love and unity at last,
And in the same these fourteen years knit fast?
Rich Grace! O then let's bless his holy name
That ever blessed Walley hither came.
We thought at first 'twas but a pleasant dream,
So great a good for us God did not mean,
To fill our hearts with laughter and a song
With others who for such a day did long:
Though Quakers mad, did 'gainst it rage and tear,
Yet Syons friends rejoyc'd both far and near;
No wonder then that now we hear sighs, groans,
Deep lamentations, cryes and dolefull moanes:
Wally, that man of matchless worth is Dead;
Our Crown, Alas! is fallen from our head:
The Glory of our Colony is gone,
O Barnstable thou art almost undone.
When such choice ones are call'd away from us,
God makes way for his hot displeasure thus.
The Charets and Horsemen of our Israel
He was, eke Father; where's his Parallel
For Wisdome, love, and friendly Courtesie,
Quick sight, sound Judgment with rare piety?
Pleasant and fruitful was his Company,
Large heart and hand, cloath'd with humility:
He fitted was with meekness for to bear
Our ill manners in th' day we froward were.
In 's Conversation was right amiable,
Ready in doing good as he was able.
In giving Counsell he was eminent;

Mens cases to resolve thato him went.
Fit to converse with men of high degree:
Converse with weak and low, yet shun'd not he.
He zealous was Gods great truths to maintain;
In less things could more lenity retain,
Truth, Peace and Order he still did pursue
Unto the last, as I can tell and you.
He had a powerfull searching Ministry,
A pattern was his life exemplary.
His care of's flock, and kids thereof was great,
In health and sickness he with them would treat.
His memory shall blessed be; his name,
Wally Peace-maker, to 's immortal fame.
Ah poor Deceived Quakers, who rejoyce
At Death of him and such as he whose voice,
In witnessing Christs truth, was your torment;
Blind Souls, with out true chang, You shall lament,
And never come into that place of joy,
Where he abides for ever and for ay.
His peace with God on 's death-bed he did see
Through Christ, and rests where true Peace-makers be.
Its no hiperbole for me to tell
In all new-England scarce his parallel.
As learnd Oakes of Shepard dear did say,
So of our Walley great and good I may;
"Here is a Subject for the loftiest verse
"That ever waited on the bravest Hearse.
His work is done, he's calld for to be Crown'd,
Whilst we'r left combating upon the ground
Bereaved of his help, who in dark day,
Did strengthen, lead and guide us in Gods way.
O Barnstable, who was renown'd of late,
Alas! now sit'st as Widow desolate:
Thy barrenness and sins, are cause of this,
Its time for thee them wholly to dismiss
With greatest hatred, and them not to save
Which brought thy Pastor dear, down to his grave
And thy most pleasant things out of thy Sight,
Because of them thou hadst esteem too light.

O Sions friends, Some pitty on us take,
And cry to God our great loss up to make
In such a guide as Walley good and wise;
Such gift of grace would greatly us Suffice,
And stop such breach, as did us soon befall,
After that bright light Lothrops Funeral.

Thomas Wall'y Anagram. O Whats my all.

O Whats my all but Christ alone,
Who is the all-Sufficient one,
Who to the uttermost can save
All that affiance in him have.
Let's Wally mind, and 's faith attend
Likewise his Conversations end.
Christ Jesus the same yesterday,
To day for ever and for aye.
As on his Death Bed he did find,
When his life past he call'd to mind,
Full forty years in th' Ministry,
Labring with 's hearts integrity;
Yet said no man did ever see
More need of Christ then now did he:
Let Christ, his all; be thine and mine:
Us, and all ours, let us resign
Into his saving hand then we
Shall sure and safe preserved be,
And shall have such supplys as he
Best mercyes for us now doth see.
Thomas Walley, alls well with thee;
But ill with me its like to be.
In the loss of such a friend a Father
And help alas! where's such another
God's will is done my loss they gain;
Which doth or may asswage my pain. T Hinkly

John Wilson II

This poem of the younger John Wilson is a simple, charming little bit of Puritan domesticity. The father, after a long and exhausting Sunday in the Medfield pulpit, sat down in the evening to write a letter in verse to his daughter Elizabeth, whose broken shoulder bone had been set. She must have been in Boston with her relatives at the time, and not with her husband, John Welde III, in Dunstable, for her father included greetings to Cousin Edward Rawson (the well known secretary of the colony), to Cousin Anne Page, to his sister Mary and her husband Joseph Rock (Mary's first husband had been the poet Samuel Danforth I). The poem probably dates from about 1685 or 86, since "little pretty Jo" is probably her infant son John who lived less than a year and a half.

A poeticall Epistle sent from my Father Wilson to my wife
after her Shoulder bone was set,
composed on Lords day evening;

Thy tyred Father unto thee doth write
And now in meter doth to thee indite
He seems to feel your pains by Sympathy
And for thy troubles greiveth dolefully.
Yet do rejoyce to hear the bone is in
And hopeth much that God who doth begin
Will perfect, strengthen, advance his praises eke
To them that wait on him, to him that seek.
I have not much to write for weariness
But humbly beg of God he would thee bless
Give comfort, joy & settlement at length
That to the joynted bone he would give strength
Ith night our sorrows wonted are to come
But in the Morn joy cometh in the room
We pilgrims are, this is a vale of Tears
A place of sorrow, pain & grizly fears.
But in the Lord is laid up our salvation
In midst of all our deepest desolation
God pitty, bless & heal thee evermore
Raise up your Spirits eke your limbs secure
My dearest Love unto my Dear I send
And all of you unto Gods grace commend

My Son & daughter, little pretty Jo
And unto thee alas, alas for wo
To Cosin Rawson & loving Cosin Page
That must be registred for a whole age
Fare well all present till that you I see
In better health & larger libertie
My brother, Sister Rock I dearly greet
I long to see them lovingly to meet
Thy loving Father now doth make an end
John Wilson that these lines to thee doth send

John James

John James' tribute to John Bunyan is one of the briefest and most tensely wrought of his poems. The "Tinker" of course refers to Bunyan's trade of tinsmith, and the whole image of the poem is that of God forging him into a fit blade and instrument for his service. "Unswaupt" (unswapt) is one of the many examples of James' eccentric word usages; it may possibly mean here unsmitten, uncut, or freed of imperfections.

Of John Bunyans Life &c

Wel mended Tinker! sans dispute
Brasse into Gold Grace can transmute.
Its hammer rings upon thy breast
so sanctifyed wert and blest
In thee an happy change was made
And thou becamest an other blad
Unswaupt, instampt & meliorate
By such means was thy wretched state
So sovereigne a Mastery
Has Grace to cure debauchery.

Nov-8-1702

Joshua Moody

John Rayner, the younger, who succeeded his father as pastor of Dover, New Hampshire, though of delicate health, had volunteered as a chaplain on one of the expeditions during King Philip's War. In the field he contracted a "cold and fever," and shortly thereafter died at the home of his father-in-law, Edmund Quincy of Braintree.

Of the broadside elegy that was published at his death only one copy, a fragment, has survived, with the last twelve or fourteen lines missing from each column. Fortunately, Samuel Sewall copied extensive excerpts from an apparently perfect copy, so that we now have nearly the whole of the elegy and also know the author's name. This reprint follows the broadside, so far as it goes, and supplements it with twenty lines from the Sewall manuscript.

LAMENTATIONS

Upon the never enough bewailed Death of the Reverend
Mr. John Reiner,
Pastor of the Church of Christ at Dover
who was gathered to his Fathers
December, 21. 1676.

When Heathen first assail'd our peaceful Land
My Comfort was, ours is Immanuels Land.
When Robbers us impov'risht thought I then
We may be poorer and not worser men.
I hope't when our young men i'th'field fell down
God brake our Arm of flesh to bare his own.
When treach'rous Foes did with success out-brave us
I said God meant to humble us, then save us.
But when that doleful word REINER is dead,
I heard, Lips quiver'd, Belly trembled,
My Spirits fail'd, Corruption seiz'd my Bones,
My Face grew pale, my heart as cold as Stones.
Mee thought I saw engraven on this Rod
Plain to be read that fatal Ichabod.
This single Death I count more wrath discovers
Then the removal of some hundred others.
Here's Anger great, Displeasure boiled up,
And that's the Gall and Wormwood in our Cup.

By former blasts our Leaves and Boughs did fall,
This terrible gust hath blown up Roots and all.
Some smarting Wounds we had receiv'd before,
This lays us welt'ring in our Blood and Gore,
Under the fifth Rib struck; you that pass by
Stand still and see, and sigh to see us dye.
Some of us saw of late our Houses burning,
Gods House lies waste now, High-way thither mourning,
Sanct'ary-doors shut up, a Famine not
of Bread, but Bread of Life's our threatned Lot.
How many hath this Right'ous Mans Lips fed,
Who now must pine, 'cause no man breaks them Bread?
So much as Heav'n exceeds the Earth, so far
As Souls than Bodies more excelling are,
So much is this more then our former wo,
These Iron Bands our Souls have pierc't into.
What ever other ailes upon us were
Had God been pleased but to spare us here
Our Bread and Water of affiliction would
Been less afflictive far, Oh that we could
Our Teacher see! but that sight of our eyes
Is gone, and He close in a corner lies,
Sure God a way for further Anger makes
When such a Man out of the way he takes.
In's latest Text too true a Prophet found,
(Not one of Samuels Words fell to the ground)
. . . . . . renew'd against us are . . .
. . . .
Elisha dies, what then? why you will hear
That Moabs Bands invade the land next year,
God could prevent if any one would be
A making up the Hedge, but ah we see
Hedge-breakers and Gap-makers do abound,
Hedge-makers and Gap-menders rarely found.
When God his worthy Father from us took
We for a night of Darkness thick did look;
But that Sunsets and yet no night ensues:
His Son a second Sun brought better news.
. . . .
. . . .

A precious Soul he was, not old but sage,
Grave, wise and prudent far above his age,
Chearful but serious, merry too but wise
(Sour Leven pleases not for Sacrifice)
His Courtesie obliged most and best,
His Innocence did stop the Mouths o'th'rest.
In Supplications mighty, fervent, bold
Like Jacob he with confidence took hold
Of God in Prayer, wrestling with him till
He wrestling got the name of Israel.
(Ah such a Moses we shall dearly miss
I'th Mount; when Amalek a fighting is)
His Sermons were Experiences, first wrought
On his own Heart, then lived what he taught.
He blameless was, unless you blame him shall
Because he was well spoken of by all.
His Life desir'd, his Death bewail'd you see
(Lord let our last end like the Righteous be)
A faithful friend, plain-open-hearted he,
His words and heart in one did well agree.
Study what should or we would wish to be,
And say 'twas here, fear no Hyperbole.
Such pregnant young one are but seldome found
Such pregnant young ones seldome stay when [found.]
Not the Worlds field but Heavens Barn is th['Place.]
For forward Souls, so early ripe in Grace.
Though green in years, yet he was gather'd in
Like shock of Corn that fully rip'ned been.
My Brother John, I am distress'd for thee,
Thou very lovely, pleasant wert to me:
I thus bewail thee, but great sorrows will
Not drein themselves dry at a little quill.
Heart full, eyes full, too full themselves to vent
By words, a little taste is only meant.
I'le not attempt his worth, our loss to write,
Unless I had some Angel to indite,
To him that gav't the former's only known,
By sad effects the latter may be shown,
And best by him that's yet unborn be told,
But Lord while we thus weep our Foes grow [bold.]

We sigh, they sing, we mourn, Blaspheme . . .
. . . . . of Vengeance and the . . . .
. . . .
. . . .
Black Pagans know this Blood shall charged be
To your Account, and you ere long Shall see
Saints Blood is dear when dregs of wrathful cup
Shall be your share to wring out and drink up.
Gods heart was toward him who willingly
Oferd himselfe to greatest jeopardy
'Gainst you the Lord to help, he hath his Meed,
His ready will's accepted for the deed.
When his blest head a Martyrs Crown shall wear
You guilt of shedding Blood shall bear
. . . .
. . . .

Joshua Moody.

Samuel Stone II

This is the only known poem of the younger Samuel Stone; it is smooth, conventional, undistinguished, with little of the character and strength of the New England elegy at its best.

William Leet Esq.
Governour of connecticot collony:
who Deceased April 16. 1683.

A sad presage of evil days,
When God into his Coffers lays,
His precious ones and now alas!
Divine prediction's come to pass,
Which us foretells thats Omen sad,
When Steers men, which we sometims had,
Are snatcht away which should us guide
In stormy tims which us abide
Heavens above and earth beneath
Portentous threatnings forth do breath:
Celestial signs do oft precede
Great mens decease, and this indeed
We find to true, of such an one,
We are bereft, and now alone,
Our commonwealth a Widdow sits,
And well may fear some swooning fits,
The other Day the Stars did frown,
The earth's now clad in sable Gown,
Upon the fall of this our LEET,
Bright Tatan did his Beams retreat;
The Heavens wept the earth did sweat
And we deplore our loss so great.
Some sad Catastrope this year,
Astrologers predict 'tis clear
Already Fatal it hath been
To us, and calls aloude for sin,
That we repent and make our peace
With God above that so may cease,
Th'aspects and effects of's anger,
Or else we are in greater danger,

Of overtures and changes here,
Which Sage and wise men now do fear:
Our Pilots gone and for to steer,
When Tempest seems to be so near,
To keep our ship from foundring now,
A task's to hard for us, we bow,
under our work, which is so great,
We miss Wise, Prudent Esquire Leet.
The seas do rage the waves do roar,
Tis time divine relief t'implore.

WILLIAM LEET Anagram.
I tell I am well.
An Acrosticon.

Well I am now, my Christian Friends beleive it
In Joy so great, you cannot well conceive it
Left have I earth, I now receive reward,
Look't for by saints, after their Labour hard,
I tell you true, I would not change my state,
And if were proferd all the gold and plate
Mins, Pearls, in all the world, I should them hate.

Let all Believers freely leave their dust,
Early in morn when God shall raise the just
Each saint his own shall take again,
Then they with Christ shall ever reign.

S Stone.

Benjamin Tompson

Tompson's elegy on Governor John Leverett celebrates him in his three-fold capacity of a leader of the army, of the church, and of the state. Leverett's military and civil services began early; eventually he rose to be Major General from 1663 to 1673, and from then to the time of his death he was governor, serving with distinction during a period of deep crisis, including King Philip's War and the ever-growing attacks on the charter privileges of Massachusetts. Of the annual "publique acts" of Harvard College headed by Leverett's name, the theses of 1678 survive as an example, also the first catalog of 1674. At his elaborate funeral (see *New England Hist. Gen. Reg.* vol 4, p. 128) the students of Harvard and the boys of the grammar schools apparently marched in procession, as well as the military companies. In the astronomical passage Tompson is referring particularly to John Foster's *Almanack* for 1679, which predicted "a great Eclipse of the Sun, March, 31. at 1. afternoon, visible to us in *New-England*," though it could not predict the graver human eclipse which occurred two weeks earlier. There had apparently been an unseasonable thunder storm a short time before Leverett's sudden death. By "John the fifth" "alias sixth," Tompson meant that four (or five) of Leverett's predecessors in the colonies had borne the name of John: Governors John Carver, Winthrop, Haynes, Endecott, Webster, and the younger Winthrop (Carver probably having been omitted on the first count, and Webster altogether).

New-Englands grand Eclips
by the withdrawing of that vast body, or Trium-virate of
Politick, Ecclesiastick, Military Light John Leverett
Governour of the Massathuset, and Moderatour of the
Confederate Colonies in NE, who disbanded the 16th: of
the 1st: 1678/9 AEtatis suae: 63.

'Tis not a vulgar straine the Learned know
Can speake the Homage which all fancies ow
To this State-Giant. Had I ne're before
Seen Monarchs in their Ermins rold in Gore,
Had I not read on tombs, where publique trust
Assures us lies the most Couragious Dust:
I should have deem'd, twixt us & him this odds
That Wormes like me might die But such turn Gods.

I place not this Grand Heroe in their Spheare
But own by such he wore his title here.
Thanks first to Heaven, next to Caesar's beams
Which still gives Light to pen these dolefull Theams.
Hee's something worse then Monster in defect
Who covers such a piece with disrespect.
Heaven did not winke & chuse. Nor did the voice
Of an whole Countrey onc repent this Choice
Form'd to this very end; sent as a Gift
To help this province at a deadly lift.
Lesse Active spirits might serve turn at helme
While th'Vulgar like the sea is still & Calme,
But for a boysterous spell, needs such an one,
Who with his Countenance could quell alone.
Goodness of extract happyly Conjoyn'd
By heavenly Marriage to an Heroe's mind:
In which if anywhere might be confest
The Lion with the Lamb did feed & rest.
Abràm in armes, well might th'acute Divine
Make application at this wine of thine.
Tall Cedars in our forrest, In whose shade
Those Sympathizeing twine so long have laid
Of State & Church. His valour set a spell
And snib'd the outrage of the Infidell.
This Holy Land was preposest before
But Joshua turnd the Heathen out of Dore.
And by the Soul of valour bolted out
Whole Nations of the tawny barbarous rout
Hee clos'd the Churchs wounds and kept the peace
When secret undermines did Increase.
When some delv'd deep their enterprize to hide
He trumpeted away their envious pride,
And cut that Gordian knot which many thought
Would our Assemblys to Confusion brought.
Tis more then Common vertue must stand here
No vulgar Art could such a vessel steer,
Whose passengers were saincts & Cabins hold
Such heavenly treasure as transcendeth Gold.
To keep the Arke so stedy yet not smitten.
In such great Earthquakes may be truely written

Among the Choicest Records: Twas a thing
Whereof from Age to Age our World may ring.
Next to that unseen hand which cannot Erre
We may the Crown of praise on him transfer.
Great were his parts, Sublimer much his grace
Some beams of Majcesty had toucht his face
Sufficient to enforme a Countrey whence
He borrow'd his Majestick Influence.
A Generall of such a noble sphear
His person & his purse both scorn'd the Reare.
So amiable both in Court & Field
His hand could Conquer while his spirits yield.
Come fellow souldiers: Chere all hearts amain
The Countreys cordiall is Soveraigne
He Honourably cry'd up all the Joy
When Boston Eccho'd loud *Vive le Roy*
Tis plaine without him we had had no sence
What meant the things call'd Royall Influence.
Twas not pure Custome but an anuall debt
Which caus'd our Alma Mater humbly set
Great Leveretts name, maine patron of her rights
In publique acts after their studious nights
A Thesis of it self so full of light
All disputations were decided by't.
He left that Marble which before was Stone
Or rather that Created which was none.
A great worke built on ruines former fame
Yet but an urne compar'd with his great name.
Next that Grand matron, creep the Infant schools
[W]hich save some naturall wits from greatest fools
Drest in the weeds of grief: And well they may
Since their Maecaenas is divorc'd away.
The Regiments, professours of the time
Lament in Ranke & file thô not in Rhime.
All quarters startled at the suddaine end
Of this brave Joshua their publique friend.
Bring floods of tears, yet some returnd as though
The numerous already would not off.
Whose big swoln Clouds are ready to disperse
Their Amber tears upon the Sable herse

This Providence hath baffled all that Art
Which to the World did heav'n's concerns impart.
Such who the most by starrs & tide did know
Could not portend this full sea of our woe.
By this prodigious stroke of Cruell fate
Which our Eclypses Scheme doth Antidate,
Who setting in our Clime has great Remarke
And proves Star-prophets sometimes in the darke.
Good Reason too wise men are patent free
And ruld great Starrs themselves & thus did hee.
When angells made a muster in the Skies
And their stupendous ordinance let flie,
Ers while what could their Loud report portend
But preparations for this Generals end.
That spacious field was cleard of that black Guard
To Convoy this up to his high reward.
Such as New Englands Annalls mind to sift
Will find him by quotation. John the fifth: alias sixth
But I recede from this Illustrious Throne
Whither my phancy roves to make my moane
Poor broken Boston, shall thy bleared eyes
And dolefull which dayly stab the Skies
Greifs Hurricanes, what shall they never o're
And force their entry at some other dore?
Must this darke Climate be the onely stage
For Nemesis to act her various rage?
This the Aceldama for wounds & gore
The publick hospitall for pox & poor?
And must that man of sin who plots our woe
And Heav'ns dishonour, always scotfree goe?
Shall the Laviathan who feasts on states
And quaffs the blood of Kings escape the fates?
Lord cast some Angry sparke into the nest
Of that blood sucking Anti Christian beast.
What yet remains New England's out of view
To pilate in such storms adventure few.
All Caesars subjects with a Common voyce
Cry God save Charles & help you in next choyce.
His diadem which now is soild with tears
So that her Lustre something disappears.

Sole Cordiall in his paines, which by his limbs
In a deep Gulf of tears before you swims
Whilst this small province in its freedome stands
Honour the dead by lending liveing hands
This will be omen of your future peace
Heaven will Create or rayse up more of these.

B. T.

* * *

Tompson's elegy on Edmund Davie and his consolatory address to his father, Humphry Davie, who had just previously lost his wife, help to unravel one of the biographical mysteries of early New England, which had defied the industry and ingenuity of both Savage and Sibley. Edmund Davie was apparently one of the most brilliant students of Harvard in the seventeenth century. Soon after his graduation in 1674 he seems to have gone to Padua, studied medicine, and attained the degree of M. D. Thence he went to London where he was apparently noted for his intense devotion to scientific learning and experiment. He would probably have attained great fame, had he not been cut off prematurely in 1681, probably at about the age of twenty five or six. His younger brother John, Harvard 1681, was, according to tradition, just hoeing the corn on his farm in Groton, Connecticut, in 1707, when word reached him that he had fallen heir to the baronetcy of Creedy in Devonshire.

Edmund Davie 1682.
anagram
AD Deum veni

To God, the Center of all Souls, I'm flown,
Having been from all eternity his own.

I'm now arriv'd the Soul desired Port
More pleasing far then glories of the Court:
My Saviour is my only Caesar: Here's
Instead of Nobles, Angels hosts, bright Peers,
Great Princes thronging round, thicker then swains
Below at publicke votes: Here each one Reigns.
Our streets are pav'd with Saphires, and we pass
Or'e streems of Christial like to fusil Glass
Heres Treasuries, the like weve never seen;
All guesses at the worth have fool'ries been.

Mountains of Rubies safe from privateers
Within the Ramphiers of these lofty Spheres.
Here's piles of Scepters, Diadems of Gold
More then the worlds vast Space at once will hold.
But that which butifies this boundless room
Is great JEHOVAH, unto whom I'm come.
Eternity's the highest link of Bliss;
Its sunshine never sets, nor clouded is.
I've hitt the very Place I wisht at heart,
I'm fixt for ever: Never thence to part.

His heart was erst inamourd with delights
In studious Solitudes, in Attick Nights
To prove the greatest avarice of his minde
After the Gems of Skill his Body pin'd.
Hating the slugards bed, and flattering sloth,
Nocturnal Wakes had brought him to vast growth.
His tender years were seasoned with a Juice,
Which might have provd, if spar'd, of gen'ral use.
He clim'd the Shrowds of Science: Now hees dead,
Hees got above the verry topmost head,
Hearing that word which set his Soul on fire
With blazing zeal of Love: Brite soul, come higher,
All that thou seest is thine, myselfe to boot;
Heres an Eternal feast of Love: fall to it.
High, we believe, this welcome Guest was seated,
And in an instant all his joys compleated.

EPITAPH

THE World was once in danger to drop out
Sidney's Remains Wits universe about.

'Here in Death's gripes a gemme of Art so rare
New-England's Poverty claimeth her share;
Since here she nurst him with a silvane teat
Untill hee's fledgd to seek a distant seat:
Gaining the naked Substance, his Intent's
From statelier Halls to gain Embellishments
Of sciences profound: Twas well essayd;
But by that means this gallant Spark hath paid

What England, Honours Throne, his place of Birth,
Did rightly claime, his soul deserted Earth.
Hee lies among that precious Dust unknown
Which with most friendly silence huggs its own.
Great Gransiers of most venerable race,
Yield this their Nephew a retiring Place
In their dark Conclave, where there hands and brains,
Under the umbrage of the grave remains.

Haec Genitoris amor, Matris reverentia possit
Carmina, Tutoris pauperis obsequio.

B. T

* * *

To my Honoured Patron
HUMPHERY Davie
A renewing the Memory of Dr Edmund Davie.
Who expired at London, Anno 1681

Bereaved Sir

Delug'd with tears, by what you heard before,
Here Unexpected meets you one stroke more.
Wave upon wave; Blows fall so thick, so fast,
Arterial blood, I fear, will come at last
Instead of tears; Methinks I feel the Smart,
Which in this hour of tryal cramps your heart.
A spouses Death, so wise, so Chast, so fair,
Would bring a Job himselfe next Door Despair:
Soon after that, the First fruits of your streangth;
I fear your patience will you fail at length.
But I recall that word, though hard no doubt
Who tends the Furnace, sure will help you out.
Had I an intrest where this Pair are gone,
The Vertuous Mother, with the Learned Son;
I'd beg a Balsom for your bleeding wound,
No where below this Climate to be found
Distance cannot be salv'd: let Simpathize
A very little space your heart suffice.

Amplitudini tuae divinctus Benjamin Tompson.
Braintry; 29 4 1682.

Perhaps Tompson's most amusing poem is his address to Lord Bellamont, that clever and popular politician, when he came to Boston in 1699 to assume the governorship. Ebenezer Parkman of Westborough, who preserved these verses, wrote thus about them to Mather Byles, August 27, 1760, just after a new governor, Sir Francis Bernard, had been welcomed: "Now you have all run thro the Ritual a la Mode, and the Congratulations & Addresses to his Excellency for his safe Arrival, are over; sit down & rest you; & I pray you heark to what Ben. Thompson sung when a former Governour came. He is supposd in Quality of a shooe-Maker to run out from his stall to pay his homely Complements to his Lordship as he passed through Dedham toward Boston. There break out, now & then, incomparable Strokes—& the 22 pastoral Lines beginning with 'Mountains bare-headed stand' &c. give me great pleasure." Parkman goes on to suggest that the poem might well be turned over to Mr. Draper for publication in his newspaper, but a careful search indicates that the poem was not published at the time.

The pagentry on the occasion of Bellamont's arrival apparently came as near to a dramatic representation as anything ever did in Puritan New England, for Tompson came out for his recitation dressed as the Simple Cobbler of Aggawam, and after the recitation apparently, a shepherdess came forward to proffer the new governor a cup of sillabub, another brought Lady Bellamont a vase of flowers, and a third sang a song of welcome. Harvard's charter difficulties at this time, to which the poem alludes amusingly, are fully described in Morison's *Harvard College*. The account of the country and Indians before European settlement is apparently based on the humorous first paragraph of the eighth chapter of Edward Johnson's *Wonder-Working Providence*. "Emmett" is the archaic word for ant. It is difficult to say what Tompson meant by his statement about Nathaniel Ward, "Fam'd Agawam, who once drew Salem Fair," unless Salem is a slip for Ipswich. The lines which follow refer to the reversal of the situation: whereas Ward fifty years previously had written his book out of a willingness "To help 'mend his Native Country, lamentably tattered, both in the upper-Leather and sole," the Simple Cobbler is now petitioning England in the person of the new governor for similar aid. The poem offers a remarkable example of the continuity of the New England literary tradition, from Nathaniel Ward, through Benjamin Tompson, to Mather Byles.

To Lord Bellamont
when entering Governour of the Massachusetts.

Were I sole sov'reign of rare Fancies now,
All to your Merits should with Rev'rence bow.

Transcendent Sir,

Your Stamp is royal; Your Commissions Rays
From loyal Hearts demand loud Thanks, high Praise.
Our Senators with publick Cares so tir'd,
With Chearfullness resign to you desird.
Accept a poor Mans Thanks, a rural Bitt,
E'er you arrive the Festivalls of Witt.
The Traveller where Wine's not to be had,
With a Cup of cold Water's often glad.
Since Harvards Libertys we fear are lost,
And Hasty Pudding's Servd instead of roast.
I've seen some feasted & placd in the Chair
And treated as I thought with Treatment rare:
But what was in the Pot he who this writ,
Tasting not once thereof, still turnd the Spit.
We hope your Grandeur, for whom all have prayd,
Shall never lack our Love, our Purse, our Aid.
We bless our King; we thank the Waves & Wind,
That to our Sinking State have been So kind:
To land that Person, Ship'd by Grace of God.
Our loyal Hearts bespeak your long Abode.
Had you arrivd some hundred Years agoe,
The naked Tribes with knotty Clubbs and Bow
Storming your canvas'd Whale, with spears Head tryd
Whether your Timber had been soul-ifyd.
An antient Chicataubuts smoaky Ghost,
Once Lord of all this Soil and dreary Coast
Awakend by the Triumph of this Day
Hearing your Lordship was to come this Way,
Beggd Pluto's Leave, but that it would affright
To testifie his Joy at this fair Sight.
Here's running, riding, pressing hard to See
A blazing Beam darting from Majesty.
And who among whole thousands can do less,

Than for this Voi'ge thank you & Heav'n bless?
Whilst to your Lordship we our Gratias render,
Poor Emmett I tremble as an Offender.
But gen'rous Souls o'er look a World of Faults.
The Heart well trimd, the Pen more rarely halts.
    Fam'd Agawam, who once drew Salem Fair
Sure prophecyd this Interview so rare.
So what in jest with his sharp Awl he wrote
Is in good Earnest to our Quarters brought.
    Mountains bare-headed Stand, Each fertile Field,
When washd with showers will rich presents yield.
Adopt this People as we ready be;
An Eden so long hid you'll quickly See.
Deep Mines their Riches tender; Gardens Flowers;
Their Sprawling Vines stretch out to make you Bowers.
Charles River swoln with Joys, o'er flows with Thanks:
And sends his golden *Trouts* up winding Banks.
Old Merimack was ne'er so glad before:
And casts up *Salmon* free cost on the shore.
Deep Conges drop the *Elm;* tall *Cedars* bow—
And Corydon to gaze deserts the Plough.
Dametas his Nown Self, had hither rid,
But that he's run with Speed to fetch a Kid.
To make this Country Treat more Solemn up
Brisk Thesylis comes panting with a Cup
Of dainty Syllabub: Sweet Amaryl
Her Flask replets with Rose & Daffodyl.
Down at your Ladys Feet her self she flings;
Whilst Daphne, in her Strains, your Welcome sings.
And not one Face in all this Grand Convent
But smiles forth Tokens of their full Content.
Brisk sons of Mars, Valours right Heirs, all round,
Your modest Arms this Day are richly crownd.
A General you have from Europe blown
Whose very sight might make Quebeck your own
Altho with Wrinkled Age my Colours furld,
Under his Conduct we'd soon storm that World.

Pardon, fair Sir, that many Thousand Meet
To lay a Province' Welcomes at your Feet.
A City Treaty for your Worth remains
By Potent Purses & more Powerfull Brains.
I'll to my Coblers Den, with Leave retire:
And if your Grandeur Frowns, there I'll expire.

William Adams

This brief excerpt is all that remains of William Adams' elegy on young Seth Flint, apparently a student at Harvard who died in 1673.

An Elegie Upon The Death of Mr. Seth. Flint.

So soon And Ripe so young and Pluckt for heaven,
Grace me adore that is so freely given.
A hardest Flint on softest Pillowes yield,
So did the tender love of God reveald
In Christ constraine him forcing him to give
Himselfe, had God so pleas'd, to him to live:
But yet his all to be at God's dispose
His sins to cover Pardon: wounds to close,
And heale: Life endlesse in his Light to see,
That Christ to him all and in all might be. &c.
Olim te fruitus Vivo, mihi candide, Chare
Certe; Iaces: Quid agam? Magni tacuere Dolores.
Aposuit William Adams.

G. H.

Richard Dummer was one of the early settlers of Newbury and a person of distinction in public affairs. The author of the elegy upon him has not as yet been satisfactorily identified, but so much is clear, that when he wrote this elegy, he borrowed freely from two elegies of the English Puritan poet, Robert Wild (1609–1679). From the elegy on Dennis Bond, the Cromwellian statesman, G. H. took over not only the couplet preceding the reference to Bond, but also about ten other lines in whole or in part. Several further lines he took from Wild's elegy "Upon the Death of So many Reverend ministers of late." Both poems can be found in Robert Wild, *Iter Boreale*, London, 1661 and 1668.

AN ELEGY Upon the Death of the Wo[r]shipfull Richard Dummer Esq. Who deceased at newbury July 4. 1689

Dummer is gone, that brave and gallant mind,
And we bereav'd and sad are left behind
For to Condole the Town and Countreys Loss;
To help bear an helpless Families sad cross.
The worthiest men are alwaies worn out first.
Those fruits that are the choicest keep the worst.
Well may the mourners go about the Streets,
When poor New England's fill'd with winding sheets.
Widows and Orphans Fingers in their Eye.
Who do need no Welch Leeks to make them cry:
Fresh 'larms now in our border heard
And private Families with rumours scar'd.

Such peerless ones, so many, dye so fast!
How precious in their Death? What maks shuch waste?
Scarce had we dry'd our Eyes from one sad Story,
Before we hear the Loss of this Towns Glory.
If that our heads were Waters, and each Eye
A fountain were now may we weep them dry.
Tremble New-England and now stand agast,
To see thy worthies leave the World so fast.

Adieu brave Dummer; Newbery she may burn
Her withering Laurel at thy sacred Urn.
Thou needst no Monument or Marble Stone

Diamonds themselves have Flaws, thy name hath none
The wicked's Name, when they are gone shall rot
Thine with the truly Righteous mans shall not.
That plott of Earth which grasps thee in her womb
Proud of her Treasure swells into a Tomb.
As wild of dennis bond, doth Elegize,
Whom the English gentry did so highly Prize.
When next this Town shall altogether come,
And miss their Moderator from his Room;
Well may presadge that Meeting will not speed
But want Success, his Prudence theyll so need.
Whose worth, if my dull fancy should aspire,
Twould want due Epithites for shuch a squire.
Just, Pious, Prudent, Sober, Grave, and Wise;
Able for councel, fit for enterprize.
His NAME forever is Embalmd in BLISS
All men such lips most ready were to Kiss.
Bles't are the Peace-Makers, our SAVIOUR notes.
Who to end strife did use to give their Votes,
His last work was to make his Neighbours even
Who were at Odds, before he went to Heaven.

Sic cecinit summo Maerore
affectus. G. H.

Printed at Boston N.E. 1689.

Anonymous

The elegy on Governor Thomas Prence was left unfinished in Sewall's manuscript copy, stopping suddenly in the middle of a couplet. No other copy of it seems to be known.

An Ellegy On Thomas Prence Esqr. Governour
of New Plimouth Colony Died March 29. 1673.

Like to Fond youth, in vanity
My younger, Years I spent.
Till the most high in his mercy
To me, me hither sent:
My Fathers House I did forego
Kindred and Friends together,
My Dear and Native Land also
To go. I knew not whether;
Unto vast Willderness I came,
But knew not well for what:
And yet I heare was found of him
Whom my poor Soul Sought not.
Ev'n of the wise Omnipotent,
Whose tender mercies ever
Are unto those that do repent;
What time, or place soever.
In Marriage state he did me mate
With blessings ev'n fourfold
Which unto me he made to be
More worth then choicest Gold.
From old from young choice favours sprung
How should I then but sing
Unto his praise ev'n all my dayes
N . . . .

Daniel Henchman

Sir William Phips (1651–1695), one of twenty-six children of a poor gunsmith in Maine, was the most famous example of the self-made man in his period. Against every external disadvantage he worked his way upward, and when his expedition in search of a sunken Spanish silver galleon turned out successfully, fame and knighthood, as well as a very modest portion of the treasure, came to him. He commanded a successful expedition against Port Royal, though he failed against Quebec. In 1692 he was appointed the first governor under the new charter, but he died a few years later, only forty-four, not having been able to carry out his projects for naval stores, for mines, and for the finding of the famous galleon of Governor Boadilla which had been wrecked with a massive table of gold aboard, weighing three thousand three hundred and ten pounds.

This elegy was appended to Cotton Mather's life of Phips without any indication of authorship, and it might well have continued to be attributed to Mather, had not Sewall left us a manuscript copy of the lost broadside with the author's name added. Mather's version lacks the first seven lines, four other lines, and also varies in a number of minor verbal details, one or two of which seem to be slips in copying on the part of Sewall. As in Tompson's elegy on Governor Leverett, 1678, the point is made that the almanacs foretold a great solar eclipse, but could not foretell this human eclipse.

LAMENTAT[I]ONS Upon The Death of
Sir WILLIAM PHIPS, Knight Governour.
Who Expired in London February 18 1694,5.

And is He Mortal too, whose Life maintain'd
The Breath and Joy of ours? He who had gain'd
His Monarchs Favour, and his country's Love
By Glorious Actions, Registred above?
HE who himself did so Immortalize
By his All made one Glorious Sacrifice
To his lov'd Peoples Weal? . . . .

Rejoyce, Messieurs; Netops, Rejoyce; 'Tis True;
Ye Philistines, None will Rejoyce, but you;
Loving of all HE dy'd; who love him not
Now have the Grace of Publicans forgot.

Our Almanack's foretold a great Eclipse.
This they foresaw not of our Greater PHIPS.
Phips, our great Friend, our Wonder, and our Glory,
The Terrour of our Foes, the Worlds rare story.
England will boast him too, whose Noble Mind,
Impell'd by Angells, did those Treasures find,
Long in the bottom of the Ocean laid,
Which her three Hundred Thousand Richer made
By Silver yet nev' Canker'd, nor defil'd
By honour, nor betray'd when Fortune Smil'd.

Since this bright Phoebus visited our Shoar
We saw no Foggs, but what were rais'd before:
Those vanish'd too; Harrass'd by bloody Wars
Our Land saw peace by his most Generous Cares.
The Wolvish Pagans at his dreaded Name
Tam'd, Shrunk before him, and his Doggs became.

Fell Moxus, and Feirce Docawando, fall,
Charm'd at the feet of our brave General.
O Dont his Death to the Blind Heathen shew,
Least they thereby, Their Courage do renew;
Nor let in Ask'lons Streets, the Deadly Voice
of it be heard, Least at it they Rejoyce.
Fly-blow the Dead, Pale Envy, let him not
(What Hero ever did?) escape a Blot.
All his distort with an Inchanted Eye;
And Height will make what's right still stand Awry.
HE was, O that he was? His faults we'l tell,
Such faults as these; we knew and lik'd 'em well
Just to an Injury; Denying none
Their Dues; but self denying oft his Own.
Good, to a Miracle; Resolv'd to do
Good unto all, whether they would or no.
To make us good, great, Wise, and all things else,
He wanted but the Gift of Miracles.
On him vain Mob, they Mischeiefs cease to throw;
Bad but in this alone, the tims were so.
Stout to a prodigy; living in pain
To send back Quebeck Bullets once again

Thunder his Musick; Sweeter than the Spheres
Chim'd Roaring Cannons in his Martial Ears.
Frigats of Armed men could not withstand
'Twas try'd, the force of his one Swordless Hand:
Hand which in one all of Briareus had,
And Hercules' Twelve Toyls but Pleasure made.
Too Humble; In brave Stature not so tall,
As low in Carriage, stopping unto all:
Raisd in Estate, in Figure, in Renown,
Not pride; Higher and yet not prouder grown.
Of Pardons full; ner' to Revenge at all,
Was that which He would satisfaction call.
True to his Mate; from whom though often flown,
A stranger yet to every love but one.
Write him not Childless, whose whole people were,
Sons, Orphans, now of his Paternal Care.
Now least Ungratfull Brands, we still incurr,
Your Salary, we'l pay in tears, Great Sir!
To England often blown, and by his Prince
Often sent laden with Preferments thence:
Preferr'd each Time He went: when all was done
That Earth could doe, Heaven fetch'd him to a Crown.
'Tis he: with him interr'd how great Designs!
Stand fearless now Ye eastern Firrs and Pines,
with naval Stores not to enrich the Nation,
Stand for the Universal Conflagration.
Mines, opening unto none but Him, now lay
Close under lock, and Key, 'till the last Day.
In this, like to the grand Aurifick Stone,
By any but Great Souls not to be known.
And thou, Rich Table, with Bodilla lost,
In the Rich Galeon, on the Spanish Coast,
In weight three Thousand and Three Hundred Pound,
But of pure Massie Gold, lye Thou not found;
Safe since He's laid under the Earth asleep,
Who learn't where thou dost under water keep.
But Thou Chief looser Poor New England, speek
Thy Dues to such as did thy Welfare seek.
The Governour, that Vow'd to Rise and Fall

With Thee, thy Fate shows in his Funeral.
Write now his Epitaph; 'twill be thy own:
Let it be this; A PUBlick Spirits gone.
or, but name PHIPS; more need's not be exprest,
Both ENGLANDS, and next Ages tell the Rest.

Sic Lamentatus est
D. Hincsman.

Printed at Boston
in new England by
B: Green. 1695.]

Bibliography of Early New England Verse

Though this study is concerned with seventeenth-century New England verse, any arbitrarily fixed terminus, such as 1700, would cut through the work of several of the most important writers. It was therefore decided to include the known verse of all the writers who were born up to the 1670's and to complete their bibliographies to the time of their death. At the other end, all the verse of the immigrants is listed, even that which was written before their arrival. The verse of the transients is included only if it was written in New England or as a result of experiences there. The verse of writers long resident in New England or educated there is also included, even though they later lived and wrote elsewhere. The anonymous verse is listed chronologically and only to the year 1700.

Usefulness for the student of early American literature has been the primary consideration in the arrangement and structure of the bibliography; bibliographical and bibliophilic points which are only an end in themselves are omitted, and the space thus saved is devoted to biographical details on the writers and the subjects of the verse, details which in many instances have an important bearing upon the attributions made or still to be made. Considerable space has been devoted to previously unsolved or erroneously solved bibliographical problems, e.g. on Peter Folger's *Looking Glasse* and on the poems in Cotton Mather's *Magnalia.* Anonymous verses for which the attributions are certain or probable are listed under their respective authors; the rest are listed together at the end, with the likely attributions whenever possible. The locations of all extant manuscripts are given so far as known, likewise the location of the early imprints, if these are unique or very rare.

The poems of each author are listed individually unless they originally appeared together in a volume or have since been adequately edited, in which case only the chief subdivisions of the volume are indicated. For example: the adequate and easily available modern editions of Anne Bradstreet's poems makes an individual listing unnecessary, whereas the varying content of the different editions of Michael Wigglesworth's *Day of Doom* makes such a listing necessary. The modern publications of the poems of John Wilson and Benjamin Tompson are incomplete and a separate listing was necessary; on the other hand, though Edward Taylor's poems have not all been published, the bibliographical references in the *Poetical Works* are adequate except in three small instances.

After careful consideration, it was decided not to omit the listing of any verse which came to the author's attention, even of such which is obviously of poor quality, for in several instances such verse turned out to be of considerable historical importance, and in a few cases further study and better understanding revealed literary qualities in a poem which were at first not apparent. The author could not escape the conclusion that other seemingly insignificant verse may turn out to be important; the final critical sifting may well be postponed to a later date when all the material evidence has been gathered and we also have a better understanding of seventeenth-century poetic intent. Thus, negligible scraps of verse and fragments, even of two or four lines, have been recorded, and in several instances they proved to be unexpectedly significant or of noteworthy quality. One of the earliest examples of English dactylic hexameter has thus been recorded, and an apparently negligible couplet by President Charles Chauncy led to the identification of his only known poem in English. Even some of the graveyard verse, which no one till now has taken seriously, turned out in a few instances to be of striking originality or quality, for instance, the free verse epitaphs by Joshua Moody and such anonymous epitaphs as those on Captain Richard Lord, 1662, and Giles Hamlin, 1689, coming from sections of Connecticut for which no early poet is as yet known. Other epitaphs, frankly, seem to be fully as bad as general opinion depicts them. Obviously derivative epitaphs have not been included.

Perfection in a bibliography is an unattainable ideal, and for some strange reason this particular field of early American verse is traditionally afflicted by all the little imps of error, to the extent that there is no important publication on the subject which does not contain its full measure of grave and occasionally funny lapses. As many as possible of these past errors have been silently corrected, attention having been called to them only where the present corrections might otherwise have been considered errors, or also where they may serve as typical instances of the pitfalls which beset this field. The fact alone that this bibliography could rely on past bibliographies for less than a fifth of its material makes it certain that errors of commission and omission have found their way into it, and the author will be grateful to have any such called to his attention.

List of Abbreviations

Locations:

AAS	American Antiquarian Society
BA	Boston Athenaeum
BM	British Museum
BPL	Boston Public Library
BrUL	Brown University Library
CHS	Connecticut Historical Society
HCL	Harvard College Library
HEH	Henry E. Huntington Library
JCB	John Carter Brown Library
LC	Library of Congress
MHS	Massachusetts Historical Society
NEHGS	New England Historic Genealogical Society
NYHS	New York Historical Society
NYPL	New York Public Library
RIHS	Rhode Island Historical Society

Books:

Ford	Worthington Chauncy Ford, *Broadsides, Ballads, &c. Printed in Massachusetts 1639–1800*, The Massachusetts Historical Society, 1922.
Kettell	Samuel Kettell, *Specimens of American Poetry*, 3 vols., Boston, 1829.
Magnalia	Cotton Mather, *Magnalia Christi Americana*, London, 1702, 2nd ed. 2 vols., Hartford, 1820, 3rd ed. 2 vols., Hartford, 1853, etc. The page references are to the 2nd ed.
Morton	Nathaniel Morton, *New Englands Memoriall*, Cambridge, 1669, facsimile ed., New York, 1937.
Murdock	Kenneth B. Murdock, *Handkerchiefs from Paul*, Cambridge, 1927.
Sibley	John Langdon Sibley, *Biographical Sketches of Graduates of Harvard University*, Cambridge, 1873–1942. 6 vol.
Winslow	Ola Elizabeth Winslow, *American Broadside Verse*, New Haven, 1930.

General:

a.	age
d.	died
Ms.a.	manuscript autograph
Ms.c.c.	manuscript contemporaneous copy
Ms.l.c.	manuscript later copy
n.s.	new series
pr.	printed
repr.	reprinted

ADAMS, HUGH (1676–1748), b. Limerick, Ireland, H.C. 1697, pastor S. Carolina, Braintree and Chatham, Mass., Durham, N. H., physician.

1. (Impromptu paraphrase of the first Psalm).
   4 lines, c. 1696, in J. Farmer and J. B. Moore, *Collections* (Concord, N. H.), vol. 2, (1823), p. 307; repr. Sibley, vol. 4, p. 322.
2. Admonishing Poem against Mens Wigs and Womens Hooped Coats.
   original apparently lost, excerpt of 16 lines, Ms.a. MHS, Belknap Papers, dated March 20, 1722; pr. 1 *Proc. M.H.S.*, vol. 3, p. 326.

ADAMS, WILLIAM (1650–1685), b. Ipswich, Mass., H.C. 1671, pastor Dedham, Mass.

1. An Elegie upon the Death of Mr. Seth Flint.
   d. Cambridge (?), May 12, 1673, H.C. student.
   excerpt of 10 lines English and 2 lines Latin, Ms.c.c. NYHS, commonplace book of Samuel Sewall; the original, or a complete copy has not yet come to light.
2. Carmen funebre in obitum viri plurimis nominibus reverendi Uriani Oakesii.
   d. Cambridge, July 25, 1681, a. 50.
   40 lines Latin, Ms.a. JCB, in Urian Oakes, *The Soveraign Efficacy of Divine Providence* (Boston, 1682), fly leaf verso.

ALLEN, JAMES (1632–1710), b. Hampshire, Eng., Magdalen Hall and New College, Oxford; N.E. 1662, pastor Boston, Mass.

A funerall Elegie upon the Lamented Death of Mr. Danielle Russell son [of] Richd. Russel Esq.
   d. Charlestown, Jan. 4, 1678/9, a. 36.
   54 lines, Ms.a. private possession, signed Ja—. Allen; accompanied by Ms.l.c. in hand of T. Walcott; cf. Anon. no. 32 below.

ARNOLD, SAMUEL (1622–1693), b. England, N.E. c. 1643, fisherman, pastor Marshfield, Mass.

Mr. Samuel Arnold . . . his last Farewell to the World.
   d. Marshfield, Sept. 1, 1693, a. 71.
   50 lines, broadside, LC, fourth column, preceded by the two elegies on Arnold by Ichabod Wiswall; facsim. Winslow, p. 15.

BACHE, SAMUEL (fl. 1662–1671) b. England, wealthy merchant of London, N.E. 1662 with Humphrey Davie, merchant New Haven, Conn.

(An Elegy upon the Death of Mr. John Wilson.)

d. Boston, Aug. 7, 1667, a. 78.

apparently lost; 14-line excerpt, *Magnalia*, vol. 1, pp. 280–1.

BACHILER, STEPHEN (1561–1660), b. England, St. John's College, Oxford, N.E. 1632, pastor Hampshire, Eng., Lynn, Yarmouth, and Newbury, Mass., Hampton, N. H., returned to England.

1. "Reioyce yow Prelates that to your side."
2. "The Phisicke maker / the Tobacco taker."

Libellous verses against the Rev. George Widley of Goodworth Clatford, Southampton.

50 & 42 lines, composed by Stephen Bachiler, Sr., and Jr., and Thomas Owen during the summer of 1613, circulated and sung by them and their friends, including the poet, George Wither.

Ms.c.c. London, Star Chamber Proc. James I, 297/25, pr. Charles Edward Banks, "Early New Englanders in Chancery," *Proc. M.H.S.*, vol. 60, pp. 134–5.

BAILEY, JAMES (1650–1707), b. Newbury, Mass., H.C. 1669, pastor Danvers, Mass., Killingworth, Conn., physician, d. Roxbury, Mass.

(Verses upon his Illness.)

apparently lost; ref. in Nicholas Noyes' poem, "May 28th, 1706. To my worthy Friend, Mr. James Bayley":

"Thou many a Death hast under-gone,
And Elegies made of thine own . . .
And I have seen thine hand, and Pen,
Play on that Cockatrices den
In Measur'd Lines, as if inspir'd
And Paroxisms had only fir'd
An holy Soul with flaming zeal,
That flesh-pains it could scarcely feel.
What, in one breath, both Live and Dye
Groan, Laugh, Sigh, Smile, Cry, Versifie?"

BAILEY, SAMUEL
farmer of Little Compton, Mass. (now R. I.)
The College Ferula. Being a Reply to the Countryman's Apocrypha.
26 lines, Ms.a. (?) formerly in City Clerk's Office, Providence, R. I., pr. *New England Hist. Gen. Reg.*, vol. 9, p. 356; addressed "To John Whipple, Providence, March 1, 1678" (error for 1670?); an answer to John Richardson's "The Country-Mans Apocrypha," in his *Almanack* for 1670, (p. 15), see below.

BAILEY, THOMAS (1653–1689), b. England, N.E. 1684, pastor Watertown, Mass.

1. In Quintum Novembris 1669. November 5, 1669.
   126 lines English, Ms.a. MHS. This and the Latin poems listed below, all juvenalia and written before he came to New England, remain unpublished.
2. Arcus nimis intensus rumpitur.
   60 lines Latin, Ms.a. MHS, dated 1668.
3. Carmina Aurea.
   6 lines Latin, Ms.a. MHS, dated 1668.
4. Carmina Asclepiadoea.
   4 lines Latin, Ms.a. MHS, dated 1668.
5. Carmina Sapphica.
   3 four-line stanzas, Ms.a. MHS, dated 1668.

BISHOP, JOHN (1612–1694), b. Dorset, England, Balliol College, Oxford, N.E. 1640, pastor Batcombe, Dorset and Stamford, Conn.
In Pium, Doctum, & Praeclarum Dorcestrensem Matherum.
(Richard Mather) d. Dorchester, April 22, 1669, a. 73.
14 lines Latin, *Magnalia*, vol. 1, p. 414.

BOSWORTH, BENJAMIN (c. 1612–1700), b. England, N.E. 1634, Higham, Mass., removed to Hull by 1660, to Stow 1682, several years later to Boston, where d.

1. *Signs of Apostacy Lamented.*
   88 lines, pages 1–3 of a four-page leaflet, (Boston), 1693, BRUL; signed at end of leaflet "Benjamin Bosworth of New-England In the 81st Year of My Age, 1693."
2. A Caution to prevent Scandal.
   16 lines, in *ibid.*, p. 4.

BRACKENBURY, SAMUEL (1646–1678) b. Malden, Mass., H.C. 1664, asst. pastor Rowley, physician Malden and Boston.

A Word of Advise to those whom it may concern.

14 lines, p. 2 of his *Almanack* for 1667, repr. (with omission of first couplet) in John Tulley's *Almanack* for 1698, pp. (15–6).

BRADFORD, WILLIAM (1590–1657), b. Yorkshire, England, to Holland 1609, N.E. 1620, governor of Plymouth Colony.

1. A few poems made by a frind on the deplored death of mr John Robinson the worthy Pastour of the Church of God att Leyden. d. Leyden, Holland, March 1, 1625.
   6 four-line stanzas, Ms.c.c. Plymouth Church Records, 1626, pr. *Plymouth Church Records 1620–1859* (New York, 1920), vol. 1, pp. 62–3; generally attributed to Bradford.
2. (On the various heresies in Old and New England and on the Congregational Way.)
   fragment 47 pp. (first leaf, with the title missing), Ms.c.c. MHS, in hand of John Willis, dated 1657 (the year of Bradford's death), unpublished, almost certainly by Bradford (cf. his *Dialogues*), followed in the Ms. by the five other poems of Bradford in the order here below listed.
3. A Word to New Plymoth.
   34 four-line stanzas, Ms.c.c., *ibid.*, pp. 49–53, pr. 1 *Proc. M.H.S.*, vol. 11, pp. 478–82.
4. A Word to New England.
   22 lines, Ms.c.c., *ibid.*, p. 55; also Ms.a. MHS, pr. 3 *Coll. M.H.S.*, vol. 7, p. 28.
5. Of Boston in New England.
   48 lines, Ms.c.c., *ibid.*, p. 55–7; also Ms.a. *MHS*, pr. 3 *Coll. M.H.S.*, vol. 7, pp. 27–8.
6. Epitaphium Meum.
   34 lines, Ms.c.c., *ibid.*, pp. 59–60; pr. (prob. from Ms.a.) Morton, pp. 144–5.
7. Some observations of God's merciful dealing with us in this wilderness, and his gracious protection over us these many years.
   431 lines, Ms.c.c., *ibid.*, pp. 61–77, pr. 1 *Proc. M.H.S.*, vol. 11, pp. 465–78; also Ms.a. fragm. MHS, pr. 1 *Coll. M.H.S.*, vol. 3, pp. 77–84 (first 79 lines lacking).

BRADSTREET, ANNE (DUDLEY) (c. 1612–1672), b. prob. Northampton, Eng., N. E. 1630, resided briefly in Salem, Charlestown, Newtown (Cambridge), Ipswich, and for the rest of her life in Andover, Mass.; wife of Governor Simon Bradstreet, daughter of Governor Thomas Dudley.

1. *The Tenth Muse Lately sprung up in America.*
   London, 1650, 12mo. pp. (14),–1–207; 2nd ed., *Several Poems Compiled with a great variety of Wit and Learning* (Boston, 1678); later editions 1758, 1867, 1897, and 1932.
2. Several other Poems . . . found among her Papers after her Death.
   first pr. in 2nd ed., 1678, and in subseq. ed.
3. To my dear Children.
   Occasionall meditations.
   Upon speciall occasions.
   Upon the burning of our house, July 10, 1666.
   Ms.c.c., 43–67, by her son Simon, in private possession, pr. by John Harvard Ellis, *The Works of Anne Bradstreet* (Charlestown, 1867), pp. 3–42 (includes also some religious meditations in prose).
4. "As weary pilgrim, now at rest."
   Ms.a., *ibid.*, pp. 97–8 (in same Ms. vol. as no. 3), in private possession, pr. by Ellis, *ibid.*, pp. 42–4.
   Note: the Meditations Divine and morall (Ms.a. *ibid.*, pp. 1–41, Ellis ed. pp. 47–76) are in prose.
5. The Romane Monarchy.
   continuation after Tarquinius Superbus, Ms. far advanced when burned by fire of 1666 (ref. Ellis ed. pp. lxi & 329).

BRADSTREET, SAMUEL (c. 1633–1682), b. prob. Newtown (Cambridge), Mass., H.C., 1653, in Eng. 1657–1661 probably studying medicine, physician Boston, removed to Jamaica, W.I.

1. Aspice venturo latentur ut omnia Seclo.
   6 six-line stanzas in English, on Apollo wooing Tellus, in his *Almanack* for 1657, t.p. verso; repr. Perry Miller and Thomas H. Johnson, *The Puritans* (New York, 1938), p. 632.
2. "The saucy Ram 'gins doss at Titans Mace."
   4 lines, in *ibid.*, under February. Note: there may have been more verse on the missing pages of the only known copy, AAS.

BRADSTREET, SIMON III (1671–1741), b. New London, Conn., H.C. 1693, pastor Charlestown, Mass.

(Epitaph on Charles Morton.)

d. Charlestown, April 11, 1698, a. 72.

17 lines rhythmic prose and 6 lines verse, Latin, on tomb, pr. William I. Budington, *The History of the First Church Charlestown* (Boston, 1845), p. 225.

BRATTLE, WILLIAM (1662–1717), b. Boston, Mass., H.C. 1680, pastor Cambridge, tutor, fellow, treasurer H.C., F.R.S.

(Calendar Verse.)

6 lines under each month, in his *An Ephemeris of Coelestial Motions . . . For the Year . . . 1682* (Cambridge, 1682).

BRIGDEN, ZECHARIAH (1639–1662), b. Charlestown, Mass., H.C. 1657, tutor and fellow, pastor Stonington, Conn.

Astra regunt mundum: at sapiens dominabitur astris.

4 lines English, in his *Almanack* for 1659, t.p. verso, repr. in John Tulley's *Almanack* for 1698, p. 15.

BROWNE, JOSEPH (c. 1646–1678), b. Salem, Mass., H.C. 1666, fellow, temp. pastor Charlestown, Mass.

1. Upon the death of that pious mother in God Mrs Katherine Chauncy.

   d. Cambridge, Jan. 23 (or 24), 1667, a. 66.

   29 lines (plus 2, apparently illegible in Ms.), Ms.a. (?) found 1856 (or earlier) by A. Harris, present location not known, pr. *New England Hist. Gen. Reg.*, vol. 10, pp. 253–4, and William Chauncey Fowler, *Memorials of the Chaunceys* (Boston, 1856), pp. 31–2; Ms. signed J.B. and attributed to Joseph Browne by Morison, *Harvard College in the Seventeenth Century*, p. 322 n.

2. An Protoplasti per lapsum amiserint Dona Naturalia?

   14 lines Latin, *Quaestiones Duae, Pro Modulo, Discutiendae* (Cambridge, 1669), broadside, repr. Sibley, vol. 2, pp. 205–6, and Morison, *op. cit.*, p. 603.

BULKELEY, EDWARD (1614–1696), b. Bedfordshire, Eng., St. Catherine's College, Cambridge, N.E., 1635, pastor Marshfield and Concord, d. Chelmsford, Mass.

1. A Threnodia upon our Churches second dark Eclipse . . . by Deaths Interposition between us and that Great Light and Divine Plant, Mr. Samuel Stone.
   d. Hartford, July 20, 1663, a. 61.
   40 lines, Morton, pp. 168–9, signed E.B., and generally attributed to Edward Bulkeley.
2. Upon the Death of that truely Godly, Reverend, and Faithful Servant of Christ, Mr. Jonathan Mitchell.
   d. Cambridge, July 9, 1668, a. 44.
   28 lines, Morton, pp. 192–3, signed E.B., and generally attributed to Edward Bulkeley.

BULKELEY, GERSHOM (1636–1713), b. Cambridge, Mass., H.C. 1655, fellow, pastor New London and Wethersfield, Conn., surgeon, physician, alchemist, deputy, d. Glastonbury, Conn.

An Voluntas semper sequatur ultimum dictamen intellectus practici?
   14 lines Latin, in *Quaestio In Philosophia Discutienda* (Cambridge, 1658), repr. Morison, *op. cit.*, p. 595; the earliest preserved of the *Quaestiones* with verse.

BULKELEY, PETER I (1583–1659), b. Bedfordshire, Eng., St. John's College, Cambridge, fellow and university preacher, N.E. 1635, pastor Litchfield and Odell, Eng., and Concord, Mass.

1. A Lamentation for the Death of that Precious and Worthy Minister of Jesus Christ, Mr. Thomas Hooker.
   d. Hartford, July 7, 1647, a. 61.
   100 lines, Morton, pp. 127–9, signed P.B., and generally attributed to Peter Bulkeley.
2. (Elegy on the death of Thomas Shepard.)
   d. Cambridge, Aug. 25, 1649, a. 44.
   apparently lost; 2 line excerpt in Latin, *Magnalia*, vol. 1, p.357.
3. (Elegy on the death of John Cotton.)
   d. Boston, Dec. 23, 1652, a. 67.
   apparently lost; 12 line excerpt in Latin, *Magnalia*, vol. 1, p. 256.
4. (Epigram on an earthquake, October 29, 1653.)
   16 lines Latin, Ms.a. Mather Mss. (?), apparently lost, pr. *Magnalia*, vol. 1, pp. 364–5.

5. (Epigram on his birth-day, Jan. 31, 1654.)
   6 lines Latin, Ms.a. apparently lost, pr. *Magnalia*, vol. 1, p. 364.
6. (Epigram on his old age, March 25, 1657.)
   10 lines Latin, Ms.a. apparently lost, pr. *Magnalia*, vol. 1, p. 364.

BULKELEY, PETER II (1643–1691), b. Concord, Mass., H.C. 1662, removed to Fairfield, Conn. with his mother c. 1663, merchant, physician.

1. "Like to the Grasse thats Green too day."
   224 lines, Ms.a. Hartford Medical Society, among the Gershom Bulkeley medical Mss., a thick quarto vol., bound in vellum, with medical recipes, theological treatises, and 37 pages of verse (and another 1¼ pp. at back of vol.) in the hand of Peter Bulkeley the Younger, youngest son of Peter Bulkeley of Concord (with medical additions by Gershom).
   Note: the five leaves just before the first poem are cut out.
2. Of the Trinity and the Unity of the Godhead.
   58 lines, Ms.a., *ibid.*
3. God so Loved the world that he sent his only begotten son into the world that &c.
   126 lines, Ms.a., *ibid.*
4. The dignity and Transcendant Excellency of Jesus Christ.
   82 lines, Ms.a., *ibid.*
5. A Loving Conference had with Christ and the deceast soule, touching the state and Joyes of the Life to Come promised to them that learne of Christ, and follow him in this life.
   354 lines, Ms.a., *ibid.*
6. The humanity of Christ.
   24 lines, Ms.a., *ibid.*
7. O Death where is Thy Sting, O Grave where is thy Victory &c.
   38 lines, Ms.a., *ibid.*
8. "Use and peruse this book, with greatest care."
   38 lines, Ms.a., *ibid.*, on the back cover and the facing fly leaf.

BURT, JONATHAN (1627–1715), b. prob. Eng., N.E., as a child, settled Springfield, Mass., deacon, selectman.

A Lamentation Occasion'd by the Great Sickness & Lamented Deaths of divers Eminent Persons in Springfield.

128 lines, broadside MHS, facsim. Winslow, p. 177; below title: "Composed by Mr. Jonathan Burt, (an Old Disciple,) in his Fourscore & Fifth year, (Since Deceased,) . . ."; under last col.: "writ, April, 1712. Printed in the Year, 1720." (date of birth given in Winslow, p. 176, as 1632.)

C., E.

Upon the Death, and much lamented loss, of that excellentlie well accomplisht Gentleman, John Winthrop Esquire.

d. Boston, April 6, 1676, a. 70.

64 lines, Ms.a. or c.c. (?), MHS, Winthrop Deeds, etc., p. 60; signed "amiculus E. C"; a Massachusetts writer (as several lines reveal), possibly Ezekiel Cheever, Elijah Corlet, or Elnathan Chauncy.

CAPEN, JOSEPH (1658–1725), b. Dorchester, Mass., H.C. 1677, pastor Topsfield, Mass.

A Funeral Elegy Upon the much to be Lamented Death and most Deplorable Expiration of the Pious, Learned, Ingenious, and Eminently Usefull Servant of God Mr. John Foster.

d. Dorchester, Sept. 9, 1681, a. 33.

52 lines, broadside (lost?), repr. from Ms.c.c., private possession, in Thomas C. Simonds, *History of South Boston* (Boston, 1857), pp. 38–9, and from same Ms. in Samuel A. Green, *John Foster* (Boston, 1909), pp. 36–7; repr. *literatim* from Green (with about a dozen lapses) in *Harper's Literary Museum*, Ola Elizabeth Winslow, ed. (New York, 1927), pp. 95–7. Though both Symonds and Green copied from the same Ms. (error in Ford, see Green, p. 35), the results show about 75 points of difference, most of them in punctuation and orthography, a few verbal. In general, Green seems to have been more accurate, though at a few points Simonds seems to have the correct version. There is apparently no evidence of the existence of the original broadside since the advertisement in William Brattle's almanac of 1682.

CHAMBERLAIN, RICHARD (c. 1630's–after 1698) b. probably London, Trinity College, Cambridge, lawyer Gray's Inn 1651, secretary of the province of New Hampshire, 1680.

To the much Honoured R.F. Esq;

20 lines (6 three-line stanzas and a couplet), dedicatory poem in his *Lithobolia: or, the Stone-Throwing Devil* (London, 1698), repr. in *Narratives of the Witchcraft Cases*, George L. Burr ed. (New York, 1914), pp. 59–60.

CHAUNCY, CHARLES (1592–1672), b. Hertfordshire, Eng., Trinity College, Cambridge, fellow, professor Hebrew and Greek, N.E. 1638, pastor Cambridge, Ware, Marston–St. Laurence, Eng., Plymouth and Scituate, Mass., President Harvard College, physician.

1. Gratulatio Academiae Cantabrigiensis in Reditum Illust. Caroli Walliae Principis.
   42 lines Latin, Cambridge, 1623, 4to, repr. William Chauncey Fowler, *Memorials of the Chaunceys* (Boston, 1858), p. 6, and *New England Hist. Gen. Reg.*, vol. 10, p. 110.
2. Epithalamium Illust. Principum Caroli Regis et H. Mariae Reginae.
   26 lines Latin, Cambridge, 1625, 4to, repr. *ibid.*, a) p. 7, b) pp. 110–1.
3. Cantabrigiensium Dolor et Solamen.
   (on the death of King James I and accession of Charles I.)
   95 and 20 lines Latin, Cambridge, 1625, repr. *ibid.*, a) pp. 7–10, b) pp. 111–3.
4. *'Εις τὸν γάμον τοῦ φαιδιμωτάτου βασιλἕως*, ΚΑΡΟ'ΛΟΥ, *ἐπιθαλάμιον.*
   (Epithalamium on the Marriage of the Most Illustrious King Charles.)
   12 lines Greek, repr. *ibid.*, a) p. 10, b) p. 113.
5. (Album verses.)
   Ms.a. in Album of Johann Friedrich Wagner of Nürnberg (matric. Cambridge, 1627), signed Carolus Chauncy, socius coll. Trin. Cantab. 1627, British Museum, Addit. Mss. 15,852.
6. Novae Angliae Lamentatio.
   12 lines and 2 lines Latin, Ms.a. BPL, Cotton Papers, vol. 3, p. 11; there listed as anonymous, though the abbreviated

signature "Charl. Chanc." with the date 1649 appears in Ms. The two lines appended and the name of the son "Isaack Chanc." under them are also in the hand of Charles Chauncy (cf. the preceding Ms., vol. 3, p. 10).

7. A Perpetuall Calender, fitted for the Meridian of Babylon, where the Pope is Elevated 42 Degr.

32 Lines, in John Richardson's *Almanack* (Cambridge, 1670), last page (16), signed "Incerti Authoris." Samuel Sewall in a letter to his brother Stephen, Dec. 24, 1680, *New England Hist. Gen. Reg.*, vol. 24, p. 122, quotes the last two lines, calling it "the verse of Mr Chauncy President" (prophecy on the fall of Rome and the rise of a Western New Jerusalem on the 42nd parallel).

CHAUNCY, ELNATHAN (c. 1639–1684), b. prob. Plymouth, Mass., H.C. 1661, studied medicine in Europe, physician Boston, d. Barbadoes.

1. (Elegy on Silvanus Walderne.)

student H.C., d. after June, 1658.

anagram, 2, 4, and 15 lines, last set with initial and medial acrostic, Ms.a. commonplace book, first leaf verso (defective), in possession of heirs of William Chauncy Fowler, pr. *Publ. Col. Soc. Mass.*, vol. 28, p. 3. (with the defects in part incorrectly restored through a disregard of the initial acrostic).

2. (Elegy on Henry Dunster.)

d. Scituate, Feb. 27, 1659.

anagram, 2, 4, 14, and 4 lines, third set with medial acrostic, Ms.a. *ibid.*, leaf 3 recto (defective), pr. *ibid.*, p. 4.

CHAUNCY, ISAAC (1632–1712), b. Hertfordshire, Eng., N.E. 1638, H.C. 1651, ret. Eng., pastor and physician (M.D.) London.

"Abstulit una Dies, qualem nec multa tulerunt."

2 lines, Ms.c.c. BPL, appended to his father's "Novae Angliae Lamentatio."

CHAUNCY, ISRAEL (1644–1703), b. Scituate, H.C. 1661, founder and trustee Y.C., pastor Stratford, Conn.

(Fragment of verse.)

his almanac for 1664, last page, of which only the inner margin remains in the unique copy at the AAS, showing some of the rhyming words of what was apparently a full page of verse.

CHAUNCY, NATHANIEL (1639–1685), b. Plymouth, Mass., H.C. 1661, tutor and fellow, pastor Windsor, Conn. and Hatfield, Mass., physician.

1. Upon the Eclipse of the Moon.
   12 lines, in his *Almanack* for 1662, p. 2.

2. New Englands Zodiake.
   12 lines, *ibid.*, p. 16 (a third poem is signed "Incerti Authoris").

CHEEVER, EZEKIEL (1616–1708), b. London, Eng., Emmanuel College Cambridge, N.E. 1637, schoolmaster New Haven, Conn., Ipswich, Charlestown, and Boston, Mass.

Poems which can with certainty be ascribed to him have not yet been brought to light. However, Cotton Mather in his epitaph on him (*Corderius Americanus*, Boston, 1708, p. 37) calls him "POETA, a quo non tantum Carmina pangere, sed et Caelestes Hymnos, Odasq; Angelicas, canere Didicerunt, Qui discere voluerunt," showing that he both wrote verse and taught his apter pupils to write it.

The commonplace book bearing his signature and containing a number of Latin and Greek poems, now at the Boston Athenaeum, is not in his handwriting, and John T. Hassam has proved for many of the poems that Cheever could not have written them, several being from classical sources and others dating from Cheever's childhood or before his birth. See John T. Hassam, *The Cheever Family* (Boston, 1896), Appendix, and *New England Hist. Gen. Reg.*, vol. 57, pp. 40–4.

CHEEVER, SAMUEL (1639–1724), b. New Haven, Conn., H.C. 1659, pastor Marblehead, Mass.

1. (Calendar Verses.)
   8 lines under each month, except last month (February) which has 10 lines, in his *Almanack* for 1660.

2. (Calendar Verses.)
   8 lines under each month, except last month (February) which has 10 lines, in his *Almanack* for 1661.

CHESTER, STEPHEN (1639–1705), b. Wethersfield, Conn. and resided there, d. Hartford.

A Funeral Elegy Upon the Death of that Excellent and most worthy Gentleman John Winthrop Esq.

d. Boston, April 6, 1676, a. 70.

60 lines, anagram, acrosticon, and epitaph, broadside MHS, facsim. Winslow, p. 9.

CLAP, ROGER (1609–1691), b. Devonshire, England, N.E. 1630, Dorchester, Mass., captain of militia, deputy, captain of the Castle, retired and d. Boston.

1. Verses made upon the death of Mr. nowell.

   (Increase Nowell), d. Charlestown, Nov. 1, 1655, a. 65.

   20 four-line stanzas, Ms.c.c. BPL, in account book of son Samuel Clap, pr. *Publ. Col. Soc. Mass.*, vol. 8, pp. 225–8.

2. Upon the death of our honourable Gouernour John Endicot esqr.

   d. Boston, Mar. 15, 1665, a. 76 or 77.

   24 four-line stanzas, Ms.c.c. *ibid.*, pr. *ibid.*, pp. 228–31.

3. Upon the death of Eldar withington.

   (Henry Withington), d. Dorchester, Feb. 2, 1667, a. 79.

   15 four-line stanzas, Ms.c.c. *ibid.*, pr. *ibid.*, pp. 231–3.

COLMAN, BENJAMIN (1673–1747), b. Boston, Mass., H.C. 1692, pastor London and Bath, Eng., Boston, Mass.

1. A Quarrel with Fortune.

   18 lines, written for Miss Ashurst, daughter of Sir Henry Ashurst, at her request, c. 1697, pr. Ebenezer Turell, *The Life and Character of The Reverend Benjamin Colman, D.D.* (Boston, 1749), pp. 24–5.

2. (Extempore poem on Miss Elizabeth Singer, "Philomela," at Bath.)

   8 lines, c. 1699, pr. *ibid.*, p. 36.

3. To Celia flying from her mother.

   35 lines, plus 3 lines, Ms.a. MHS, Colman Papers, vol. 1, p. 3.

4. On content.

   6 lines, Ms.a. MHS, *ibid.*

5. *A Poem on Elijahs Translation, Occasion'd by the Death of the Reverend and Learned Mr. Samuel Willard.*

   d. Boston, Sept. 12, 1707, a. 67.

273 lines, t.p. & 14 pp., appended to Ebenezer Pemberton, *A Funeral Sermon on The Death of That Learned & Excellent Divine The Reverend Mr. Samuel Willard* (Boston, 1707), AAS, MHS; repr. Kettell, vol. 1, pp. 55–61.

6. "Laetum Rus genuit, Cultos Academia Morit."
   9 lines Latin, followed by transl., "The farm-house boasts his Birth with humble pride," 11 lines; later dated in pencil: (1712), Ms.a. MHS, Colman Papers, vol. 1.
7. "Joy of my Life! is this thy lovely Voice?"
   22 lines, in his *Reliquiae Turellae, et Lachrymae Paternae* (Boston, 1735), Appendix, Ebenezer Turell, *Memoirs of the Life and Death of the Pious and Ingenious Mrs. Jane Turell* (sep. t.p. but contin. pag.), p. 64, AAS, MHS, BPL, etc.; addressed by Colman to his daughter, Jane, Jan. 1718, in answer to her first effort in verse in her eleventh year.
8. "Thrice I have heard your tuneful Voice."
   29 lines, pr. *ibid.*, p. 67; addressed to his daughter, Jane, in response to three poems by her; dated June 7, 1725.
9. A Hymn of Praise On a recovery from sickness.
   6 four-line stanzas, Ms.a. MHS, Colman Papers, vol. 1, p. 2; added a Latin translation, 6 four-line stanzas by William Welsteed, Colman's assistant from 1728.
10. To Urania on the death of her first child.
   74 lines, pr. Ebenezer Turell, *The Life and Character of The Reverend Benjamin Colman, D.D.*, pp. 188–90.
11. Another to Urania, &c.
   51 lines, pr. *ibid.*, pp. 190–1.
12. "The generous Tho't awakes my youthful Fire."
   38 lines, plus 3 lines, Ms.a. MHS, Colman Papers, vol. 2, draft of Colman's reply to a gracious letter from Jonathan Belcher, Sept. 27, 1739, pr. *ibid.*, pp. 192–3 (only 31 lines).
13. The Transport. To Mr. Pope, on looking again into his Essay on Man.
   37 lines (plus 1 cancelled), Ms.a. MHS, *ibid.*, dated "Febr. 14. 1739. America."

CORLET, ELIJAH (c. 1610–1688), b. London, Eng., Lincoln College, Oxford and Pembroke College, Cambridge, N.E. by 1642, schoolmaster Eng., and Cambridge, Mass.

1. (Elegy on Thomas Hooker.)
   d. Hartford, July 7, 1647, a. 61.
   31 lines Latin, *Magnalia*, vol. 1, p. 319.
2. In Obitum . . . John Hull.
   d. Boston, Sept. 30, 1683, a. 59.
   48 lines Latin, in Samuel Willard, *The High Esteem which God hath of the Death of the Saints* (Boston, 1683).

COTTON, JOHN I (1584–1652), b. Derbyshire, Eng., Trinity and Emmanuel College, Cambridge, fellow and head lecturer, N.E. 1633, pastor Boston, Eng. and Boston, Mass.

1. Another Poem . . . upon his removal from Boston to this Wilderness.
   8 four-line stanzas, in John Norton, *Abel being Dead yet Speaketh* (London, 1658), pp. 29–30.
2. A thankful Acknowledgment of God's Providence.
   5 four-line stanzas, in *ibid.*, pp. 28–9.
3. On my Reverend and dear Brother, Mr. Thomas Hooker.
   d. Hartford, July 7, 1647, a. 61.
   8 four-line stanzas, prefixed to Thomas Hooker, *A Survey of the Summe of Church-Discipline* (London, 1648); also in Morton, pp. 125–6.
4. In Saram. In Rolandum. In Utrumque.
   3 stanzas of six, eight, and twelve lines, on the death of his two children, Jan. 20 & 29, 1649–50, in the *Magnalia*, vol. 1, pp. 260–1.
5. To my Reverend Dear Brother, M. Samuel Stone.
   30 lines, prefixed to Samuel Stone, *A Congregational Church Is a Catholike Visible Church* (London, 1652).

COTTON, JOHN II (1640–1699), b. Boston, Mass., H.C. 1657, pastor Wethersfield, Conn., Edgartown and Plymouth, Mass., Charleston, S. C., where d.

1. (Verses on the Death of Noah Newman.)
   d. Rehoboth, April 16, 1678, a. 47.
   broadside, apparently lost, ref. letter of Samuel Wakeman to John Cotton, Fairfield, Apr. 16, 1680 (Ms. BPL, Cotton Papers, vol. 8, p. 18), which mentions "two papers of verses upon the deaths . . . of mr Walley & mr Newman the one of

which was endorsed with the harty respects of the author" (the other on Thomas Walley is probably the extant one written by Thomas Hinckley).

2. Upon the Death of that Aged, Pious, Sincere-hearted Christian, John Alden, Esq.
   d. Duxbury, Sept. 12, 1687, a. 89.
   100 lines, broadside, unique copy BA, signed J.C., repr. *The Mayflower Descendant*, vol. 9, pp. 194–6, with facsim. facing p. 193; also repr. by Timothy Alden, Jr., in a broadside of 1806 and in his *Collection of American Epitaphs* (New York, 1814), vol. 3, pp. 271–4.

CROWNE, JOHN (c. 1640–1712), b. prob. Shropshire, Eng., N.E. 1657, H.C. 1657–1660 (not grad.), in Maine summer of 1658, ret. Eng. late Dec. 1660, dramatist and poet.

1. "Like me that list, my honest Prose and Rimes."
   couplet, in his *Pandion and Amphigenia: or, the History of the Coy Lady of Thessalia* (London, 1665), "To the Reader."
2. "Then must I live, and will none pitty lend."
   42 lines, in *ibid.*, pp. 4–5.
3. "Though cruel fortune make us part."
   couplet, in *ibid.*, p. 6.
4. "If thou'lt preserve thy tottering Kingdoms fall."
   couplet, in *ibid.*, p. 34.
5. "Who Honor and these Arms would win."
   4 lines, in *ibid.*, p. 59.
6. "What strange untrained passions do controle."
   46 lines, in *ibid.*, pp. 93–4.
7. The Song.
   "Phaebus lend me thy flulgent rays."
   6 ten-line stanzas in, *ibid.*, pp. 110–1.
8. "You Angels that reside above."
   8 thirteen-line stanzas, in *ibid.*, pp. 123–6.
9. "Were I immur'd in flesh and blood."
   9 six-line stanzas, in *ibid.*, pp. 128–30.
10. "Fair Venus Queen of Beauty's dead."
   8 eight-line stanzas, in *ibid.*, pp. 176–8.

11. The Antiphone.
"Sweet day, so calm, so cool, so bright."
95 lines, in *ibid.*, pp. 189–92; a cantata for chorus, treble, and bass, on Sol wooing Tellus.
12. *Juliana, or, the Princess of Poland.*
London, 1671, a tragi-comedy in blank and rhymed verse and in prose; includes three "Songs"; repr. in *The Dramatic Works of John Crowne* (Edinburgh, 1873), vol. 1, pp. 15–116 (here and following the vol. and p. ref. are given from this ed.).
13. "Lo, behind a scene of seas."
4 nine-line stanzas, in *ibid.*, pp. 23–4.
14. "Awake, awake! thou warlike genius of our state."
2 stanzas of nine and thirteen lines, in *ibid.*, pp. 61–2.
15. "How nobly heaven doth receive."
3 ten-line stanzas, in *ibid.*, pp. 99–100.
16. *The History of Charles the Eighth of France.*
London, 1672, a drama in rhymed couplets, repr. vol. 1, pp. 127–8; includes two songs.
17. The Song sung to Julia in the Garden.
"Oh love! if e'er thou'lt ease a heart."
3 ten-line stanzas, in *ibid.*, pp. 182–3.
18. The Song of Spirits sung to Isabella as she sits asleep.
"They call! They call! what voice is that?"
3 ten-line stanzas, in *ibid.*, pp. 198–9.
19. *Calisto: or, The Chaste Nimph. The late Masque at Court . . . With the Prologue, and the Songs betwixt the Acts.*
London, 1675, a verse drama with lyric prologue and songs, repr. vol. 1, pp. 232–326.
20. Prologue.
132 lines, in lyric form, in *ibid.*, pp. 241–6.
21. Chorus of Shepherds.
"Hark, hark, I hear the merry hunter's horn."
19 lines, in *ibid.*, pp. 261–2.
22. An entry of Basques.
"Kind lovers, love on."
6 lines, in *ibid.*, p. 262.
23. Chorus of Shepherds.
"Come Shepherds quickly hasten to the shades."
29 lines, in *ibid.*, pp. 273–4.

24. Chorus of Shepherds, An Entry of Gypsies, An Entry of Satyrs.
"Oh whither does my lovely Daphne fly?"
29 lines, in *ibid.*, pp. 288–9.
25. Daphne and Sylvia (Concerted piece).
"Oh! whither are our poor despairing shepherds gone?"
33 lines, in *ibid.*, pp. 304–6.
26. Chorus of Shepherds, followed by Bacchusses.
"Joy, Shepherds joy! Diana's disgrac'd."
2 five-line stanzas, in *ibid.*, p. 306.
27. Chorus of Shepherds . . . African Women.
"Happy lovers! happy live."
49 lines, in *ibid.*, pp.321–2.
28. *The Country Wit.*
London, 1675, a comedy mostly in prose, but with prologue, epilogue, and several passages in the play in verse, and with one song, vol. 3, pp. 11–130.
29. "A pox of impertinent age."
2 eight-line stanzas, in *ibid.*, pp. 48–9.
30. *The Destruction of Jerusalem by Titus Vespasian. In Two Parts.*
London, 1677, a drama in rhymed couplets, with prologue and epilogue to each part, and two songs, vol. 2, pp. 231–396.
31. A Song to be sung by Levites at the Temple Gates.
"Day is dismounted on the watery plain."
14 lines, in *ibid.*, p. 242.
32. "Come pious mourner, pray no more!"
2 twelve-line stanzas, in *ibid.*, p. 358.
33. *The Ambitious Statesman, or the Loyal Favorite.*
London, 1679, a tragedy in blank verse, rhymed prologue and epilogue, and one song, vol. 3, pp. 141–241.
34. "Long, long had great Amintor lain."
4 stanzas, 2 of eight lines, 2 of nine, in *ibid.*, pp. 200–1.
35. *The Miseries of Civil-War* (Henry the Sixth, Second Part).
London, 1680 & 1681; no modern reprint, drama in verse, adapted from Shakespeare.
36. *Henry the Sixth, the First Part.*
London, 1680; no modern reprint, drama in verse, adapted from Shakespeare.
37. *Thyestes.*
London, 1681; a tragedy in blank verse with rhymed prologue and epilogue, and two songs, vol. 2, pp. 13–80.

38. The Song at Atreus his Banquet.
"A lovely pair endowed by fate."
6 five-line stanzas, in *ibid.*, pp. 14–5.

39. A Chorus of Priests.
"Goddess Minerva, wise, austere."
2 ten-line stanzas, in *ibid.*, p. 15.

40. *City Politiques.*
London, 1688, a comedy mostly in prose, but with prologue, last part of epilogue, and several passages in the play in verse, vol. 2, pp. 95–213.

41. *Sir Courtly Nice; or, It Cannot be.*
London, 1685, a comedy, mostly in prose, but with prologue, epilogue, and several passages in the play in verse, and with two songs and a poem, vol. 3, pp. 254–355.

42. A song to be Sung in Dialogue between a man and a woman.
"Oh! be kind, my dear, be kind."
4 six-line stanzas, in *ibid.*, pp. 290–1.

43. A Dialogue Sung between an Indian man and woman.
"Thou lovely Indian sea of charms."
4 stanzas, of six, eight, eight, and ten lines, in *ibid.*, pp. 329–30. Note: not American but East Indians.

44. "As I gaz'd unaware."
10 lines, in *ibid.*, p. 340, adapted from the Stop thief! poem in Moliere's *Precieuses Ridicules.*

45. *A Poem on the lamented death of our late gratious Sovereign, King Charles the II, of ever blessed memory. With a congratulation to the Happy succession of King James the II.*
London, 1685, in rhymed couplets.

46. *Darius, King of Persia.*
London, 1688, a tragedy in blank verse, with rhymed prologue and epilogue, vol. 3, pp. 369–457.

47. *The English Frier: or, the Town Sparks.*
London, 1690, a comedy, mostly in prose, but with prologue, epilogue, and several passages in the play in verse, and with three songs, vol. 4, pp. 14–121.

48. Airy dancing and singing.
"When the kind wanton hour."
8 lines, in *ibid.*, p. 41.

49. Airy sings.
"Oh, the wakings."
6 lines, in *ibid.*, p. 101.

50. Airy Sings.
"I once had virtue, wealth, and fame."
4 four-line stanzas, in *ibid.*, p. 102.

51. *Daeneids, or the Noble Labours of the Great Dean of Notre-Dame in Paris.*
London, 1692, mock-heroic poem in four cantos.

52. *The History of the Famous and Passionate Love between a Fair Noble Parisian Lady and a Beautiful Young Singing-Man.*
London, 1692, mock-heroic poem; repr. by Dryden in *Miscellany Poems* (London, 1716), part 3, p. 352.

53. A Song set by Mr. Henry Purcell, the Words by Mr. J. Crown.
"Ah me! to many Deaths decreed."
2 five-line stanzas, in the *Gentleman's Journal, or Monthly Miscellany*, ed. by Motteaux, London, August, 1692, pp. 27–30.

54. *Regulus.*
London, 1694 (first performed 1692), a tragedy in blank verse and prose, with rhymed prologue and epilogue, and two songs, vol. 4, pp. 133–222.
Note: the first song, p. 155, is no. 53 above, "Ah me! to many Deaths decreed."

55. "Down with your sprightly wine, boys."
5 seven-line stanzas, in *ibid.*, pp. 186–7.

56. *The married Beau: or, the Curious Impertinent.*
London, 1694, a comedy in blank verse, with rhymed prologue and epilogue, and two songs, vol. 4, pp. 232–336.

57. "Oh, fie! what mean I, foolish maid."
10 three-line stanzas, in *ibid.*, pp. 272–3.

58. "See! where repenting Celia lyes."
2 nine-line stanzas, in *ibid.*, p. 318.

59. *Caligula.*
London, 1698, a tragedy in rhymed couplets (a few unrhymed lines), with rhymed prologue, and one song, vol. 4, pp. 355–426.

60. "Hail! mighty Prince, whose loud renown."
3 stanzas, of thirteen, eleven, and ten lines, in *ibid.*, pp. 378–9.

61. *Justice Busy, or the Gentleman Quack.*
produced probably in 1700, never printed and apparently lost. About one song in it there is this report: "Mrs Bracegirdle, by a potent and magnetic charm, in performing a song in't, caus'd *the stones of the street to fly in the men's faces*" (vol. 4, p. 345).

DANE, JOHN (c. 1612–1684), b. Hertfordshire, Eng., N.E. by 1638, chirurgeon of Ipswich, Mass., brother of the Rev. Francis Dane.
By John Dane, senner, of Ipshwitch, And Chiriergen, in the yer of our Lord, 1682; Containing sum poems in waie of preparation for death, besides the obsarvaton of seavarall provedensis in the Cose of his lyfe, and aded seaverall meditations.
with prefatory verse of 4 lines; Ms.a. NEHGS (cannot now be located), Ms. is described in *New England Hist. Gen. Reg.*, vol. 8, p. 147, and the prose autobiography from it is published, pp. 149–56, but of the verse only the four prefatory lines are printed. The autobiography in verse, as well as the religious meditations and advice to his children in rhyme remain unpublished.

DANFORTH, JOHN (1660–1730), b. Roxbury, Mass., H.C. 1677, fellow, pastor Dorchester, Mass.

1. (Calendar Verse.)
8 lines under each month, except last month (February) which has 10 lines, in his *Almanack* for 1679.
2. "What if a day or a month or a year."
4 twelve-line stanzas, Ms.a. (?) MHS, on the first, badly worn leaf of a volume of sermon notes and lectures by John and Benjamin Eliot, Samuel Willard, and others, 1679–1680, kept by John Danforth; broadside JCB, "The Vanity of the World, A Poem," no place, date, printer, or author indicated, probably second half of 18th century, possibly a reprint of an earlier, lost broadside; 4 eight-line stanzas (short lines pr. as double lines), with considerable revision and rearrangement.
3. (Epitaph on Josiah Flint.)
d. Dorchester, Sept. 15, 1680, a. 35.
18 lines, gravestone, Dorchester, pr. *New England Hist. Gen. Reg.*, vol. 2, pp. 382–3, and in *History of the Town of Dorchester*

(Boston, 1859), pp. 240–1; possibly but not certainly by Danforth.

4. A Poem. Upon the Triumphant Translation of a Mother in Our Israel, Viz. Mrs. Anne Eliot.
   d. Roxbury, March 24, 1687, a. 84.
   5 ten-line stanzas, in his *Kneeling to God, At Parting with Friends* (Boston, 1697), pp. 64–5, AAS.
5. A Poem. To the Blessed Memory of the Venerable Mr. John Eliot.
   d. Roxbury, May 20, 1690, a. 86.
   195 lines, in *ibid.*, pp. 66–72.
6. Ad Politum Literaturae, atque Sacrarum Literaturum Antistitem, . . . D. Cottonum Matherum . . . Epigramma.
   2 lines Latin and 5 lines English, among prefatory verse, *Magnalia*, vol. 1, p. 19.
7. A Funeral Elegy Humbly Dedicated to the Renowned Memory of the Honorable, Thomas Danforth Esq.
   d. Cambridge, Nov. 5, 1699, a. 77.
   156 lines, broadside in three columns, private possession, signed John Danforth; Ms. at top: "For the Revd. Mr. Nath: Clappe."
8. A few Lines to fill up a Vacant Page.
   4 seven-line stanzas, in his *The Right Christian Temper In every Condition* (Boston, 1702), p. (29), AAS.
9. (Epitaph on Miriam Wood.)
   d. Dorchester, Oct. 19, 1706, a. 73.
   8 lines, gravestone, Dorchester, pr. *History of the Town of Dorchester*, p. 554; probably by John Danforth.
10. A Pindarick Elegy Upon the Renowned, Mr. Samuel Willard.
    d. Boston, Sept. 12, 1707, a. 68.
    73 lines, broadside, unique copy NYHS (erroneously attributed to Samuel Danforth in Wegelin).
11. Upon the decease of the pious Mr. Thomas Bromfield, aged twelve years, the second son of the Honourable Edward Bromfield, Esq.
    d. Boston, Feb. 8, 1709/10, a. 12.
    13 four-line stanzas, broadside, in 1871 in possession of Daniel Denison Slade, M.D., present location unknown; 3 stanzas repr. in *New England Hist. Gen. Reg.*, vol. 25, pp. 334–5.
12. Profit and Loss. An Elegy upon the Decease of Mrs. Mary Gerrish.

d. Wenham, Nov. 17, 1710, a. 19.
104 lines, broadside, BPL, signed J.D.

13. Love and Unity Encouraged, and Contention and Division Disswaded, in a Poem.
264 lines, in Peter Thacher, *Christ's Forgiveness Of True Christians* (Boston, 1712), pp. 119–28, AAS.

14. (Elegy on the Death of Captain Jonathan Danforth.)
d. Billerica, Sept. 7, 1712, a. 84.
broadside or Ms. (?), apparently lost, excerpt of 7 lines & ref. in Henry A. Hazen, *History of Billerica* (Boston, 1883), Genealogical Register, p. 35, where attrib. to Jonathan's nephew, John Danforth.

15. Honour and Vertue Elegized: in an Poem, Upon . . . Madame Elizabeth Hutchinson.
d. Boston, Feb. 2, 1712/3, a. 71.
93 lines, broadside, BA.

16. A Poem, Upon the much Honoured and very Exemplarily Gracious Mrs. Maria Mather.
d. Boston, April 4, 1714, a. 73.
broadside, HCL, Ford, no. 368.

17. Memento Mori. Remember Death. Greatness & Goodness Elegized, In a Poem, Upon the much Lamented Decease of . . . Madam Hannah Sewell.
d. Boston, Oct. 19, 1717, a. 60.
67 lines, broadside, BPL, NYPL, facsim. Winslow, p. 31.

18. A Funeral Poem in Memory of Mr. Hopestill Clap.
d. Dorchester, Sept. 2, 1719, a. 72.
63 lines, broadside, in 1876 mentioned as having been "in the possession of the late Dea. James Humphreys, of Dorchester," probably unique; no later reference has been found; repr. in Ebenezer Clapp, *The Clapp Memorial* (Boston, 1876), pp. 13–4.

19. (Epitaph on Hopestill Clap.)
8 lines, gravestone, Dorchester, pr. in Thomas Prince ed. of *Memoirs of Captain Roger Clap* (Boston, 1731, 2nd ed. 1766), Appendix by James Blake, Jr.; "copied verbatim from the gravestone," in *The Clapp Memorial*, p. 12.

20. The Mercies Of the Year, commemorated: A Song for Little Children in New England. December 13th 1720.

9 four-line stanzas (followed by Isaac Watts, A Psalm for New England), broadside JCB, facsim. Winslow, p. 179.

Note: this broadside has remained unidentified to date, though it is almost certainly the broadside referred to by Samuel Sewall, *Letter Books*, vol. 2, p. 131, as Danforth's "Verses on the New Year," which he sent to Edward Taylor, March 18, 1720/1.

21. An Elegy upon the much Lamented Decease of Mrs. Elizabeth Foxcroft.
    d. Cambridge, July 4, 1721, a. 56.
    105 lines, appended to Thomas Foxcroft, *A Sermon Preach'd at Cambridge* (Boston, 1721), pp. 52–5.
22. An Elegy Upon the much Lamented Decease of the Reverend and Excellent Mr. Joseph Belcher.
    d. Roxbury, April 27, 1723, a. 53.
    58 lines, in Cotton Mather, *A Good Character* (Boston, 1723), pp. 25–7, repr. in the *Dedham Pulpit* (Boston, 1840), pp. 217–8.
23. The Divine Name Humbly Celebrated On Occasion of the Translation to Heaven of . . . Madam Susanna Thatcher.
    d. Milton, Sept. 4, 1724, a. 59.
    64 lines, broadside, MHS.
24. Two vast Enjoyments commemorated, and two great Bereavements lamented, in two excellent Persons, viz. the Reverend Mr. Peter Thacher . . . And the Reverend Mr. Samuel Danforth.
    d. Milton, Dec. 17, 1727, a. 77.
    d. Taunton, Nov. 14, 1727, a. 61.
    136 lines, 5 pp. appended to his *A Sermon Occasioned by the Late Great Earthquake* (Boston, 1728), also printed separately (ref. Sibley, vol. 2, p. 514, Ford, no. 530); repr. Samuel Hopkins Emery, *The Ministry of Taunton* (Boston, 1853), vol. 1, pp. 288–91.

DANFORTH, SAMUEL I (1626–1674), b. Suffolk, Eng., N.E. 1634, H.C. 1642, fellow, pastor Roxbury, astronomer.

1. (Calendar Verse.)
    6 lines of verse for each month from March to February, in his *An Almanack for the Year of Our Lord 1647* (Cambridge, 1647); repr. Murdock, pp. 101–4.

2. (Almanac Poem.)
   96 lines, in his *An Almanack for the Year of Our Lord 1648* (Cambridge, 1648); repr. Murdock, pp. 104–7.
3. (Almanac Poem.)
   88 lines, in his *An Almanack for the Year of Our Lord 1649* (Cambridge, 1649); repr. Murdock, pp. 108–11.
4. A Prognostication.
   8 lines, in *ibid.*, repr. Murdock, p. 111.
5. & 6. (Two anagrams and poems on William Tompson.)
   d. Braintree, Dec. 10, 1666, a. 68.
   12 & 12 lines, Ms. journal of Joseph Tompson of Billerica, pr. 2. *Proc. M.H.S.*, vol. 10, pp. 283–4, and Murdock, pp. 19–20.
   Note: the first of these is erroneously included by Hall among Benjamin Tompson's works, p. 108.

DANFORTH, SAMUEL II (1666–1727), b. Roxbury, Mass., H.C. 1683, pastor Taunton, Mass., physician.
1. Ad Librum.
   97 lines, in his *The New England Almanack For The Year of our Lord 1686* (Cambridge, 1686), pp. 2–3.
2. An Elegy in the Memory of the Worshipful Major Thomas Leonard, Esq.
   d. Taunton, Nov. 24, 1713, a. 73.
   11 six-line stanzas, broadside BA, repr. *New England Hist. Gen. Reg.*, vol. 22, p. 141.

DRAKE, FRANCIS (c. 1650–after 1668), possibly son of Capt. Francis Drake of Portsmouth, N. H., H.C. during 1668; father and brothers (?) to Piscataway, N. J., c. 1666 or 67; to England with a Harvard-educated Indian (ref. Daniel Gookin, "Historical Collections of the Indians in New England," 1 Coll. M. H. S., vol. 1, p. 173).

To the Memory of the learned and Reverend, Mr. Jonathan Mitchell.
   d. Cambridge, July 9, 1668, a. 44.
   74 lines plus a 4 line Epitaphium, in Morton, 193–6, signed F. D.; repr., with the omission of 14 lines, in Cotton Mather, *Ecclesiastes* (Boston, 1697), pp. 109–11 and in his *Magnalia*, vol. 2, pp. 94–6, in the latter signed F. Drake, and with these prefatory words: "When our Mitchel was dying, he let fall

such a speech as this unto a young gentleman, that lodg'd in his house, and now stood by his bed . . . The speech had a marvellous impression upon the soul of that young gentleman; who then compos'd the ensuing lines."

DUDLEY, JOSEPH (1647–1720), b. Roxbury, Mass., H.C. 1665, politician, Chief Justice, Mass. and N.Y., Governor Mass.

1. An detur in Deo scientia Media?
   8 lines of Latin verse under the second of the *Quaestiones in Philosophia Discutiendae* (Cambridge, 1668), repr. Sibley, vol. 2, p. 164, and Morison, *Harvard College in the Seventeenth Century*, p. 602.
2. Upon the Suns Eclipse.
   8 lines in his *Almanack* for 1668.

DUDLEY, THOMAS (1576–1653), b. Northampton, Eng., administrator for the Earl of Lincoln, N.E. 1630, Deputy Governor and Governor Mass., d. Roxbury, Mass.

1. (The State of Europe.)
   apparently lost; ref. "Life of Thomas Dudley," Ms. MHS, pr. 1 *Proc. M.H.S.*, vol. 11, pp. 207–22: "A paper of verses, describing the state of Europe in his time, which having passed the royal test in King James's time . . ." (p. 221).
2. (On the Four Parts of the World.)
   apparently lost; ref. Anne Bradstreet's poem inspired by it, "To her most Honoured Father Thomas Dudley Esq;" *Works*, Ellis ed., p. 97. Apparently written in America, a short time before his daughter's poem, which is dated March 20, 1642,
   "Dear Sir of late delighted with the sight
   Of your four Sisters cloth'd in black and white. . . .
   Yours did contest for wealth, for Arts, for Age. . . ."
3. The Verses following were found in his Pocket after his death.
   "Dim Eyes, deaf Ears, cold stomach show . . ."
   20 lines, Morton, p. 140, repr. with two words changed in the *Magnalia*, vol. 1, pp. 122–3; variant version in "Life of Thomas Dudley" (see above under 1.), p. 221.

DUNSTER, HENRY (1609–1659), b. Lancashire, Eng., Magdalene College, Cambridge, schoolteacher, N.E. 1640, President H.C., pastor Scituate, physician.

The Psalms, Hymns, and Spiritual Songs of the Old and New Testament, Faithfully Translated into English Metre.

Cambridge, (Eng.), 1648, and over fifty subsequent editions.

Only the *Psalms* were revised by Henry Dunster and Richard Lyon from the Eliot-Welde-Mather version *The Whole Booke of Psalmes*. . . (Cambridge, Mass., 1640); the *Hymns and Spiritual Songs* . . . are new additions by Dunster and Lyon. Thomas Prince describes the collaboration thus: Dunster, "one of the greatest Masters of the oriental Language that has been known in these Ends of the Earth: who was helped as to the Poetry, by Mr. Richard Lyon, an ingenious Gentleman . . . ." (Preface to Prince revision of Psalm Book, dated May 26, 1758.)

DUNTON, JOHN (1659–1733), b. Huntingtonshire, Eng., bookseller, N.E. during 1686, returned to Eng.

1. "Neither of Fortune nor of Love complain."

   3 four-line and a six-line stanza (an expanded sonnet), addressed by him, playing the part of a fortune teller, to Miss Whitemore, a young lady of Boston, distracted with love, 1686, pr. in *The Life and Errors of John Dunton* (London, 1705, 2nd ed., London, 1818), vol. 1, p. 113.

2. "Kind Boston, adieu; part we must, though 'tis pity."

   4 lines on his departure from Boston, 1686, pr. in *ibid.*, vol. 1, p. 137.

   Note: his voluminous and widely scattered verse before and after his New England stay has no proper place in this bibliography.

EASTON, PETER (1622–1687), b. Eng., N.E. 1638, Pocasset (Portsmouth), N. H., Newport, R. I., 1639, commissioner, deputy, general treasurer, attorney general.

1. "There is suche a force in Complaining."

   4 lines, unrhymed, 1663, Ms.a. AAS; a series of leaves originally bound with eight early almanacs (1662–1670) with notes and sayings, including examples of lettering, verses, proverbs,

accounts of dreams, notes on the history of Newport, calendar calculations, etc., all but the historic notes remaining unpublished.

2. "Egypt sorley Issaraill did Greeve."
   6 lines, *ibid.*, 1665.
3. "When John Shews Richard how to wrong Tom."
   couplet, repeated with variation, *ibid.*, 1668, again 1668 in second version.
4. "if it be not right."
   couplet, *ibid.*, 1668.
5. "heer lies Peter Easton."
   3 lines, *ibid.*, 1668, repeated, humorous self-epitaph.
6. "why great mens wills should be ther only la[w]."
   couplet, *ibid.*, 1668.
7. "God is the God of order and right."
   22 lines, *ibid.*, 1669, preceded by an unrhymed version of 14 lines.
8. "Give the signall let us trye."
   4 lines, *ibid.*, 1669.
9. "When mine is thine."
   3 seven-line stanzas, of which the last two lines are missing, and two preceding partly illegible, *ibid.*, 1670.
10. "I pray to you . . . ."
    fragment, 5 lines, *ibid.*, 1670, apparently translated from Ovid.
11. "when Rich men their riches doe not affect."
    4 lines, *ibid.*, 1670.
12. "When Rich [me]n their Riches doe not so muce respect."
    8 lines, a much improved revision of 11, *ibid.*, 1670.
13. "When men affect great gain neglect."
    5 lines, Ms.a. in John Richardson's *Almanack* (Cambridge, 1670), t.p. margin; revised and rearranged from 9, stanza 1, with third line new.

EDWARDS, JONATHAN the Elder
of Weymouth

"Spina vir ille Dei, pastor pius ille, fidelis."
4 lines Latin, appended to a letter written to Increase Mather, Weymouth, May 11, 1686, Ms. BPL, misc. collec.

ELEAZAR, an Indian, probably d. 1678/9, "Indus Senior Sophista" at Harvard.

In obitum Viri vere Reverendi D. Thomae Thacheri.

d. Boston, Oct. 15, 1678, a. 58.

24 lines Latin, 4 lines Greek, pr. in *Magnalia*, vol. 1, p. 448.

ELIOT, BENJAMIN (1647–1687), b. Roxbury, Mass., H.C. 1665, asst. pastor Roxbury.

Utrum detur causa aliqua externa volitionis divinae.

8 lines of Latin verse under the first of the *Quaestiones in Philosophia Discutiendae* (Cambridge, 1668), repr. Sibley, vol. 2, pp. 163–4, and Morison, *Harvard College in the Seventeenth Century*, p. 602.

ELIOT, JOHN (1604–1690), b. Hertfordshire, Eng., Jesus College Cambridge, school teacher in Essex, N. E., 1631, pastor Roxbury, Mass., and to the Indians.

1. *The Whole Booke of Psalmes Faithfully Translated into English Metre.*

   Cambridge, Mass., 1640; he collaborated in this translation with Richard Mather and Thomas Welde I.

2. *Wame Ketoohomae uketoohomaongash David.*

   the Psalms in meter, translated into the Massachusetts Indian language; some translated as early as 1651; a selection published 1658 (lost), pr. with *Old Testament*, 1663, and separately (lost), and again with the Bible of 1685.

FIRMIN, GILES (1615–1697), b. Suffolk, Eng., Emmanuel College Cambridge, N. E. 1632, et. Eng., pastor and physician.

To his Ingenious Friend, Mr. Zerobabel Endecott, Upon his Treatise, entituled Synopsis Medicinae.

24 lines, signed G**** F***** D** (i.e. Giles Firmin Dr.), in Zerobabel Endecott, *Synopsis Medicinae or A Compendium of Galenical and Chymical Physick*, Ms. in private possession, pr. Salem, 1914, George Francis Dow, ed.

FISKE, JOHN (1608–1677), b. Suffolk, Eng., Peterhouse College, Cambridge, N.E. 1637, pastor and schoolmaster Salem, Mass., pastor Wenham and Chelmsford, Mass., physician.

1. Upon the much-tobe lamented desease of the Reverend Mr. John Cotton.
   d. Boston, Dec. 23, 1652, a. 68.
   98 lines, Ms.a. BRUL, in a commonplace book of John Fiske and descendants.
2. In obitum Reverendissimi Viri . . . Domini Joannis Cottoni.
   2 lines Latin, 8 lines English, Ms.a., *ibid.*
3. Ad Matronam pientissimam spectatissimam Ipsius . . . John Cotton.
   2 eight-line stanzas, Ms.a., *ibid.*
4. Reverendo viro Domino Joanni Wilsono.
   2 four-line stanzas, Ms.a., *ibid.*, consolatory verses addressed to John Wilson upon the death of his colleague, John Cotton, dated Wenh(am) 7 of 11th 52 (Jan. 7, 1652/3), with anagram.
5. Thomas Parkerus.
   2 lines Latin, Ms.a., *ibid.*, with anagram.
6. Upon the decease of the Reverend Mr. Tho: Hooker &c.
   d. Hartford, July 7, 1647, a. 61.
   4 lines, Ms.a., *ibid.*, with anagram.
7. To his very good freind Mr Snelling phisitian.
   4 lines, Ms.a., *ibid.*, anagram and epigram, followed by other anagrams to Margaret and William Snelling.
8. In obitum viri tum pietatis tum integritatis probate, . . . Domini Samuelis Sharpij . . . Carmen funebrae.
   d. Salem, May 3, 1655, a. 71.
   4 lines Latin, 4 lines English, Ms.a., *ibid.*, with anagram.
9. Upon the departure of The worthy aged useful servant of god mr Sa: Sharp.
   anagram, couplet, and 12 four-lines stanzas, Ms.a., *ibid.*
10. Ezechiel Rogersius.
    2 lines Latin, Ms.a., *ibid.*, with anagram.
11. Upon the decease of the Reverend Learned and faithful servant of Christ, Mr Nathaniel Rogers.
    d. Ipswich, July 3, 1655, a. 57.
    25 four-lines stanzas, Ms.a., *ibid.*
12. Upon the decease of Mris. Anne Griffin (the wife of Mr Richard Griffin . . . in Concord).
    d. Chelmsford, Dec. 23, 1655, a. ca. 96.
    12 four-line stanzas, Ms.a., *ibid.*

FISKE, MOSES (1642–1708), b. Wenham, Mass., H.C. 1662, pastor Westfield and Braintree, Mass.

An ulla substantia creata sit immaterialis.

8 lines of verse, Latin, in *Quaestiones in Philosophia Discutiendae* (Cambridge, 1665), repr. Sibley, vol. 2, p. 102, and Morison, *Harvard College in the Seventeenth Century*, 601.

FLYNT, JOSIAH (1645–1680), b. Braintree, Mass., H.C. 1664, pastor Dorchester, Mass.

(Calendar Verse.)

6 lines over each month, except last month which has 8 lines, in his *Almanack* for 1666.

FOLGER, PETER (1618–1690), b. Norwich, Norfolk, Eng., N.E. 1635, missionary to Indians on Martha's Vineyard, to Nantucket 1663, where d.

A Looking Glasse for the Times.

8 line introduction and 105 four-line stanzas, Ms.a. Nantucket Historical Society, dated at end April 23, 1676, one leaf with 10 stanzas now missing; pr. with added Quaker material (of 1724) possibly at Newport, in 1763, JCB; this ed. repr. in *Rhode Island Historical Tracts*, no. 16, Providence, 1883; the AAS fragment differs only in slight typographical details from the JCB copy and probably dates from about the same year; repr. from orig. Ms. (with a few obvious mistakes in transcription) in Florence Bennett Anderson, *A Grandfather for Benjamin Franklin* (Boston, 1940), pp. 306–19.

Note: it is highly improbable that this work was printed in Boston or Cambridge during the 17th century, and there is no contemporaneous evidence that it was. Benjamin Franklin's statements in his *Autobiography* are apparently from a faulty memory (e.g. the misquoting), and his date of printing, 1675, the year before the poem was written, may have been a slip of the pen for 1765 (a vaguely remembered 1763). The date 1676 is only the date of writing appended to the Ms., and the date of printing, 1677, found in many bibliographies, is entirely apocryphal. The only possibility for printing at the time would have been in England, for the only presses then in the American colonies were under the strict supervision of the Massachusetts authorities, who would certainly not have permitted the publication of such incendiary material. The one bit of internal evidence on the matter is ambiguous and can be interpreted in opposite ways, according to one's concept of Folger's use of the subjunctive. The fifth stanza from the end reads:

"If that you doe mislike the uerse
for its uncomely dress
I tell you tru I neuer thought
that itt would pass the press"

The book inventory of Ralph Wormeley of Virginia, dated Nov. 1, 1701 (*Va. Mag. Hist. Biog.*, vol 36, p. 285) lists one title as "a looking Glass for the times." Whether this is Peter Folger's poem or another book with the same title, cannot now be ascertained, though the British Museum catalogue does not list any such title. If it refers to Folger's poem, this is the first material evidence that has come to light that the poem was issued contemporaneously, presumably in England.

The Ms. was apparently for a long time in Dartmouth, Mass., a Quaker center (previous to its return to Nantucket it was owned by Jesse Tucker, of North Dartmouth), and this may account for its publication in 1763 with appended Quaker material. The 1763 version, in addition to its normalized spelling and the addition of punctuation, exhibits many verbal changes from the Ms., a few of them involving important changes of meaning (e.g. *I* for *ye*, *you* for *God*, *quiet* for *quits*).

FOSTER, JOHN (1648–1681), b. Dorchester, Mass., H.C. 1667, schoolteacher Dorchester, printer Boston, mathematician, astronomer.

1. (Calendar Verse.)
   4 lines under each month (except March & April) of his *1676. An Almanack* . . . (Boston, 1676); "Signs of Rain are thus described," 12 lines, *ibid.*, p. 30.
2. The Dominion of the Moon in Man's Body.
   12 lines in his *1678. An Almanack* . . . (Boston, 1678).
3. (Calendar Verse.)
   6 lines under each month of his *MDCLXXIX. An Almanack* . . . (Boston, 1679).
4. "'Tis fear'd a thousand Natives, young and old."
   couplet, *ibid.*, p. (23), in chronological table under Dec. 19, 1675.

5. "Metior, atque meum est: emit mihi dives Iesus."
   Latin couplet written as his death approached, in answer to a couplet from Increase Mather both engraved on headstone of John Foster in Dorchester, pr. Sibley, vol. 2, p. 228, and Samuel A. Green, *John Foster* (Boston, 1909), p. 49.

FOX, JABEZ (1647–1703), b. Concord, Mass., H.C. 1665, pastor Woburn, Mass., d. Boston.

An omne bonum sit necessario sui communicativum?
   6 lines of Latin verse under the third of the *Quaestiones in Philosophia Discutiendae* (Cambridge, 1668), repr. Sibley, vol. 2, p. 163, and Morison, *Harvard College in the Seventeenth Century*, 602.

FRANKLIN, BENJAMIN the Elder (1650–1727), b. Northamptonshire, Eng., silk-dyer of London, N.E. 1715, Boston, Mass.

1. (Poetical Works.)
   2 quarto volumes, Ms.a., belonging c. 1840 to Mrs. Emmons of Boston, a descendant of the author; used by Jared Sparks for his *The Life of Benjamin Franklin* (Boston, 1844), pp. 6 & 540–2; present location unknown, all subsequent references derive from Sparks. "His thoughts run chiefly on moral and religious subjects. Many of the Psalms are paraphrased in metre. The making of acrostics on the names of his friends was a favorite exercise. There are likewise numerous proofs of his ingenuity in forming anagrams, crosses, ladders, and other devices." "He continued to make verses, and to turn the Psalms into rhyme after he came to New England."
2. Sent to his Namesake, upon a Report of his Inclination to Martial Affairs, July 7th, 1710.
   10 lines, Ms.a. *ibid.*, pr. *ibid.*, p. 541; verses addressed to his nephew Ben when the latter was 4½ years old.
3. Acrostic, Sent to Benjamin Franklin in New England, July 15th, 1710.
   2 eight-line stanzas, Ms.a. *ibid.*, pr. *ibid.*, p. 541.
4. Sent to Benjamin Franklin, 1713.
   14 lines, Ms.a. *ibid.*, pr. *ibid.*, p. 542.
5. A peny line sent to my Daughter Eliz. at Mr Honybourns 16 Dec. 1713.

28 lines, Ms.a. commonplace book, fragm. in private possession, pr. *Publ. Col. Soc. Mass.*, vol. 10, pp. 199–200, signed B. F.

Note: the editor does not identify the poem on p. 194–5, "When Indians hear that some there be"; it is by Roger Williams (no. 23).

6. On Tobacco.

"O Nasty black pipe, art thou crept in here."

13 lines, *ibid.*, pr. *ibid.*, p. 201, signed B.F.

7. On Fasting.

"The Sick Man Fasts because he cannot Eat."

6 lines, Ms.a. *ibid.*, pr. *ibid.*, p. 204, unsigned and possibly not by Franklin.

FULLER, THOMAS (16 –1698), b. England, N.E. 1638, Salem Village, founded second iron works in New England.

(Autobiographical Verses.)

16 four-line stanzas, Ms.l.c. recorded from oral tradition by his great grandson, the Rev. Daniel Fuller, of Gloucester, pr. in the *Diary of the Revd. Daniel Fuller* (New York, 1894), pp. 23–6: selection of 11 stanzas in *New England Hist. Gen. Reg.*, vol. 13, p. 351; obviously not written in 1638, as here stated, but much later, probably in his old age.

GARDINER, SIR CHRISTOPHER, b. Eng., probably a Knight of the Holy Sepulchre, N.E. 1631, back to Eng.

1. The Sonnet.

12 lines, rhymed in triplets, written by Sir Christopher after he had survived an Indian skirmish incited by "Master Temperwell," pr. in Thomas Morton, *New English Canaan* (Amsterdam, 1637), repr. by Peter Force (Washington, 1838), and by Prince Society, 1883, vol. 14, p. 341.

2. Sir Christoffer Gardiner, Knight. In laudem Authoris.

19 lines, *ibid.*, p. 112.

GIBBS, HENRY (1668–1723), b. Boston, Mass., H.C. 1685, pastor Watertown, Mass.

Attempt at Versification on the Word of God.

144 lines, Ms.a. Essex Institute, appended to a Ms. collection of his sermons.

GOOKIN, DANIEL II (1650–1718), b. Cambridge, Mass., H.C. 1669, fellow, librarian, pastor Sherborn and Natick, Mass., missionary to Indians.

1. Upon the Death of the reverend, pious, incomparably learned, and faithful servant of Christ . . . Mr. Urian Oakes.
   d. Cambridge, July 25, 1681, a. 50.
   19 six-line stanzas, Ms.a. AAS, pr. *Publ. Col. Soc. Mass.*, vol. 20, pp. 249–52, with facsim. betw. pp. 248 & 249; excerpt of 2 stanzas first pr. in Samuel Kettell, *Specimens of American Poetry* (Boston, 1829), vol. 1, pp. xliv–xlv.
2. A Few Shadie Meditations occasioned by the Death of the Deservedly Honoured John Hull Esqr.
   d. Boston, Sept. 30, 1683, a. 59.
   74 lines, Ms.a., endorsed by Samuel Sewall "Cous. Danl Gookin on my Father Hull"; in 1857 it was in the possession of the Rev. Mr. Sewall, who transcribed it for publication at the close of the *Diary of John Hull*, *Trans. A.A.S.*, vol. 3, pp. 255–7.

GORTON, SAMUEL (c. 1592–1677), b. Lancashire, Eng., clothier London, N.E. 1637, Boston and Plymouth, Mass., Pawtuxet and Warwick, R. I., mystic, founder of Gortonist sect.

A lover of peace, and one of eminent respect, viewing this treatise at the presse, kindly added this verse prefixed, which hath both sodainly and unexpectedly drawn from my thoughts as here followeth. . . .

116 lines, prefixed to his *Simplicities Defence against Seven-Headed Policy* (London, 1647), and evoked by the commendatory verses of a stranger, R.B., who read the treatise while it was still in press.

H., G.

AN Elegy Upon the Death of the Worshipfull Richard Dummer Esq.

d. Newbury, July 4, 1689, a. 39.

44 lines, broadside, "Printed at Boston N.E. 1689," apparently lost and completely unknown except for Ms.c.c. NYHS, Samuel Sewall's commonplace book, pp. 15–6, signed G.H. (could be either Gershom Hobart (1645–1707) pastor of Groton, Mass., or with greater likelihood, if the G. stands for Guilielmus, William Hubbard (1621–1704) pastor of Ipswich, Mass.

HALE, ROBERT (1668–1719), b. Beverly, Mass., H.C. 1686, asst. pastor Beverly, and Preston, Conn., school teacher and physician Beverly.

1. (Epitaph on Nathaniel Mather.)
   d. Salem, after Sept. 25, 1688, a. 19.
   22 lines, in Cotton Mather, *Early Piety, Exemplified in the Life and Death of Mr. Nathanael Mather* (London, 1689), p. 60, and in *Magnalia*, vol. 2, pp. 150–1; in former signed "R. Hale" in latter "R.H."

2. Amici, quum legisset, Carmen Gratulatorium.
   31 lines Latin, in Cotton Mather, *Thoughts for the Day of Rain* (Boston, 1712), pp. 35–6, signed R.H.

HARRIS, BENJAMIN (c. 1640's–1720), b. Eng., London printer, bookseller, journalist, N.E. 1686–1695, Boston, Mass., ret. Eng.

1. (The Rhymed Alphabet.)
   24 couplets in his *The New-England Primer*, Boston, c. 1687–1690, 2nd ed. 1690, earliest preserved ed. 1727, and numerous ed. through the 18th and 19th centuries, with many variants; also in his *New English Tutor*, London, c. 1702–1714; derived in part from Harris' *The Fables of Young Aesop* (earliest preserved ed. London, 1700). See Paul Leicester Ford, *The New-England Primer* (New York, 1899), pp. 53–68 and preceding and succeeding illustrations, and those after p. 113.

2. A Dialogue between Christ, Youth and the Devil.
   218 lines, in *ibid.*, attributed to Harris by Ford, *op. cit.*, pp. 93–5. Other verses, such as the famous "Now I lay me down to sleep" were added later in the 18th century.

3. A Prognostication For the Year 1688.
   82 lines, in John Tulley's *Almanack* for 1688, pp. 15–22, interspersed with prose; mock-prophetic verses, very likely by Harris, to judge from their tone and content and from later performances in Tulley's almanacs; cf. also Tulley's later statement (1696) about the verse in the 1694 almanac.

4. To Their Most Sacred Majesties King William and Queen Mary.
   20 lines, in the *Boston Almanack* for 1692, p. (15), 1st impression no signature, 2nd signed B.H.

5. "God Save The King, that King that sav'd the land."
   in John Partridge, *Monthly Ovservations* (Boston, 1692), on King William.
6. "The Throne's not Vacant now; but fill'd with those."
   7 lines, in John Tulley's *Almanack* for 1693, p. (15).
   Note: the verses on the following page, "Some few Lines by another Hand," 4 stanzas of 4, 5, 6, and 7 lines, anti-Catholic, may be by Harris or by Samuel Sewall.
7. Of the French Kings Nativity.
   20 lines, in John Tulley's *Almanack* for 1694, p. (19), anti-French, anti-Catholic, at the head of a prose essay. In his 1696 almanac Tulley defended himself against Christian Lodowick by asserting that this section was added during publication without his knowledge and consent. Tulley seems in all cases to have confined his labors to the almanac proper, leaving the literary embellishments to his Boston publishers.
8. *Divine Poems for Youths; Containing Forty Remarkable Scripture Histories turned into common English Verse.*
   apparently lost, advertisement at end of *ibid.* Can this be a New England predecessor of his *The Holy Bible in Verse* (London, 1699)?
9. An Account of the Cruelty of the Papists.
   12 lines (2 couplets and an octave) in John Tulley's *Almanack* for 1695, pp. (18, 21, 23), included in a prose essay.
   Note: his voluminous and widely scattered verse before and after his New England stay has no proper place in this bibliography.

HAWKINS, JOHN, of Boston.

Epigram on Providence.

4 lines, quoted by Samuel Kettell, *Specimens of American Poetry* (Boston, 1829), vol. 1, p. xlv, without any information as to its provenience, or as to the author, except that he was of Boston. This might be the John Hawkins, mariner, who was admitted to the First Church in 1630, or the John Hawkins, weaver, who appeared in Boston at the end of the century.

HAYDEN, ANNA TOMPSON (1648–after 1720), b. Braintree, Mass., daughter of the Rev. William Tompson, and sister of Benjamin.

1. Upon the Death of that desirable young virgin, Elizabeth Tompson.
   d. Boston, Aug. 24, 1712, a. 22.
   28 lines, Ms.c.c., journal of Joseph Tompson of Billerica, pr. in Murdock, pp. 6–7.
2. Verses on Benjamin Tompson, by his sister, Anna Hayden.
   d. Roxbury, April 10, 1714, a. 72.
   57 lines, Ms.c.c., *ibid.*, pr. *ibid.*, pp. 20–2.

HENCHMAN, DANIEL (1677–1708), b. Boston, Mass., H.C. 1696, to South Carolina, where died, scientist, correspondent of James Petiver.

Lamentations Upon the Death of Sir William Phips, Knight Governour.
   d. London, Eng., Feb. 18, 1694/5, a. 44.
   93 lines, broadside, "Printed at Boston in New England by B: Green. 1695. Sic Lamentatus est D. Hincsman." No copy of this broadside is known to exist, but Ms.c.c. NYHS, in Samuel Sewall's commonplace book, pp. 20–2; repr. with the first 7 lines, 4 other lines, and author's name omitted, in Cotton Mather's *Pietas in Patriam* (London, 1697), 6 pp. at end, and in the *Magnalia*, vol. 1, pp. 207–8. The elegy has generally and erroneously been attributed to Cotton Mather, in part because of the two ambiguous paragraphs of Mather's preceding the poem. It is possible that Sewall, often careless in his copying, wrote D. instead of R. Hincsman, for Daniel's brother, Richard (sons of Daniel, d. 1685), several times exchanged verses with his friend Samuel Sewall and wrote a long poem to his patroness, Lady Phips (see below).

HENCHMAN, RICHARD (c. 1655–1725), b. Boston, schoolmaster Yarmouth 1686, to Boston by 1697, North Writing School 1700–c. 1719.

1. In Consort to Wednesday Janr. 1st, 1701. Before Break of Day.
   2 lines Latin, 95 lines English, Ms.a. BPL, an ode in four parts, dedicated to Samuel Sewall, and called forth by Sewall's "Wednesday January 1. 1701 . . ." of which the third part of the ode is an elaborate paraphrase.

2. Vox Oppressi. To the Lady Phipps.
   105 lines, Ms.a. BPL, after receiving a large gift of silver from her.
3. "Sewall our Israel's Judge and Singer Sweet."
   55 lines, Ms.a. BPL, pr. Sewall, *Letter Book*, vol. 1, pp. 316–7, translation of Nehemiah Hobart's Latin verses on Samuel Sewall (March 27, 1712) and of Sewall's added couplet.
4. "Tho' Sternhold and Hopkins."
   8 lines, Ms.a. BPL, pr. *ibid.*, p. 317.

HIGGINSON, JOHN (1616–1708), b. Leicestershire, Eng., N.E. 1629, pastor Saybrook, Hartford, and Guilford, Conn., Salem, Mass.

Epigramma Matheros.

7 lines Latin, in "An Attestation to this Church-History of New-England," prefixed to *Magnalia*, vol. 1, p. 13, and dated Mar. 25, 1697.

HINCKLEY, THOMAS (1618–1706), b. Eng., N.E. by 1635, Barnstable, Governor of Plymouth Colony.

1. Mr. Thomas Walley, the Reverend Pastor of the Church of Christ at Barnstable.
   d. Barnstable, March 14, 1677/8, a. 61.
   130 lines, broadside, apparently lost, Ms.c.c. NYHS, in Samuel Sewall's commonplace book, pp. 25–30; mentioned (without author ref.) in Samuel Wakeman's letter to John Cotton II, Fairfield, Apr. 16, 1680, in connection with Cotton's broadside on Newman (cf. above).
2. Upon the Death of the Honourable and highly esteemed Josiah Winslow, Esq.
   d. Marshfield, Dec. 18, 1680, a. 52.
   96 lines English, 2 lines Latin, Ms.a. (?) BPL, Hinckley Papers, pr. 4 *Coll. M.H.S.*, vol. 5, pp. 53–5.
3. (Upon the death of his wife, Mary Smith Hinckley.)
   d. Barnstable, July 29, 1703, a. 72.
   169 lines, Ms.a. (?), Thomas Prince Papers, in 1847 in the possession of the Rev. Chandler Robbins of Boston, pr. *New England Hist. Gen. Reg.*, vol. 1, pp. 92–5.

HOAR, LEONARD (1630–1675), b. Gloucestershire, Eng., H.C. 1650, to Eng. 1653, A.M. and M.D. Univ. of Cambridge, ret. N.E. 1672, president H.C., d. Boston.

"En regis magni diploma insigne Jacobi!"

22 lines, broadside, *Catalogus* (Cambridge, Mass., 1674), facsim. in Morison, *Harvard College in the Seventeenth Century*, facing p. 411, repr. with transl. *ibid.*, pp. 413–4.

HOBART, NEHEMIAH (1648–1712), b. Hingham, Mass., H.C. 1667, fellow, pastor Newton, Mass.

1. ("Lines . . . on the dreadful fire at Boston.")
   Ms.a. lost; sent to Nicholas Noyes for criticism during the winter of 1711/2, according to a letter from Hobart to Noyes (Ms. AAS) dated "Newtown, Mar. 29, 1712."
2. Martij 27. 1712.
   37 lines Latin (with couplet added by Samuel Sewall), broadside BA and MHS, repr. Sewall, *Letter Book*, vol. 1, p. 315, with Richard Henchman's translation, pp. 316–7; numerous ref. to broadside in Sewall, *Letter Book* and *Diary*.

HOPKINS, ANNE YALE (16 –1698), b. Eng., wife of Edward Hopkins, Gov. of Conn., became insane c. 1645, left in Boston with her brother, David Yale, a merchant.

"Mr. Hopkins, the governor of Hartford upon Connecticut, came to Boston, and brought his wife with him (a godly young woman, and of special parts), who was fallen into a sad infirmity, the loss of her understanding and reason, which had been growing upon her divers years, by occasion of her giving herself wholly to reading and writing, and had written many books . . . ." John Winthrop, *Diary* (Savage ed., Boston, 1853), vol. 2, pp. 265–6, April 13, 1645.

HUBBARD, SAMUEL (1610–c. 1697), b. Suffolk, Eng., N.E. 1633, Salem and Watertown, Mass., Windsor and Wethersfield, Conn., Springfield, Mass., Wethersfield, Conn., turned Baptist, later Seventh Day Baptist, 1648 to Newport R. I., preacher, missionary to New Netherlands, 1665.

(Elegy on Philip Eades?)

d. Newport, March 16, 1681/2.

original lost, 8 line excerpt, Ms.l.c. RIHS, Register of Mr. Samuel Hubbard, copied by Isaac Backus, p. 150, in Hubbard's letter to Gov. William Leete, Dec. 20, 1682; verses not certainly by Hubbard.

HUTCHINSON, SAMUEL (c. 1618–1667), b. Lincolnshire, Eng., N.E. c. 1633 (brother-in-law of Anne Hutchinson), Lynn and Boston, Mass.

"The Lord must Reign, let all the World be still."

36 lines signed S.H. in his *A Declaration of a Future Glorious Estate of a Church to be here upon Earth* (London, 1667), pp. 33–4 (see below under Thomas Tillam for the verses, pp. 3 and 18–9, signed T.T.), AAS.

J., W.

Some short but serious Meditations upon tyme death Judgment & Eternity.

47 six-line stanzas, Ms.a. MHS, signed "by W. J. 1695"; no satisfactory explanation of these initials has been found.

JAMES, JOHN (1633–1729), b. Eng., N.E., c. 1657, H.C. (Hon. A.M.) 1710, pastor Haddam and Derby, Conn., Brookfield, Mass., to Wethersfield, Conn. where d.

1. Memor . . . Monumentum . . . .
   (on an infant, d. at birth, Derby, March 2, 1695/6)
   15 lines, Ms.a. Harris Collection, Brown Univ., on blank pages and margins of a large paper edition of the poems of William Drummond, 1616, blank verso of "To the Author" (title of poem badly worn and partly illegible).
2. To the Memory off Grace Nichols.
   d. Derby, March 2, 1701/2, a. 29.
   56 lines, Ms.a., *ibid.*, sign. K. lb.
3. On Jno Bunyans Life.
   10 lines, Ms.a., *ibid.*, sign. A 3a, dated Nov. 8, 1702.
4. To the Memory off The Worthy & much bewail'd Mrs Esther Buckinghame & Mrs [Est]her Beaumont.
   1. (mother), d. Saybrook, Conn., June 3, 1702.
   2. (daughter), d. late in May, 1702, a. 34.

188 lines and 2 lines Latin, Ms.a., *ibid.*, sign. K 2a -K 4a, 5 pp., addressed to the Rev. Mr. Tho. Buckingham of Hartford.

5. On the Decease of the Religious & Honourable John Haynes Esq.
   d. Hartford, Nov. 25, 1713, a. 44.
   22 lines, Ms.a. (?) CHS, pr. *Annual Report* CHS, 1908, pp. 20–1.
6. On the Death of the very Learned, Pious and Excelling Gershom Bulkley Esq. M.D.
   d. Glastonbury, Conn., Dec. 2, 1713, a. c. 78.
   68 lines, broadside, New London, 1714, unique copy BA, with top of second column cut out.
7. (Epitaph on Noadiah Russell)
   d. Middletown, Dec. 3, 1713, a. 53.
   mentioned in *Annual Report*, *supra.*

JOHNSON, EDWARD (1598–1672), b. Canterbury, Eng., N.E. 1630, ret., N.E. 1636, Charlestown and Woburn, Mass., var. offices in town and colony, historian.

1. "In peniles age I woburne Towne began."
   32 lines, Ms.c.c. (by his son William Johnson), first page of *Records For the Towne of Woburne From the year 1640*, facsim. Jameson ed. of no. 3, facing p. 212, and pr. *ibid.*, pp. 7–8.
2. *Good news from New-England: with An exact relation of the first planting that Country.*
   London, 1648, repr. 4 *Coll. M.H.S.*, vol. 1, pp. 195–218.
   The poetic-epic sections are as follows:
   1) Of the reasons moving this people to transplant themselves and Families to those remote parts.
      90 lines.
   2) Of the Transportation of people and goods to the Mattachusetts bay, and other adjacent Collonies.
      82 lines.
   3) Of the arrivall of our English Nation at the Mattachusets Bay, &c.
      58 lines.
   4) A briefe description of the Land, Beasts, Birds, Trees, and Fruits.
      70 lines, four separate sections on the New England seasons.

5) Of their building, planting, and giving out of Lands.
   44 lines.
6) "To populate this howling desart Land."
   92 lines, under the section Of their Civill Government.
7) "What creature man that is so apt to take."
   102 lines, under the section, Of the planting of the Gospel . . .
8) "Yet unto God this people feeling sayes."
   46 lines, under *ibid.*
9) "Church-covenant Band brought in with liberty."
   4 lines, under *ibid.*

Note: the *Good News*, 1648, should not be confused with Edward Winslow's *Good Newes from New England: or a true Relation* (London, 1624), as it frequently is, even as recently as Perry Miller and Thomas H. Johnson, *The Puritans* (New York, 1938), pp. 788 f. The 1648 *Good News* was obviously written by a Massachusetts Bay and not a Plymouth man, and though anonymous is here attributed to Edward Johnson on the basis of style, content, and underlying philosophy, this being an earlier, lighter, preliminary version of his *History* of 1654. The whimsical humor of *Good News*, likewise so apparent in the Woburn poem, also occasionally shows through the high seriousness of the later *History*.

3. *A History of New-England. From the English planting in the Yeere 1628. untill the Yeere 1652.*

London, 1654, generally referred to as the *Wonder-Working Providence of Sions Saviour in New England;* latest ed. by J. Franklin Jameson, New York, 1910. Anonymous, but attributed to Johnson by Thomas Prince on the basis of a statement made by William Johnson, a son of Edward, to Samuel Sewall. A large number of verses on the various New England leaders, and a few other poems are scattered through the volume, as follows (ref. to the Jameson ed.):

1) Matthew Craddock, Thomas Goffe, and other members of the Massachusetts Bay Company (Thomas Mayhew mentioned), 6 lines, p. 38.
2) John Endicott, Salem, 10 lines, pp. 44–5.
3) Francis Higginson, Salem, 8 lines, pp. 47–8.
4) Samuel Skelton, Salem, 8 lines, p. 48.
5) Isaac Johnson, Charlestown, 8 lines, pp. 65–6.

6) John Wilson, Boston, 20 lines, pp. 67–8.
7) John Maverick, Dorchester, 8 lines, p. 70.
8) John Eliot, Roxbury, 20 lines, pp. 72–3.
9) Stephen Bachiler, Lynn, etc. 8 lines, pp. 72–4.
10) George Phillips, Watertown, 16 lines, p. 75.
11) John Winthrop, Boston, 18 lines, p. 76.
12) Thomas Dudley, Newtown (Cambridge), etc., 12 lines, p. 81.
13) Thomas James, Charlestown, 16 lines, pp. 82–3.
14) Thomas Welde, Roxbury, 14 lines, pp. 83–4.
15) Increase Nowell, Boston, 10 lines, p. 86.
16) John Cotton, Boston, 28 lines, pp. 88–9.
17) Thomas Hooker, Newtown (Cambridge) and Hartford, 16 lines, pp. 90–1.
18) Samuel Stone, Newtown (Cambridge) and Hartford, 12 lines, p. 93.
19) Nathaniel Ward, Ipswich, 16 lines, p. 97.
20) Richard Bellingham, Boston, 10 lines, pp. 97–8.
21) Thomas Parker, Newbury, 12 lines, pp. 99–100.
22) Zechariah Symmes, Charlestown, 12 lines, p. 101.
23) Sir Henry Vane, Boston, 4 lines, p. 102.
24) Sir Richard Saltonstall, Boston, 12 lines, pp. 102–3.
25) Roger Harlackenden, Cambridge, 6 lines, p. 103.
26) John Norton, Ipswich and Boston, 16 lines, p. 104.
27) Richard Mather, Dorchester, 16 lines, p. 105.
28) John Warham, Dorchester and Windsor, 12 lines, p. 107.
29) Thomas Shepard, Cambridge, 24 lines, pp. 107–8.
30) Hugh Peter, Salem, 12 lines, p. 109.
31) Peter Bulkeley, Concord, 16 lines, pp. 110–1.
32) John Jones, Concord and Fairfield, 12 lines, pp. 112–3.
33) Peter Hobart, Hingham, 12 lines, p. 117.
34) Henry Flynt, Braintree, 6 lines, p. 117.
35) George Fenwick, Saybrook, 6 lines, p. 118.
36) Ralph Partridge, Duxbury, 12 lines, p. 119.
37) Nathaniel Rogers, Ipswich, 24 lines, pp. 119–20.
38) Samuel Whiting, Lynn, 16 lines, pp. 120–1.
39) Simon Bradstreet, Ipswich and Andover, 10 lines, p. 141.
40) John Davenport, New Haven, 20 lines, p. 177.
41) Theophilus Eaton, New Haven, 10 lines, p. 178.
42) Edward Hopkins, Hartford, 6 lines, p. 179.

43) John Allen, Dedham, 20 lines, pp. 179–80.
44) Thomas Thacher, Weymouth and Boston, 24 lines, pp. 181–2. (also addressed to the people of Weymouth).
45) Ezekiel Rogers, Rowley, 16 lines, p. 184.
46) John Miller, Rowley, etc., 12 lines, p. 184.
47) John Harvard, Charlestown, 12 lines, pp. 187–8.
48) Herbert Pelham, Cambridge, 6 lines, p. 188.
49) Timothy Dalton (Doulton), Hampton, 12 lines, p. 189.
50) William Worchester (not Thomas Woster) Salisbury, 12 lines, p. 190.
51) John Knowles, Watertown, 16 lines, p. 191.
52) Jonathan Burr, Dorchester, 8 lines, p. 192.
53) (An omnium-gatherum for John Rayner of Plymouth and Dover, William Hook of Taunton and New Haven, Samuel Eaton of New Haven, Charles Chauncy of Plymouth and Cambridge, Ephraim Hewett (Huet) of Windsor, Henry Smith of Wethersfield, Henry Whitefield of Guilford, Robert Peck of Hingham, Peter Saxton of Scituate, Richard Denton of Stamford, and Hempstead), 16 lines, p. 196.
54) Edmund Browne, Sudbury, 16 lines, p. 196.
55) Henry Flynt and William Tompson, Braintree, 16 lines, p. 198.
56) "You that have seen these wondrous works by Sions Savior don," 56 lines, pp. 203–4.
57) Henry Dunster, Cambridge, 16 lines, p. 205.
58) Richard Blinman, Marshfield, etc., 12 lines, p. 206.
59) Thomas Carter, Woburn, 16 lines, p. 218.
60) Henry Green and Samuel Hough (Hoph), Reading, 12 lines, p. 226.
61) John Fiske, Wenham and Chelmsford, 12 lines, p. 227.
62) John Ward, Haverhill, 12 lines, p. 235.
63) George Moxon, Springfield, 14 lines, p. 237.
64) To Andover and Francis Dane, 12 lines, pp. 249–50.
65) Marmaduke Matthews, Yarmouth, etc., 12 lines, p. 251.
66) Of the wonder-working providences of Christ.
"From silent night, true Register of moans."
22 six-line stanzas, pp. 257–61.
67) "Oh King of Saints, how great's thy work, say we."
21 six-line stanzas, pp. 272–5.

4. "This lonesome lake, like to a sea, among the mountains lies."
   32 lines, on Lake Winnepesaukee, supposedly written by Edward Johnson in 1652 while on the exploring and surveying trip with Simon Willard, Jonathan Ince, and John Sherman; in John Greenleaf Whittier, *Margaret Smith's Journal*, *Prose Works*, vol. 1, pp. 157–8.

   Note: the external evidence for and against its authenticity is about even: of the other nine poems in *Margaret Smith's Journal* attributed to seventeenth-century New England authors, five are authenticated: the verses from the Bay Psalm Book, Samuel Danforth, Benjamin Tompson (the first poem), Roger Williams, and Anne Bradstreet, though Whittier cannot refrain from revising and "improving" them; the other four, the three ballads and the second poem attributed to Benjamin Tompson, are very obviously products of nineteenth-century Romanticism. If the "Lonesome Lake" is by Johnson, it is almost certain that Whittier tampered with it, for a few phrases do not ring quite true, if it is entirely by Whittier, it is, in contrast to the four other fabrications, a most successful evocation of seventeenth-century New England, and of Edward Johnson's thought and expression. Mr. T. Franklin Currier, who called my attention to this poem, suggests that, if the poem is genuine, Whittier might have obtained it from his friend, Joshua Coffin, the ardent New England antiquarian.

J(OHNSON), M(ARMADUKE) (c. 1630–1674), b. Eng., stationer and citizen of London, N.E. 1660, printer Cambridge, Mass., to Boston 1674, where d.

(see under J.T.)

JOSSEYLN, JOHN (c. 1610's–prob. after 1692), b. Essex, Eng., N.E. 1638–1639 and 1663–1671, chiefly at Scarborough, Maine, naturalist, probably physician, ret. Eng.

1. The Poem.
   20 lines, in his *New-England's Rarities. Discovered* (London, 1672), pp. 101–2, repr. *Trans. A.A.S.*, vol. 4, p. 232; repr. Boston, 1865.
2. "And the bitter storm augments; the wild winds wage."
   10 lines, in his *An Account of two Voyages to New-England*,

London, 1674, 2nd ed. 1675, pp. 30–1, repr. 3 *Coll. M.H.S.*, vol. 3, p. 233.

3. "Swift is't in pace, light poiz'd, to look in clear."
   4 lines, *ibid.*, p. 44, repr. *ibid.*, p. 241; on the water of New England.

JOY, GEORGE, Mariner. A Quaker, probably English.

Innocency's Complaint against Tyrannical Court Faction in Newengland.

100 lines, broadside, MHS, signed George Joy, Mariner, 1677, protesting the persecution of the Quakers in New England. The MHS broadside was, to judge from paper and type, obviously printed in the late 18th or early 19th century, though Ford and other bibliographers fail to mention this fact. Apparently no contemporaneous copy is known, though one certainly existed, for John Whiting, in his *Truth and Innocency Defended* (London, 1702), quoted extensively from the poem "in a paper lately come to my hands," a common way at the time of referring to a broadside.

KNIGHT, RICHARD (1602–1683), b. Hampshire, Eng., merchant tailor, N.E. 1635, Newbury, Mass., deacon.

(Verses addressed to his children.)

apparently lost; belonged c. 1845 to Joshua Coffin, who quoted 4 lines in his *A Sketch of the History of Newbury* (Boston, 1845), p. 395, saying "It is too long for insertion."

KNIGHT, SARAH KEMBLE (1666–1727), b. Charlestown, Mass., school-teacher, shopkeeper, drafter of legal documents.

1. "Fair Cynthia, all the Homage that I may."
   18 lines, Ms.a. lost, pr. in *The Private Journal Kept by Madam Knight, On a Journey From Boston to New-York, In the Year 1704*, New York, 1825, new ed. New York, 1935, pp. 14–5.
2. "Here stood a Lofty church—there is a steeple."
   5 lines, *ibid.*, p. 16.
3. "I ask thy Aid, O Potent Rum!"
   7 lines, *ibid.*, p. 19.
4. "May all that dread the cruel feind of night."
   9 lines, *ibid.*, p. 21.

5. "Tho' ill at ease, A stranger and alone."
   12 lines, *ibid.*, pp. 24–5.
6. "Through many Trials and many frights."
   4 lines, Ms.a., scratched on a pane of glass in the old Knight mansion, later occupied by Samuel Mather. The lines were later rehearsed by Mather to Isaiah Thomas, who recorded them; repr. *Bostonian Society Publications*, vol. 9, p. 103.

LAWSON, DEODATE (16 –1698), b. Norfolk, Eng., N.E. 1680, pastor Scituate, Edgartown, Danvers, Mass., ret. to Eng. c. 1698, where d.

Threnodia, Or a Mournfull Remembrance, of the much to be Lamented Death of the Worthy & Pious Capt. Anthony Collamore.
   d. at sea, off Scituate, Dec. 16, 1693.
   27 six-line stanzas, in private possession, facsim. Winslow, p. 19, facsim. & repr. *Mayflower Descendant*, vol. 11, pp. 65–9.

LOWELL, PERCIVAL (1571–1664), b. Somersetshire, Eng., merchant in Bristol, N. E. 1639, Newbury, Mass.

A Funeral Elegie (Written many years since) On the Death of the Memorable and Truly Honourable John Winthrope, Esq:
   d. Boston, March 26, 1649, a. 61.
   98 lines, broadside (prob. Boston, John Foster, 1676), facsim. Winslow, p. 3; signed "Perciful Lowle," though "Lowell" occurs at the beginning of the last section of verse.

LYNDE, BENJAMIN (1666–1745), b. Boston, Mass., H.C. 1686, Middle Temple, Counsellor at Law 1697, ret. N.E. 1697, res. Salem, Judge of Superior Court, Councillor.

1. (Lines descriptive of Thomson's Island.)
   108 lines, Ms.a. in private possession, pr. in *The Diaries of Benjamin Lynde and of Benjamin Lynde, Jr.* (Boston, 1880), Appendix B, p. 216.
   Note: *ibid.*, p. xii: "Among Judge Lynde's papers are . . . a few short poems of a descriptive character, or suggested by local events."
2. (Poem.)
   broadside, apparently lost; ref. Sewall, *Letter Book*, vol. 1, p. 175 sent to Seth Shove Sept. 16 & 18, 1724 "Mr. N. Hobart's

Verses, Judicis Officium, Merrimac River 2 copies, Judge Lynd's Poem 2 Copies..."

3. (Verses.)

broadside, apparently lost; ref. Sewall, *Letter Book*, vol. 2, p. 194: to John Winthrop, Jan. 8, 1725/6: "Inclosed one Renatus, the only one had by me, 2 or 3 Judge Lynd's verses."

Note: this reference is a year and four months later than 2; it may refer to the same broadside, but more likely refers to another.

LYON, RICHARD, b. Eng., N.E. 1644–1651 as tutor of William Mildmay (H.C. 1647), lived with President Dunster.

The Psalms, Hymns, and Spiritual Songs of the Old and New Testament, Faithfully Translated into English Metre.

Cambridge (Eng.), 1648, and over fifty subsequent editions. The *Psalms* revised from the Eliot-Welde-Mather version, the *Hymns and Spiritual Songs* . . . in new translation, for which the philological work is ascribed to Dunster, the versification to Lyon (cf. above under Dunster).

MATHER, COTTON (1663–1728), b. Boston, Mass., H.C. 1678, fellow, pastor Boston, Mass., S.T.D. Glasgow, F.R.S.

1. *A Poem Dedicated to the Memory of The Reverend and Excellent Mr. Urian Oakes.*

d. Cambridge, July 25, 1681, a. 50.

Boston, 1682, 427 lines, preceded by 30 lines "To the Reader," BRUL, HCL, repr. *III. Early American Poetry*, The Club of Odd Volumes, Boston, 1896.

2. *An Elegy On The Much-to-be deplored Death Of That Never-to-be-forgotten Person, The Reverend Mr. Nathanael Collins.*

d. Middletown, Dec. 28, 1684, a. 42.

Boston, 1685. 388 lines and 2 lines Latin, BRUL, NYPL, repr. *ibid.*, 1896.

3. X. Commandments.

10 lines, in his *A Scriptural Catechism* (Boston, 1691), t.p. verso, BA, etc., repr. in his *Maschil* (Boston, 1702), p. 188, BPL, etc. Another version, not rhymed in his *Another Tongue Brought In* (Boston, 1707), JCB, NYPL, etc.

4. Epitaph (on Shubael Dummer.)
   d. York, Me., Jan. 25, 1691/2, a. 56.
   4 six-line stanzas, in his *Fair Weather* (Boston, 1692), pp. 92–3, AAS, MHS, etc.; revised to 16 lines in his *Decennium Luctuosum* (Boston, 1699), p. 86, BA, etc., and in his *Magnalia*, vol. 2, p. 531.
5. "Health, Bread, with Life, my God mee sends."
   2 four-line stanzas, Ms.a. AAS, Diary, winter 1692, pr. *Diary*, vol. 1, 7 *Coll. M.H.S.*, vol. 7, p. 154.
6. "Lord, bought by thy All-worthy Blood."
   3 four-line stanzas, Ms.a. AAS, *Diary*, winter, 1692, pr. *ibid.*, vol. 1, p. 155.
7. "I stript of earthly, Comforts am."
   2 six-line stanzas, Ms.a. AAS, Diary, Feb. 28, 1695/6, pr. *ibid.*, vol. 1, pp. 185–6.
8. A Preparatory Thanksgiving-Song, fetch'd from the Beginning and Conclusion of the Hundred and Third Psalm.
   32 lines, in his *The Christian Thank-Offering* (Boston, 1696), t.p. verso, JCB unique copy.
9. Hymn.
   32 lines, in *ibid.*, p. 32.
10. (Note on the Verses Scattered through the *Magnalia Christi Americana*, completed 1696/7, pr. London, 1703.)

A careful critical examination reveals that, contrary to generally accepted opinion, not one of the longer poems in the *Magnalia* can with any likelihood be attributed to Cotton Mather. The elegy on William Tompson, (vol. 1, pp. 397–8) has long since been known to be Benjamin Tompson's, though previously Mather's ambiguous introductory words, "A short flight of our Poetry shall tell the rest," had led a number of scholars astray. The same ambiguity has till now led every one astray about the elegy on Governor William Phips (vol. 1, pp. 207–8), previously printed at the conclusion of Mather's *Pietas in Patriam* (London, 1697), and it is only the finding of Samuel Sewall's Ms. copy of the lost broadside that reveals it as the work of Daniel Henchman.

There is less excuse for attributing the long elegy on John Wilson, "Some offers . . ." (vol. 1, pp. 291–2, previously pr. in *Johannes in Eremo*, Boston, 1695, pp. 42–5, repr. *IV. Early American Poetry*, The Club of Odd Volumes, Boston, 1896), to Mather, for the preceding matter makes it quite clear that he is not the author. He states that the shortcomings of his prose account "might be made up with several expressive passages, which I find in elegies written and printed upon his death. . . . But waving the rest, let the following poem, never before printed, offer some odours"; i.e. this was one of the elegies which had not been printed but had remained in manuscript, perhaps in the large Mather collection of New England material.

All the facts of the case are against his having written the elegy on Jonathan Mitchel (vol. 2, pp. 94–5, previously pr. in his *Ecclesiastes*, Boston, 1697, pp. 107–9), though it is attributed to him in the Holmes bibliography (p. 298). The introductory matter shows that it was written shortly after Mitchel's death by "a young Gentleman, that lodg'd in his House." Mather at that time was only five and a half years old and certainly living with his father in Boston. The elegy almost surely belongs with the Epitaph which immediately follows it (elegy plus epitaph is a standard combination of the time); F. Drake, whose name appears at the end of the epitaph, is therefore most probably the author.

The epitaph on President John Rogers (vol. 2, p. 13), attributed in the *Magnalia* to "one of the scholars in Harvard-College," also cannot be by Mather, as Sibley states (vol. 1, p. 169), since he was then six years out of college.

Most puzzling is the fine excerpt from a poem hailing Urian Oakes' return to America in 1671 (vol. 2, p. 97). Morison attributes this to Mather (*Harvard College in the Seventeenth Century*, p. 419), saying "on his arrival he was thus greeted with an ode by Cotton Mather." Here again a chronological check would have revealed that Mather was only seven years old at the time. Eleven years later, however, Mather did write an elegy on the death of Oakes in which a loose paraphrase of these lines occurs. Whether Mather, as so often, here tinkered with another man's lines, or later in the *Magnalia* pushed his own revised lines farther back into the past, we do not know. If they are by another, Samuel Sewall or Benjamin Tompson appears as the most likely authors.

Indeed, it comes down to this: the Epitaph on Shubael Dummer (vol. 2, p. 531; our no. 3 above) of 16 lines, and perhaps also the eight line Latin epitaph on John Winthrop the Younger (vol. 1, p. 147) are the only sets of verses of any length in the *Magnalia* which can be attributed to Mather.

As for the shorter snatches of verse scattered through the book, their number is legion; and separating Mather's own from those quoted from his vast storehouse of Classical and Renaissance verse would be a nearly impossible task, especially since he habitually changed and adapted other men's verses to his own uses. There are about twenty such, for instance, taken from epitaphs in Melchior Adam's *Vitae Germanorum theologorum* (Heidelberg, 1620, etc. one of Mather's chief models for the *Magnalia*), and applied to the various New England divines. There are about thirty odd further short sets of verses, which may or may not be by Mather. The rest fall into the following groups: 1. from the Classical poets, 2. from Renaissance poets, 3. from English poets, 4. from known or anonymous older New England poets.

11. *Songs of the Redeemed, A Book of Hymns.*
    Boston, 1697, no copy is known to have survived; ref.: Samuel Mather's list of his father's published works.
    Note: there was a copy of the work in the library of William Adams at Yale College in 1726; see 4 *Coll. M.H.S.*, vol. 1, p. 44.
12. (Metrical Translation of the 26th Chapter of Isaiah.)
    1 four-line and 15 eight-line stanzas, in *Appendix to the Psalms Hymns and Spiritual Songs of the Old and New Testaments* (tenth ed., Boston, 1702); ref. *Diary*, vol. 1, p. 300, May 2, 1699.
13. The Song of the Pardoned.
    6 four-line stanzas, in his *The Everlasting Gospel* (Boston, 1700), p. 74, AAS, MHS, NYPL, etc.; the first of the "Divine Hymns."
14. Good inferences.
    5 four-line stanzas, in *ibid.*, p. 75.
15. The Lessons of the Gospel.
    5 four-line stanzas, in *ibid.*, pp. 75–6.
16. Evening Thoughts.
    4 lines, in *ibid.*, p. 76.
18. Little Children Brought unto the Lord Jesus Christ.
    5 four-line stanzas, in his *A Token, for the Children of New-England* (Boston, 1700), pp. 29–30, AAS, JCB, etc.; the first of "Some Scriptural Hymns for Children."
18. Early Religion.
    6 four-line stanzas, in *ibid.*, pp. 30–1.
19. The Consent of the Believer unto the Ten Commandments.
    6 four-line stanzas, in *ibid.*, pp. 31–2.
20. The Lords Prayer.
    8 four-line stanzas, in *ibid.*, pp. 32–4.

21. The Lords-Day.
    7 four-line stanzas, in *ibid.*, pp. 34–5.
22. Prayer Encouraged.
    5 four-line stanzas, in *ibid.*, pp. 35–6.
23. An Hymn. The Right Understanding of much Affliction.
    4 four-line stanzas, in his *A Companion for the Afflicted* (Boston, 1701), p. 56, AAS, BPL, etc.
24. *A Poem of Consolations under Blindness.*
    Boston, 1701, no copy is known to have survived; ref. *Diary*, vol. 1, p. 408, Nov. 20, 1701.
25. A Little Body of Divinity Versifyed.
    54 lines, in his *Maschil, Or, The Faithful Instructor* (Boston, 1702), pp. 129–31, BPL, etc.; repr. in his *Cares about the Nurseries* (Boston, 1702), pp. 4–5, BPL, etc.; in his *Much in a Little* (Boston, 1702), McG–WGM; in his *The Man of God Furnished* (Boston, 1708), 2 unnumb. pp. after p. 140, BPL, NYPL, etc., repr. as *The Way of Truth Laid Out* (Boston, 1721), 2 unnumb. pp. after p. 95, JCB; and in the publication of some hymns of Isaac Watts', *Honey out of the Rock* (Boston, 1715), pp. 22–4, HEHL.
26. The Lords Prayer.
    32 lines, in his *Maschil* (Boston, 1702), p. 189 (following repr. of "The Ten Commandments" in verse, p. 188); repr. in his *The Negro Christianized* (Boston, 1706), pp. 34–5, BPL, and in his *The Instructor* (Boston, 1726), pp. 10–2, BPL.
27. "I did lift up my Voice to Jah."
    3 four-line stanzas, Ms.a. MHS, pr. *Diary*, vol. 1, pp. 431–2.
28. *Conversion Exemplified.*
    Boston, 1703, 78 lines, unique copy of sep. pr. AAS, also appended to his *Agreeable Admonitions for Old & Young* (Boston, 1703), pp. 43–8, MHS; repr. with the title "The Covenant Consented to" in his *A Monitor for the Children of the Covenant* (Boston, 1715), p. 28, BPL (fragm.), 2nd ed., 1725, pp. 28–30, HCL, and in his *Baptismal Piety* (Boston, 1727), pp. 47–8, AAS, BPL, etc.
29. My Satisfaction.
    4 four-line stanzas (on death of son), in his *Meat out of the Eater* (Boston, 1703), p. 31, AAS, NYHS, etc.
30. My Resignation.
    6 four-line stanzas, in *ibid.*, pp. 67–8.

31. My Resolution.
    3 four-line stanzas, in *ibid.*, p. 108.
32. Songs in such a Night.
    4 four-line stanzas, in *ibid.*, p. 142 (misprinted 124).
33. My Text Paraphrased, and Faith Exhibited.
    6 four-line stanzas, in *ibid.*, pp. 181–2.
34. "Go then my Dove, but now no longer Mine!"
    14 lines (on death of his wife), in *ibid.*, p. (186); first issued as a small broadside of 12 lines, pasted in the beginning of books presented at her funeral to those who had watched during her long illness (ref. *Diary*, vol. 1, pp. 449–50).
35. A Lacrymatory; Design'd for the Tears let fall at the Funeral of Mrs. Sarah Leverett.
    d. Boston, Jan. 2, 1704/5, a. 75.
    120 lines, in his *Monica Americana* (Boston, 1705), pp. 29–32, MHS, etc.
36. Epitaph (on Michael Wigglesworth).
    d. Malden, June 10, 1705, a. 73.
    8 lines, in his *A Faithful Man, Described and Rewarded* (Boston, 1705), p. 48, BPL, NYPL, etc.
37. *Good Lessons for Children.*
    Boston, 1706, 2nd ed., New London, 1722 or 23; all in verse, no copy of either edition is known to have survived; ref. *Diary*, vol. 1, pp. 555–6.
38. On the Graves of My Young Brethren.
    (an elegy upon the early death of seven young ministers)
    170 lines, in his *Vigilantius. Or, A Servant of the Lord Found Ready* (Boston, 1706), pp. 29–34, MHS, BPL, etc., repr. *IV. Early American Poetry*, The Club of Odd Volumes, Boston, 1896.
39. Epitaphium (on Fitz-John Winthrop).
    d. Boston, Nov. 27, 1707, a. 68.
    9 lines Latin, in his *Winthropi Justa* (Boston, 1708), p. 40, MHS, CHS, etc. 2nd & 3rd ed. London, 1709 & 1710.
40. Gratitudinis Ergo. An Essay On the Memory of my Venerable Master, Ezekiel Cheever.
    d. Boston, Aug. 21, 1708, a. 93.
    209 lines, plus a 44 line Latin Epitaphium, in his *Corderius Americanus* (Boston, 1708), pp. 26–33, and pp. 33–4, AAS,

MHS, NYPL, etc.; repr. *IV. Early American Poetry*, The Club of Odd Volumes, Boston, 1896, and frequently in biographies of Ezekiel Cheever, etc.

41. Upon the Wars of Europe.
10 lines, poetic dialogue, Latin and Eng., between "Sevallus" (Samuel Sewall) and "Matherus," in his *Theopolis Americana* (Boston, 1710), lower half of p. (53) in the HCL copy.
Note: this composition may be by Sewall, added by him to a few copies while the pamphlet was in press.

42. "Soul, when the Worlds Fatigues do make to groan."
couplet, transl. from Latin "Taedia quem mundi teneant. . . ." in his *Nehemiah. A Brief Essay on Divine Consolations* (Boston, 1710), p. 17, MHS, NYHS.

43. The Sons of God shouting for Joy at the Arrival of the Lord's-day.
8 lines, Ms.a. AAS, Diary for 1711, under Dec. 7, pr. *Diary*, vol. 2, p. 138.

44. A Short Hymn, Tried and Coming forth as Gold.
4 four-line stanzas, in his *A Soul Well-Anchored* (Boston, 1712), verso of t.p., JCB.
Note: Sibley (vol. 3, p. 109) gives the title as "A Short Hymn to Assist the Pauses of Self-Examination," possibly the revised title of another issue, BPL.

45. "His lip dropt language, than sweet Honey, sweeter abundance."
1 line of English hexameter, tr. from the Iliad (on Nestor), Ms.a. MHS, Belknap Papers, letter to Samuel Penhallow, Boston, Oct. 21, 1713.
Note: the use of the dactylic hexameter in English verse seems to go back much farther than has ever been suspected; the above and Edward Johnson's, here noted for the first time, seem to be the earliest so far recorded.

46. Instructions for children.
98 lines, in his *The A, B, C. of Religion* (Boston, 1713), pp. 37–42, HEHL, JCB.

47. Epitaphium (on Wait Winthrop).
d. Boston, Nov. 7, 1717, a. 76.
69 lines Latin, in his *Hades Look'd Into* (Boston, 1717), pp. 43–6, AAS, MHS, etc.; repr. *IV. Early American Poetry*, Club of Odd Volumes, Boston, 1896.

48. *Psalterium Americanum. The Book of Psalms, . . . in Blank Verse.*
    Ms.a. NYPL, pr. Boston, 1718, verse text of 410 pages (incl. notes), plus prefatory and appended material, AAS, MHS, NYPL, etc.
49. Epitaphium (on Increase Mather).
    d. Boston, Aug. 23, 1723, a. 84.
    137 lines Latin, in his *Parentator* (Boston, 1724), 5 pp. after p. 239, AAS, MHS, NYPL, etc.
50. "O Glorious Christ of God; I live."
    3 four-line stanzas, Ms.a. MHS, Diary for 1724/5, pr. *Diary*, vol. 2, p. 786.
51. Singing at the Plow.
    20 lines, in his *Agricola. Or, The Religious Husbandman* (Boston, 1727), p. 21, AAS, MHS, etc., the first of "The Plain Songs of the Pious Husbandman."
52. The Sower a Singer.
    1 four-line and 4 eight-line stanzas, in *ibid.*, pp. 96–7.
53. The Rain gasped for.
    7 four-line stanzas, in *ibid.*, p. 131.
54. The Song of the Sithe.
    7 four-line stanzas, in *ibid.*, pp. 151–2.
55. The Sons of God, Singing among The Trees of God.
    8 four-line stanzas, in *ibid.*, pp. 190–1.
56. The Songs of Harvest.
    7 four-line stanzas, in *ibid.*, p. 212.
57. "Fleres si scires unum tua tempora Mensem."
    2 lines Latin, followed by a 4 line English paraphrase, on t.p. of his *Ignorantia Scientifica* (Boston, 1727), AAS, MHS, etc.
58. "What was conceal'd from thee, O Saint below."
    couplet, tr. and adapted from the epitaph on Cyprian, and applied to Peter Thacher, in his *The Comfortable Chambers, Opened and Visited* (Boston, 1728), p. 31, AAS, MHS, etc.; 2nd ed. Boston, 1796, p. 24, AAS, MHS, etc.
59. The Pidgeon Py. A Poem in Imitation of the Monumental Gratitude.
    26 lines and 2 additional coupletes, Ms.a. with many cancellations and revisions, on last blank leaf and t.p. of John Hubbard, *A Monumental Gratitude* (New London, 1727), copy in private possession, facsim. in *Photostat Americana*, and there handwriting identified as Mather's.

MATHER, INCREASE (1639–1723), b. Dorchester, Mass., H.C. 1656, Trinity College, Dublin, pastor Boston, fellow and president H.C., S.T.D. Harvard.

1. (Elegy on Jonathan Mitchell.)

d. Cambridge, July 9, 1668, a. 44.

apparently lost; ref. Cotton Mather, *A Poem Dedicated to . . . Urian Oakes* (Boston, 1682), p. 10.

"... what
Of thy forerunner Mitchell, Mather wrote,
I'le truly add, now Oakes is dead, to mee
Life will less sweet and Death less bitter be."

2. "Astra Colis Vivens; Moriens, super Aethera Foster."

2 lines Latin, addressed to John Foster as he lay dying, and inscribed on his gravestone at Dorchester, with the 2 line answer of Foster; pr. Samuel A. Green *John Foster* (Boston, 1909), p. 49; Sibley, vol. 2, p. 228.

MATHER, NATHANIEL (1669–1688), b. Boston, Mass., H.C. 1685, d. Salem, Mass.

Hymn.

24 lines, in Cotton Mather, *Early Piety, Exemplified in the Life and Death of Mr. Nathanael Mather* (London, 1689), pp. 26–7; repr. *Magnalia*, vol. 2, p. 139 and again p. 420.

MATHER, RICHARD (1596–1669), b. Lancashire, Eng., Brazenose College Oxford, N.E. 1635, pastor Dorchester, Mass.

1. *The Whole Booke of Psalmes Faithfully Translated into English Metre.*

Cambridge, Mass., 1640, collaborated in this translation with John Eliot and Thomas Welde I.

2. Ad Lectorem.

10 lines, Latin hexameter, Ms.a. blank leaf in a Hebrew Psalter (lacking t.p.), gift to his son Samuel, to whom the verses are addressed; ownership of vol. not stated and unknown; pr. in *The Historical Magazine*, vol. 4, p. 148.

MATTHEWS, MORDECAI (c. 1635–after 1715), b. Wales (?), N.E. 1638, H.C. 1655, returned Great Britain, pastor Glamorganshire, Wales.

The Christians daily Exercise.

Boston, reprinted, 1730, 12 pages, MHS, repr. Newport, 1738. The original edition probably appeared somewhere in Great Britain, though there seems to be no record of any copy.

MIGHILL, THOMAS (1639–1689), b. Rowley, Mass., H.C. 1663, schoolmaster, Rowley, pastor Milton and Scituate, Mass.

Utrum Malum sit privativum.

10 lines Latin, in *Quaestiones in Philosophia Discutiendae* (Cambridge, 1666), repr. Sibley, vol. 2, p. 134, and Morison, *Harvard College in the Seventeenth Century*, pp. 601–2.

MITCHELL, JONATHAN (1624–1668), b. Yorkshire, Eng., N.E. 1635, H.C. 1647, tutor and fellow, pastor Cambridge, Mass.

1. (Elegy on President Henry Dunster.)

   d. Scituate, Feb. 27, 1658/9, a. 49.

   original lost, selection of 5 four-line stanzas in Cotton Mather, *Ecclesiastes. The Life of the Reverend & Excellent, Jonathan Mitchel* (Boston, 1697), pp. 70–1; repr. *Magnalia*, vol. 2, p. 80.

2. Upon the Death of that Reverend, Aged, Ever-honoured, and gracious Servant of Christ, Mr. John Wilson.

   d. Boston, Aug. 7, 1667, a. 78.

   22 four-line stanzas, in Morton, pp. 185–8, signed J.M.

   Note: generally attributed to Joshua Moody; however, in form, style, attitude, and temperament it is quite similar to the Dunster verses and different from Moody's elegy on Reiner.

3. On the following Work and Its Author.

   8 six-line stanzas, prefixed to Michael Wigglesworth, *The Day of Doom* (Cambridge, 1662 or 63, fragm. of first ed. NEHGS), and in subsequent editions through 17th and 18th century.

   Note: in the 7th ed. the original "J. Mitchel" is erroneously expanded into "the Rev. Mr. John Mitchel."

MOODY, JOSHUA (1633–1697), b. Suffolk, Eng., N.E. 1634, Ipswich, Mass., H.C. 1653, fellow, pastor Portsmouth, N. H., and Boston, Mass.

1. Lamentations Upon the never enough bewailed Death of the Revered Mr. John Reiner.

d. Braintree (on sojourn), Dec. 21, 1676, a. 33.

c. 108 lines, broadside fragment, unique copy BA, lower part missing, facsim. Winslow, p. 11; Ms.c.c. NYHS, Samuel Sewall's commonplace book, pp. 30–2, with author's name and most of the lines missing in the broadside fragm. (Sewall indicates several passages omitted in his copy with "etc."). Note: Winslow confuses father and son John Reiner; this elegy is on the son; the better known father died in 1669.

2. (Epitaph on Thomas Bailey.)

d. Watertown, Jan. 21, 1688/9, a. 35.

12 lines unrhymed, in a series of balanced epithets, on gravestone, old burying ground, Watertown, Ms.c.c. by brother John Bailey (with ascription of authorship) pr. in *Watertown Records*, vol. 4, p. 110.

3. (Epitaph on Lydia Bailey.)

d. Watertown, April 16, 1691, a. 38.

3 double lines unrhymed, in a series of contrasting epithets, on gravestone, Ms.c.c. by husband John Bailey, pr. in *ibid.*

MORRELL, WILLIAM (c. 1590–after 1626), b. Eng., Magdalene College Cambridge, N.E. 1623–24, ret. to Eng.

New England. or A Briefe Enarration of the Ayre, Earth, Water, Fish and Fowles of that Country. With a Description of the Natures, Orders, Habits, and Religion of the Natives; in Latine and English Verse.

London, 1625, 309 lines Latin, 372 lines English, fascim. ed. Boston, The Club of Odd Volumes, 1895.

MORTON, CHARLES (1627–1698), b. Cornwall, Eng., Wadham College, Oxford, fellow, teacher at Newington Green, Middlesex; N.E. 1686, pastor Charlestown, Mass., vice-president H.C.

1. *Some Meditations on the History recorded in the first fourteen Chapters of Exodus, in Meeter.*

543 lines, 16 pp. without title page, date, or place of printing, copy AAS, Mather library, bound together with five other tracts of Morton, Ms. notes by Cotton Mather. Another copy at HCL, cataloged as anonymous.

2. *The Ark, its Loss and Recovery; Or some Meditations on the History recorded in the beginning of 1 Sam. in Meeter.*

576 lines, 16 pp. without t.p., d., or p., copy AAS, Mather

library, bound with 1, outer half of last leaf torn off with considerable loss of text; no other copy as yet located.

Note: proof of Morton's authorship in the "Advertisement," last unnumbered leaf (verso) of Morton's *The Spirit of Man* (Boston, 1693), HEHL, where the two titles are listed among his works.

MORTON, NATHANIEL (1613–1685), b. Leyden, Holland, N.E 1623, secretary of Plymouth Colony, historian.

1. (Elegy on Governor William Bradford.)
   d. Plymouth, May 9, 1657, a. 69.
   40 lines, in his *New Englands Memoriall* (Cambridge, 1669), pp. 149–50; anonymous, "by one that was well acquainted with the Worth of . . ."; generally attributed to Morton.

2. Upon the life and death of that godly matron, Mistris Alice Bradford.
   d. Plymouth, March 27, 1670, a. c. 80.
   64 lines, Ms.a. (?), pasted inside the cover of William Bradford's Ms. *History of Plymouth Plantation*, pr. 4 *Coll. M.H.S.*, vol. 3, pp. 460–2, with the omission of the suffixed initials, partly illegible (AK, AB, or AR), the meaning of which is not clear. The internal evidence, however, makes it very likely that Morton was the author.

MORTON, THOMAS (c. 1580's–1646), b. Eng., lawyer Cliffords Inn, N. E. 1622, to Wollaston (present Quincy), Mass., shipped back to Eng. 1628, again 1630, ret. N.E. 1643, imprisoned Mass., d. Maine.

1. New English Canaan, or New Canaan. The Authors Prologue.
   20 lines, in his *New English Canaan* (Amsterdan, 1637), repr. by Peter Force (Washington, 1838), and by Prince Society (Boston, 1883), vol. 14, p. 114.

2. New Canaans Genius. Epilogus.
   34 lines, in *ibid.*, pp. 241–2.

3. Epitaph (to a child born about Buzzard's Bay).
   8 lines, *ibid.*, p. 266.

4. Carmen Elegiacum.
   26 lines, *ibid.*, p. 275.

5. The Poem.
   "Rise Oedipus, and, if Thou canst, unfould."
   23 lines, *ibid.*, p. 277–8.
6. The Songe.
   "Drinke and be merry, merry, merry boyes."
   4 four-line stanzas and a four-line refrain repeated five times (first and last), *ibid.*, pp. 279–80.
7. The Poem.
   "I sing th' adventures of nine worthy wights."
   88 lines, *ibid.*, pp. 290–4.
8. The Poem.
   "What ailes Pigmalion? Is It Lunacy?"
   10 lines, *ibid.*, p. 315.

MOXON, GEORGE (1602–1687), b. Yorkshire, Eng., Sidney Sussex College Cambridge, N.E. 1637, pastor Springfield, Mass. 1637–51, returned Eng.

(Latin lyrics.)

"He was so good a *Lyrick* Poet, that he could imitate *Horace* so exactly, as not to be distinguish'd without Difficulty." Edmund Calamy, *An Account of the Ministers* (London, 1713), vol. 2, pp. 128–9, the reference being apparently to Moxon's university years. No further information about this verse, or about any American verse has as yet come to light. However, on the front and back fly leaves of the AAS copy of John Cotton, *The Powring out of the Seven Vials* (London, 1642), William Robie has copied three hymns (17 stanzas, beginning missing; 12 stanzas, and 20 stanzas) with this note on the second fly leaf verso: "Mr Mossens verses Novemb: 1670." This may just possibly be a variant spelling of Moxon; or it may refer to some other Yorkshire minister (Robie was also from Yorkshire, and later a merchant of Boston).

NORTON, JOHN I (1606–1663), b. Hertfordshire, Eng., Peterhouse Cambridge, N. E. 1635, pastor Ipswich and Boston, Mass.

A Funeral Elegie upon the death of the truely Reverend Mr. John Cotton.

d. Boston, Dec. 23, 1652, a. 68.

28 lines, Morton, pp. 136–7, also with many othographic and some verbal differences in Joshua Scottow, *A Narrative of the Planting of the Massachusetts Colony* (Boston, 1694), pp. 75–6, repr. 4 *Coll. M.H.S.*, vol. 4, pp. 331–2.

NORTON, JOHN II (1651–1716), b. Ipswich, Mass., H.C. 1671, pastor Hingham, Mass., (nephew of John Norton I).

A Funeral Elegy, Upon that Pattern and Patron of Virtue, the truely pious, peerless & matchless Gentlewoman Mrs. Anne Bradstreet.

d. Andover, Sept. 16, 1672, a. 60.

96 lines, in Anne Bradstreet, *Several Poems* (2nd ed., Boston, 1678), pp. 252–5, repr. John Harvard Ellis ed. (Charlestown, 1867), pp. 409–13.

NOYES, NICHOLAS (1647–1717), b. Newbury, Mass., H.C. 1667, pastor Haddam, Conn. and Salem, Mass.

1. A short Discourse about 66.

   36 lines in Josiah Flynt, *An Almanack . . . for the ensuing Year 1666* (Cambridge, 1665), signed N.N.

   Note: probably by Noyes, though N.N. was a common designation of anonymity at the time.

2. To his worthy Friend, The Reverend Mr. William Hubbard.

   38 lines, prefixed to William Hubbard, *The Benefit of a Well-Ordered Conversation* (Boston, 1684), signed N.N.

3. A Prefatory Poem, on that Excellent Book, Entituled Magnalia Christi Americana.

   107 lines, *Magnalia*, vol. 1, pp. 14–6.

4. Reverendo Domino D. Cottono Madero.

   2 Latin poems of 8 lines each, each preceded by two anagrams, *ibid.*, p. 16.

5. (An Elegy on Thomas Hooker.)

   unknown except for ref. in Sibley, vol. 2, p. 245, with no further statement as to its whereabouts. It hardly seems probable that Noyes wrote a poem on Thomas Hooker. Could this have been an elegy on Samuel Hooker, d. 1697? The reference may go back to the erroneous statement in the *Historical Collections of the Essex Institute*, vol. 8, p. 168, "He wrote an elegy on Thomas Hooker, in which he says . . . ." The couplet quoted actually comes from Noyes' elegy on John Higginson.

6. (Prefatory Poem.)

   118 lines, in Cotton Mather, *Christianus per Ignem* (Boston, 1702), pp. 2–6, MHS, HCL, etc.

7. A Consolatory Poem Dedicated unto Mr. Cotton Mather; Soon after the Decease of his Excellent and Vertuous Wife . . . Mrs. Abigail Mather.

   d. Boston, Dec. 1, 1702, a. 32.

   111 lines, in Cotton Mather, *Meat out of the Eater* (Boston, 1703), pp. 187–90, repr. E. C. Stedman and E. M. Hutchinson, *A Library of American Literature* (New York, 1889), vol. 2, pp. 206–8.

8. May 28th, 1706. To my worthy Friend, Mr. James Bayley, living (if living) in Roxbury.

   132 lines, broadside (Boston, 1707), BPL, facsim. Winslow, 21; also in the *Boston News-Letter*, Aug. 11, 1707.

9. (On Cotton Mather's Endeavors toward the Christian Education of Negro Slaves.)

   23 lines, Ms.a. MHS (?), pr. 1 *Proc. M.H.S.*, vol. 9, pp. 484–5, in a letter from Nicholas Noyes to Cotton Mather, dated Salem, Aug. 15, 1706.

10. An Elegy upon the Death of the Reverend, Mr. John Higginson.

    d. Salem, Dec. 9, 1708, a. 92.

    236 lines, broadside in private hands (typed copy MHS); and in Cotton Mather, *Nunc Dimittis, Briefly Descanted On* (Boston, 1709), pp. 1–8, repr. *New England Hist. Gen. Reg.*, vol. 7, pp. 237–40.

11 Upon the Much Lamented Death, of that Pious and Hopeful Young Gentlewoman, Wife of Mr. Samuel Gerrish.

   d. Wenham, Nov. 17, 1710, a. 19 (Mary Sewall Gerrish).

   45 lines, broadside BPL, fasim. Winslow, p. 29.

12. An Elegy Upon The Much Lamented Death Of the Reverend Mr Joseph Green.

    d. Salem Village (Danvers), Nov. 26, 1715, a. 40.

    284 lines in Thomas Blowers, *The Deaths of Eminent Men, and Excellent Friends* (Boston, 1716), pp. 25–33, "An Epitaph," p. 34; "second edition" in Joseph Capen, *A Funeral Sermon Occasioned by the Death of Mr. Joseph Green* (Boston, 1717), pp. 37–45, "An Epitaph," p. 46. Title and ref. in Wegelin erroneous. Repr. in the *Historical Collections of the Essex*

Institute, vol. 8, pp. 168–74, and in *The Historical Collections of the Topsfield Historical Society*, vol. 12, pp. 39–47.

13. (Riddle upon a Silk Patch-work Quilt.)
    4 lines, oral tradition, pr. in *Historical Collections of the Essex Institute*, vol. 2, p. 47.

14. An Elegy upon the Death of Severall Worthy Pious Persons
    d. during 1716 & 1717.
    40 lines, and one unrhymed line, Ms.a. or c.c., EI, Curwen Mss., vol. 1, p. 73; on several members of the Sewall family, etc. of Boston, and on the Rev. George Curwin, Noyes' young colleague, d. Salem, Nov. 23, 1717, a. 35, 20 days before Noyes' own death. Internal evidence makes it likely, though not certain, that Noyes was the author.

O.,L. (believed to be Lawrence Oakes (c. 1661–1679), probably a son of Urian Oakes and a student at H.C.

To the Sacred Memory of N.E.'s Heroe, Mars his Generall, Vertues standard-bearer, & Learning's glory . . . the deservedly Worshipfull Jno Leverett.

d. Boston, March 16, 1678/9, a. 62.

150 lines, signed L. O., Ms.c.c., MHS, John Leverett II's commonplace book, pp. (8–11), pr. *New England Hist. Gen. Reg.*, vol. 4, pp. 129–31, where tentatively attributed to Lawrence Oakes; no ref. to Ms. source, or to the Benjamin Tompson poem on Leverett which precedes it.

OAKES, URIAN (1631–1681), b. Eng., N.E. 1634, H.C. 1649, fellow, pastor Hampshire, Eng., ret. N.E. 1671, Cambridge, Mass., president H. C.

An Elegie upon The Death of the Reverend Mr. Thomas Shepard, Late Teacher of the Church at Charlestown in New-England.

d. Charlestown, Dec. 22, 1677, a. 43.

Cambridge, 1677, 16 pp., 52 six-line stanzas, BRUL, repr. Boston, Club of Odd Volumes, 1896, and Perry Miller and Thomas H. Johnson, *The Puritans*, pp. 641–50.

PAIN, PHILIP (16 –c. 1667 or 68), "Who lately suffering Shipwrack was drowned," presumably very young, c. 18–20.

Daily Meditations: Or, Quotidian Preparations for, and Considerations of Death and Eternity. Begun July 19, 1666.

Cambridge, 1668. Contents: "The Porch" 22 lines, 64 six-line "Meditations," and 16 couplets, one at the bottom of each page (an extra unrhymed line on p. 4); "A Postscript to the Readers," 7 six-line stanzas, signed F. T. (not identified); first ed. HEHL, unique copy, facsim., San Marino, California, 1936; 2nd ed., Cambridge, 1670, MHS unique copy, with a few small changes, and with the "Postscript" signed M. J., presumably Marmaduke Johnson, the printer of the poems "which may represent either a confession or a pretense to authorship by Marmaduke Johnson." No *Philip* Pain has been found among the numerous Paines of New England at this time. Is it possible that the *Philip* is an erroneous resolution of the initial P., on the part of the editor of the first edition?

PAINE, JOHN (1661–1731), b. Eastham, Mass., lived and died there; leading man of town, deacon.

1. (Fragment of an elegy.)
   on a woman, probably of Eastham, d. before June, 1695 (the next dated entry.)
   27 lines, Ms.a. journal of Deacon John Paine, prose and verse, fragment from 1695–1718, 1906 in private possession, pr. serially in *The Mayflower Descendant*, vols. 8 and 9; this elegy, vol. 8, p. 181.
2. (On the death of the wife of John Freeman, and on the death of Joseph Rogers.)
   d. Eastham, April 21 and 24, 1696.
   24 lines, Ms.a., pr. *ibid.*, vol. 8, p. 182.
3. (On the deaths within the past year.)
   entry, July 19, 1697.
   couplet, Ms.a., pr. *ibid.*, vol. 8, p. 183.
4. (On the death of Joshua Moody.)
   d. July 4, 1697, a. 65.
   couplet, Ms.a., pr. *ibid.*, vol. 8, p. 184.
5. (On the birth of a daughter, Sarah Paine.)
   b. April 14, 1699.
   couplet, Ms.a., pr. *ibid.*, vol. 8, p. 227.
6. (On his wife's illness and recovery.)
   4 lines, Jan. 28, 1701, Ms.a., pr. *ibid.*, vol. 8, p. 228.

7. (On the death of Robert, the son of Mr. Samuel Treat.)
   d. Eatham, April 30, 1701, a. 16.
   27 lines, Ms. a., pr. *ibid.*, vol. 8, p. 228.
8. (On the death of his mother, Mary Paine.)
   d. Eastham, April 28, 1704.
   32 lines, Ms.a., pr. *ibid.*, vol. 8, pp. 230–1.
9. (Upon entering the forty eighth year of his life.)
   March 14, 1707/8.
   8 lines, Ms.a., pr. *ibid.*, vol. 9, pp. 50–1.
10. (On the birth of a daughter Rebekah.)
   b. Oct. 30, 1709.
   8 lines, Ms.a., pr. *ibid.*, vol. 9, p. 51.
11. March the 14th, 1709/10.
   24 lines, Ms.a., pr. *ibid.*, vol. 9, p. 51.
12. March the 14th, 1713/4 are run fifty three years of my Short time.
   12 lines, Ms.a., pr. *ibid.*, vol. 9, p. 136.
13. "A wreched Sorry fruitless worm am I."
   6 lines, Ms.a., pr. *ibid.*, vol. 9, p. 136.
14. (On the death of his infant son Benjamin.)
   d. Jan. 14, 1716/7.
   6 lines, Ms.a., pr. *ibid.*, vol. 9, p. 139.

PARRIS, SAMUEL (1653–1720, b. London, Eng., H.C. (not grad.), pastor Danvers (Salem Village) and Dunstable, school teacher.

(Epitaph for his wife Elizabeth.)
   d. Danvers, July 14, 1696, a. c. 48.
   4 lines, on tombstone, with initials S.P. in lower right corner; pr. *New England Hist. Gen. Reg.*, vol. 8, p. 74, and vol. 44, p. 279.

PAYSON, EDWARD (1657–1732), b. Roxbury, Mass., H.C. 1677, pastor Rowley, Mass.

A Small Contribution to the Memorial of that Truely Worthy, and Worthily Man of God, Mr. Samuel Phillips.
   d. Rowley, April 22, 1696, a. 71.
   140 lines, in five parts, broadside, private ownership, possibly now lost, repr. in Thomas Gage, *History of Rowley* (Boston, 1840), pp. 79–84.

PETER, HUGH (1599–1660), b. Cornwall, Eng., Trinity College, Cambridge, pastor London, Eng., Rotterdam, Holland, N.E. 1635, pastor Salem, Mass., ret. Eng. 1641, prominent in Cromwellian government, executed at Restoration.

1. (Epitaph on Sir Edward Harwood.)
   d. 1632.
   in *The Advice of that Worthy Commander Sir. Ed. Harwood, Colonel . . . also a Relatione of his Life and Death.* (London, 1642). See S. E. Morison, "Sir Charles Firth and Master Hugh Peter with a Hugh Peter Bibliography," in *Harv. Grad. Mag.*, vol. 39, pp. 121–40.
2. (Epitaph on Henry Ireton.)
   d. 1651. *Op. cit.*
3. "Union with Christ/and Knowledge sound."
   60 short lines, in his *A Dying Fathers Last Legacy to an Only Child*, London, 1660, and numerous subseq. ed., e.g. Boston, 1717, pp. 72–4.
4. My Wishes.
   3 stanzas of 12 short lines each, *ibid.*, pp. 89–90.
5. For England, &c.
   3 stanzas of 12 short lines each, *ibid.*, pp. 90–1.

PIERSON, ABRAHAM (c. 1608–1678), b. Yorkshire, Eng., Trinity College, Cambridge, N. E. 1639, pastor Lynn, Mass., Southampton, L. I., Branford, Conn., Newark, N. J.

On the Honoured Theophilus Eaton, Esquire, Governour of New Haven Colony.
   d. New Haven, Jan. 7, 1657/8, a. 67.
   31 four-line stanzas in English and 1 six-line stanza in Latin, Ms.a. MHS, Winthrop Papers, pr. 4 *Coll. M.H.S.*, vol 7, pp. 477–81.

POLE, WILLIAM (1593–1674), b. Devonshire, Eng., Oriel College Oxford, N. E. 1637, Taunton and Dorchester, Mass., schoolmaster and town clerk.

1. (Epithalamion.)
   Latin, no. 221 in the *Epithalamia* (Oxford, 1613); upon the marriage of the Princess Elizabeth to Frederick Count Palatine.

2. The Epitaph of William Pole Which He Himself Made.
    8 lines, engraved on tombstone at Dorchester, pr. *New England Hist. Gen. Reg.*, vol. 2, p. 381; 12 lines (4 lines added in the middle), Ms.c.c. BPL, account book of Samuel Clap, pr. *Publ. Col. Soc. Mass.*, vol. 8, p. 233 and note.

RAWSON, GRINDALL (1659–1715), b. Boston, Mass., H.C. 1678, pastor Mendon, Mass.

1. Upon the Death of his much Esteemed friend Mr Jno Saffin Junr. d. Boston, Dec. 9, 1678, a. 17, student H. C.
    62 lines, Ms.c.c., RIHS, commonplace book of John Saffin, pr. *John Saffin His Book* (New York, 1928) pp. 23–5.
2. To the Learned and Reverend Mr. Cotton Mather, on his Excellent Magnalia.
    10 lines (couplet in English, Latin anagram, 8 lines English), *Magnalia*, vol. 1, p. 9.

RAYNER, JOHN (1643–1676), b. Plymouth, Mass., H.C. 1663, pastor Mendon, Mass., Dover, N. H., d. Braintree, Mass.

Utrum omnes Disciplinae tendant ad ἐνπραξίαν.
    10 lines Latin, in *Quaestiones in Philosophia Discutiendae* (Cambridge, 1666), repr. Sibley, vol. 2, pp. 133–4, and Morison, *Harvard College in the Seventeenth Century*, p. 601.

RICHARDSON, JOHN (1647–1696), b. Boston, Mass., H.C. 1666, tutor and fellow, pastor Newbury, Mass.

1. An Homo sit Causa libera suarum Actionum.
    16 lines Latin, in *Quaestiones Duae, Pro Modulo, Discutiendae* (Cambridge, 1669), repr. Sibley, vol. 2, p. 206, and Morison *Harvard College in the Seventeenth Century*, p. 603.
2. The Country-Mans Apocrypha.
    36 lines in his *Almanack* for 1670, p. 15 (answered by Samuel Bailey's "The College Ferula").

ROGERS, EZEKIEL (c. 1590–1661), b. Essex, Eng., Bennet & Christ's College, Cambridge, N. E. 1638, pastor Rowley, Mass.

1. In sepulchrum Reverendissimi viri, fratris charissimi M. Tho. Hookeri.

8 lines English, the third of the prefatory poems in Thomas Hooker, *A Survey of the Summe of Church-Dicipline* (London, 1648), repr. *Magnalia*, vol. 1, p. 318.

2. Epitaph (on Governor Thomas Dudley).
   d. Roxbury, July 31, 1653.
   8 lines English, 8 lines Latin, pr. Charles M. Ellis, *The History of Roxbury Town* (Boston, 1847), p. 103, here attributed to Nathaniel Rogers; the Latin lines repr. from *Magnalia*, vol. 1, pp. 123–4, signed E. R.

ROGERS, JOHN (1630–1684), b. Essex, Eng., N.E. 1636, H.C. 1649, pastor Ipswich, Mass., president H.C., physician.

Upon Mrs. Anne Bradstreet Her Poems, &c.
9 seven-line stanzas and a couplet, prefatory poem in the 2nd ed. of her poems, *Several Poems* (Boston, 1678), pp. xii–xiv, in John Harvard Ellis ed., Charlestown, 1867, pp. 93–6.

ROWLANDSON, JOSEPH (1632–1678), b. Eng., N.E. by 1637, Ipswich and Lancaster, Mass., H.C. 1652, pastor Lancaster, Mass., and Wethersfield, Conn.

"O God from heaven looke thou down."
13 four-line stanzas, libellous verses posted upon the meeting house in Ipswich, July, 1651, Ms.c.c. in court records at Salem, pr. in *Narrative of the Captivity and Removes of Mrs. Mary Rowlandson* (Lancaster, 1828), and in Sibley, vol. 1, pp. 311–2.

RUSSELL, DANIEL (1642–1679), b. Charlestown, Mass., H.C. 1669, fellow, pastor New London, Conn., and Charlestown, Mass.

(Calendar Verse)
8 lines under each month, in his *Almanack* for 1671, repr. Perry Miller and Thomas H. Johnson, *The Puritans*, pp. 633–5.

SAFFIN, JOHN (1632–1710), b. Exeter, Devonshire, Eng., N.E. by 1644, Scituate, Mass., trip to Va. 1654, Boston c. 1659, Bristol, Mass. (now R. I.) 1688, merchant, deputy, councillor, judge, d. Boston.

1. A Dialogue between John and Martha or Exonus and Plimothenia.
   54 lines, Ms.a. RIHS, commonplace book of John Saffin, pr. in *John Saffin His Book*, pp. 185–7.

2. (Fragment of a poem upon his departure for Virginia 1654.)
"Sweetly (my Dearest) I left thee asleep."
52 lines, Ms.a. pr. *ibid.*, pp. 181–2.

3. To her[,] comeing home.
"Sayle gentle Pinnace Zepherus doth not faile."
8 lines, Ms.a., pr. *ibid.*, p. 182.

4. A Letter to his Dear Martha 1660.
76 lines, Ms.a., pr. *ibid*, pp. 182–5.

5. Martha Saffin.
couplet, 2 versions, following 2 anagrams, Ms.a., pr. *ibid.*, p. 11.

6. An Acrostick on the truly Loving & Dearly Beloved, Mrs Abigail Collins. Anno 1663.
14 lines, Ms.a., pr. *ibid.*, p. 111.

7. An Elegie on that Reverend man of God Mr John Wilson.
d. Boston, Aug. 7, 1667, a. 78.
anagram and 40 lines, Ms.a., pr. *ibid.*, pp. 115–6. Note by Saffin: "this is in Print"; no copy of the imprint is known to have survived, but the anagram and first 4 lines are quoted in a much changed version in the *Magnalia*, vol. 1, p. 284.

8. An Elegie upon the Deplorable, or rathe Deplored Death of that Super-Eminent Minister of the Gospell Mr Jonathan Mitchel.
d. Cambridge, July 9, 1668, a. 44.
2 anagrams with 4 lines of verse, and 60 lines, Ms.a., pr. *ibid.*, pp. 111–3. Note by Saffin: "this is in Print"; no copy of the imprint is known to have survived, but the "Epitaph" (last 12 lines) was repr. in Morton, p. 196, signed J.S., and till now erroneously attributed to John Sherman.

9. An Epitaph on that Eminent and truly pious Materon Mrs Mary Willett wife to the Worppfull Thomas Willett.
d. Plymouth, Jan 8, 1669.
18 lines, Ms.a., pr. *ibid.*, pp. 19–20, repeated with slight changes, pp. 114–5.

10. An Elegie on that Profound Divine Mr Charles Chancey.
d. Cambridge, Feb. 19, 1671, a. 82.
22 lines, Ms.a., pr. *ibid.*, pp. 14–5.

11. An elegie on his Dear and truely pious Mother Mrs Grace Saffin.
d. London, "in a good old age."
24 lines, Ms.a., pr. *ibid.*, pp. 15–6.

12. An Epitaph on Mrs Eliza Buttler.
    d., Jan. 12, 1672/3.
    12 lines, Ms.a., pr. *ibid.*, p. 34.
13. To His Dear Friend W. T. January the 15th 1672[/3].
    134 lines, Ms.a., pr. *ibid.*, pp. 29–33.
14. An Acrostick on Mrs Elizabeth Hull.
    12 lines, Ms.a., pr. *ibid.*, p. 27.
15. On presenting a rare Book to Madame Hull Senr: his Vallintine.
    10 lines, Ms.a., pr. *ibid.*, pp. 27–8.
16. An Acrostick on Mrs. Winifret Griffin.
    16 lines, Ms.a., pr. *ibid.*, p. 28.
17. An Acrostick on Mrs Lettice Corbin.
    12 lines, Ms.a., pr. *ibid.*, p. 28–9.
18. An Epistle To a Young Lady upon the Presenting an Acrostick on her Name.
    22 lines, Ms.a., pr. *ibid.*, p. 33.
19. An Epitaph on the Worppfull Thomas Willett Esqr.
    d. Seekonk, June, 1674, a. 64.
    16 lines, Ms.a., pr. *ibid.*, pp.22–3, and a much revised version, pp. 113–4.
20. To the Revd: Mr Wm Hubbard on his Exact History of New Englands Troubles &c.
    34 lines, Ms.a., pr. *ibid.*, pp. 110–1; also in William Hubbard's *A Narrative of the Troubles with the Indians* (Boston, 1677), after the "Epistle Dedicatory," signed J.S. and till now wrongly attributed to John Sherman or to Jeremiah Shepard.
21. A lamentation on my Dear Son Simon.
    d. Boston, Nov. 23, 1678, a. 12½.
    18 lines, Ms.a., pr. *ibid.*, p. 21.
22. A brief Elegie on my Dear Son John.
    d. Boston, Dec. 9, 1678, a. 17½.
    8 lines, Ms.a., pr. *ibid.*, p. 25, after Grindall Rawson's elegy on him.
23. An Epitaph on his truly loveing and Dearly beloved Wife Martha Saffin.
    d. Boston, Dec. 11, 1678, a. 39.
    14 lines, Ms.a., pr. *ibid.*, p. 20.
24. Another on His Dear Martha.
    16 lines, Ms.a., pr. *ibid.*, pp. 20–1.

25. An Epitaph on the Honble John Leverett Esqr Late Governor of his Majestys Colony of the Massathusetts.
    d. Boston, Mar. 16, 1678/9, a. 62.
    29 lines, Ms.a., pr. *ibid.*, pp. 116–7. Note by Saffin: "this is in Print"; no copy of the imprint is known to have survived.
26. (Fragment of an elegy on Governor Josiah Winslow.)
    d. Marshfield, Dec. 18, 1680, a. 51.
    68 lines, Ms.a., pr. *ibid.*, pp. 172–4 (beginning missing). Note by Saffin: "This Elegie was put in print by T. Maccarty the great Admirer of his vertues." No copy of this imprint is known to have survived. Maccarty was a Boston merchant, but is not known to have been a printer or publisher.
27. [Diagram of a flaming corona] This was seen and Special not is taken of, by Divers Credible persons in Anno 1681.
    28 lines, Ms.a., pr. *ibid.*, p. 189.
28. An Epithalmium or wedding Song.
    24 lines, Ms.a., pr. *ibid.*, p. 191 (by Saffin or copied?)
29. "Cankers touch fairest fruites, by their Infection."
    10 lines. Ms.a., pr. *ibid.*, p. 191 (by Saffin?)
30. On a Rogue that abus'd the people of N.E. of all Ranks and sexes, in a printed Scurrillous pamphlett.
    4 lines, Ms.a., pr. *ibid.* p. 192.
31. On the Deploreable Departure of the Honered and truely Religious Chieftain John Hull Esqr.
    d. Boston, Sept. 30, 1683, a. 59.
    106 lines, Ms.a., pr. *ibid.*, pp. 117–20.
32. Pious Contemplations on Divers Heads.
    36 lines, Ms.a., pr. *ibid.*, pp. 120–1.
33. Consideratus Considerandus.
    39 lines, Ms.a., pr. *ibid.*, pp. 122–3.
34. (Epitaph on son, Thomas Saffin).
    d. Stepney, Eng., June 18, 1687, a. 24.)
    12 lines, on gravestone, pr. *New England Hist. Gen. Reg.*, vol. 4, p. 109; judging from its style and from the family references in it, almost certainly by John Saffin.
35. A Memoriall of the Deplorable Death of that most Excellent Super-Eminent and Profound Divine the Revd: Mr Samuel Lee.
    d. St. Maloe, France, Dec. 1691, a. 66.
    43 lines (and one line variant), Ms.a. RIHS, pr. *John Saffin His Book*, pp. 46–8.

36. In a Letter to a Friend, in which was Inclosed a Manuscript.
    8 lines, Ms.a., pr. *ibid.*, p. 48.
37. A Charracteristicall Satyre on a proud upstart.
    14 lines, 2 versions, and a third version of the conclusion with 2 lines added, Ms.a., pr. *ibid.*, pp. 82–3, dated March 4th Anno 1698[/9].
38. A Charracter of a Pernicious Backbiter.
    24 lines, Ms.a., pr. *ibid.*, pp. 150–1.
39. A Charracter of a Proud man.
    18 lines, Ms.a., pr. *ibid.*, p. 151.
40. A true Discription of a meek Spirited Peace Maker.
    28 lines, Ms.a., pr. *ibid.*, p. 152.
41. To his Excellency Richard Earle of Bellamont Capt: Genll: & Governor in Chief.
    26 lines, Ms.a., pr. *ibid.*, pp. 77–8, dated Bristol the 20th October 1699.
42. An Elegy On the Late Deplorable Expiration of the Honorable Thomas Danforth Esqr.
    d. Cambridge, Nov. 5, 1699, a. 77.
    79 lines, Ms.a., pr. *ibid.*, pp. 137–9. Note by Saffin: "This was committed to the press, by his son in law Capt Fran: Foxcraft." No copy of the imprint is known to have survived.
43. "Here's Miscellanies in this Book compris'd."
    15 lines, Ms.a., pr. *ibid.*, p. 1; opening verses of Saffin's commonplace book.
44. To his Excellency Joseph Dudley Esqr Govr: &c.
    69 lines, and variant concluding couplet, Ms.a., pr. *ibid.*, pp. 65–7, dated Bristol 18th December 1703.
45. (On his Grievance against Gov. Dudley.)
    4 lines, Ms.a., pr. *ibid.*, p. 76.
46. A Revived Elegiac Lamentation of the Deplorable, and Irripairable Loss of his truely Loving and Dearly Beloved Consort Martha Saffin.
    54 lines, Ms.a., pr. *ibid.*, pp. 83–5, dated Bristol the 2d of February 1703/4.
47. A Thankfull Memoriall October 6th 1704.
    49 lines, with variant 4 lines for last 2, second version 53 lines, Ms.a., pr. *ibid.*, pp. 85–7 and pp. 104–6.
48. "There's nothing Glorious but is hard to gett."
    8 lines, Ms.a., pr. *ibid.*, p. 87.

49. On fair weather.
 4 lines, Ms.a., pr. *ibid.*, p. 87.
50. On fowle weather.
 4 lines, Ms.a., pr. *ibid.*, p. 88.
51. Eligie on the Deplored Decease of that truly Pious and Religious Matron Mrs Sarah Leveret Relict of the Late Honble John Leveret Esqr.
 d. Boston, Nov. 2, 1704, a. 75.
 96 lines, preceded by anagram, Ms.a., pr. *ibid.*, pp. 91–4; Ms.a. (?) HCL, a manuscript "broadside," 2 couplets missing, till now incorrectly attributed to Cotton Mather.
 Note: in the Ms. the title runs across the top of both pages; in the printing (pp. 91 & 93), it is cut in half to the total loss of the meaning. Cotton Mather (no. 35) gives date of her death as "2d 11m.1704,5," which then meant *Jan.* 2, 1704/5.
52. To his Excellency Joseph Dudley Esqr Govr: &c.
 50 lines, Ms.a., pr. *ibid.*, pp. 80–1, dated Bristol 22th January 1704[/5].
53. To the Reader upon the Government, and Improvement of Mirth.
 14 lines, Ms.a., pr. *ibid.*, pp. 167–8; penned upon the cover of the Rev. Mr. Benjamin Colman's book *The Government and Improvement of Mirth* (Boston, 1707), and sent to Colman with letter of July 16, 1708.
54. To the Reverend Author, (Mr Benja Coleman &c).
 44 lines, Ms.a., pr. *ibid.*, pp. 168–9, sent with above.
55. New England Lamented.
 97 lines, second version, "New England's Lamentation of her Present State &c" 1708/9, 100 lines (3 lines added before last 4 lines), Ms.a., pr. *ibid.*, pp. 98–101 and pp. 164–7.
56. "As Reason Chiefly Differs Man from Beast."
 4 lines, Ms.a., pr. *ibid.*, p. 103.

SEWALL, SAMUEL (1652–1730), b. Hampshire, Eng., N.E. 1661, H.C. 1671, fellow, merchant, Chief Justice of Mass., diarist, res. Boston.

1. "The Humble Springs of stately Sandwich Beach."
 6 lines, Ms.a. MHS Sewall Papers, pr. *Diary*, vol. 1, p. 27 (Oct. 28, 1676), revised version pr. *Boston News-Letter*, March 28, 1723, repr. *Diary*, vol. 3, p. 322.

2. "O great Menasseh, were it not for thee."
 2 lines, Ms.a. MHS, pr. *Diary*, vol. 1, p. 37 (March 6, 1677).
3. Mrs. Mehitable Holt. A Person of Early Piety.
 d. Eng. Sept. 30, 1677, a. 38 (Sewall's aunt).
 6 lines, Ms.a. NYHS Sewall commonplace book; broadside MHS with Ms. note of Sewall (prob. pr. Boston, 1689–90).
4. "Si Christum discis, nihil est si caetera discis."
 2 lines Latin, pr. book plate c. 1690's, NHYS in his commonplace book.
5. Mrs. Judith Hull.
 d. Boston, June 22, 1695. (Sewall's mother-in-law.)
 a) 10 lines, broadside BPL, b) 12 lines, broadside AAS, repr. *Trans*, *A.A.S.*, vol. 3, p. 272.
6. (Lines on his still-born son.)
 4 lines Latin, Ms.a. MHS, pr. *Diary*, vol. 1, p. 426 (May 18, 1696).
7. To be engraven on a Dial.
 4 lines, Ms.a. MHS, Sewall commonplace book, leaf 112b, c. 1690's.
8. "To horses, swine, neat cattle, sheep, and deer."
 couplet, pr. Joshua Coffin, *A Sketch of the History of Newbury* (Boston, 1845), p. 166.
9. (To Capt. Josias Crow, with a piece of his daughter's Bride-Cake.)
 4 lines Latin, Ms.a. MHS, pr. *Letter Book*, vol. 1, p. 245 (Oct. 18, 1700).
10. Upon Mr. Samuel Willard . . . after a long and dangerous Fit of Sickness; November 21, 1700.
 a) 8 lines, Ms.a. MHS, pr. *Diary*, vol. 2, p. 26; b) 3 four-line stanzas, broadside, 2 issues, 1700 and 1720, both MHS, 2nd with dithyrambic prose passages added, repr. 2 *Proc. M.H.S.* vol. 2, pp. 42–3.
11. Wednesday, January 1. 1701. A little before Break-a-day at Boston of the Massachusetts.
 a) 3 four-line stanzas, Ms.a. MHS, pr. *Diary*, vol. 2, p. 28, and broadside MHS; b) 6 four-line stanzas (st. 2, 4, & 5 added), broadside BPL & AAS, and appended to his *Proposals Touching the Accomplishment of Prophecies* (Boston, 1713), repr. 2 *Proc. M.H.S.*, vol. 1, p. 14; facsim. Winslow, p. 175.

12. (Epitaph on granddaughter, Sarah Sewall.)
    apparently lost, mentioned *Diary*, vol. 2, p. 69.
13. "Superanuated Squier, wigg'd and powder'd with pretence."
    4 lines, Ms.a. MHS, pr. *Diary*, vol. 2, p. 79; a satire, June 8, 1703, against John Saffin in connection with his lawsuit to bring Adam, a negro, back into slavery (the Index *Diary*, vol. 3, p. 562 erroneously calls them "Verses on Gov. Dudley").
14. (Verses to Richard Henchman, with a copy of Calvin on the Psalms.)
    a) 4 lines Latin, Ms.a. MHS, pr. *Diary*, vol. 2, p. 136; b) 6 lines, pr. *Letter Book*, vol. 1, p. 314 (Aug. 24, 1705).
15. "Oceani fluctus Anna moderante superbos."
    2 lines Latin, Ms.a. MHS, pr. *Diary*, vol. 2, p. 137 and *Letter Book*, vol. 1, p. 314; sent to Cotton Mather, Sept. 10, 1705, and at his suggestion *Anna* was changed to *Christo*, and this new version was translated into English, *Diary*, vol. 2, p. 140.
16. "Roma simul coelebsque ruunt in tempore Petrus."
    2 lines Latin, Ms.a. MHS, pr. *Letter Book*, vol. 1, p. 318 (sent to Richard Henchman, Oct. 13, 1705).
17. "Roma inhonesta jacet, Sanctae gaudete puellae."
    2 lines Latin, Ms.a. MHS, pr. *Diary*, vol. 2, p. 140 (Oct. 15, 1705), and revised *Letter Book*, vol. 2, p. 139 (1722).
18. "Desine Belshazzar Templo Omnipotentis abuti."
    2 lines Latin, Ms.a. MHS, pr. *Diary*, vol. 2, p. 141 (early Nov., 1705).
19. "Sound! Sound! the Jubilean Trumpet sound."
    2 lines, Ms. a. MHS, pr. *Diary*, vol. 2, p. 141 (early Nov., 1705).
20. On the burning of the Quebec Cross.
    a) 2 lines Latin and 4 lines English paraphrase *Diary*, vol. 2, p. 143 (Nov. 25, 1705); b) 4 lines Latin *Diary*, vol. 2, p. 150 (Dec. 24, 1705) ("Iddum," line 3 should be Idolum"); pr. *Boston News-Letter*, Dec. 24, 1705, with title "In Obitum Crucis."
21. (On Tom Child, the Painter.)
    d. Boston, Nov. 10, 1706.
    4 lines, Ms.a. MHS, pr. *Diary*, vol. 2, p. 170.
22. Feria Septima, Martij 8°. 1707. Anno Regni Annae Reginae Angliae &c. Sexto.
    2 lines Latin, 4 lines English, Ms.a. MHS, pr. *Diary*, vol. 2, p. 181.

23. Feria Sexta; Quintilis quarto, 1707.
    broadside, apparently lost; *Diary*, vol. 2, p. 191: "July 4, 1707. I printed *Feria Sexta* . . . ."

24. Deo Servatori.
    4 lines Latin, Ms.a. MHS, pr. *Letter Book*, vol. 1, p. 350 (July 14, 1707, in remembrance of Ipswich and to Mr. George Jaffrey's memory, d. Feb. 13, 1707).

25. Upon the Reverend Mr. Francis Goodhue.
    d. Rehoboth, Sept. 15, 1707, a. 29.
    8 lines Latin, broadside (?, see *Diary*, vol. 2, p. 199), pr. *Boston News-Letter*, Feb. 28, 1723, repr. *Diary*, vol. 3, p. 321.

26. (Verses on Mr. Clap.)
    broadside, mentioned *Diary*, vol. 2, p. 243 (gave Madam Brown two copies, Nov. 20, 1708); no copy known; may not be by Sewall.

27. Stylo Juliano, Bostoniae Novanglorum Feria Septima, Decembris 17, 1709.
    a) 2 lines Latin, Ms.a. MHS, pr. *Letter Book*, vol. 1, p. 387, inscription sent with the Commentaries on Job written by a learned Spanish Divine, to Mr. Charles Sucre, Governor of Carthagena, then in Boston; b) 2 lines English, upon the same subject, *Letter Book*, *ibid.*; c) 2 lines Latin, inscribed at the end of the book, *Letter Book*, *ibid.*

28. In deditionem Castelli Portus Regalis Imperatori Excellentissimo Francisco Nicholsono armigero, Octob. 2, 1710.
    a) 16 lines Latin, Ms.a. MHS, pr. *Letter Book*, vol. 1, pp. 399–400, signed S.S.; b) 20 lines (4 lines added before last 2), *Letter Book*, *ibid.* note; c) 22 lines English translation by Sewall, *Letter Book*, vol. 1, pp. 406–7 note; another freer translation (by Simon Willard?) *Letter Book*, vol. 1, p. 406. The original may have been published as a broadside.

29. (Distich for Jonathan Sewall, Jr.)
    2 lines Latin, Ms.a. MHS, pr. *Diary*, vol. 2, p. 311 (May 16, 1711). (error: "mihi" should be "mi," vocative of meus".)

30. (With gift of Edward Tompson's *Heaven the best Country*.)
    2 lines Latin, Ms.a. MHS, pr. *Diary*, vol. 2, p. 339 (March 8, 1712); also *Diary*, vol. 3, p. 392 (Sept. 10, 1728), dream: distich engraved on his watch.

31. (Couplet added to Nehemiah Hobart's verses on Sewall "Martij 27. 1712.")
    2 lines Latin, broadside BA, repr. *Letter Book*, vol. 1, p. 315.

32. (Couplet added to Benjamin Larnell's verses.)
    2 lines Latin, Ms.a. MHS, pr. *Diary*, vol. 2, p. 369 (Dec. 20, 1712).

33. To the Rev'd Mr. Jno. Sparhawk on the Birth of his Son, Augt. or Sept. 1713.
    12 lines English, 2 lines Latin, Ms.a. MHS, pr. *Diary*, vol. 3, p. 408.

34. (Distich left for Mr. Stanton the Chaplain who was gone a Gunning.)
    2 lines Latin, Ms.a. MHS, pr. *Diary*, vol. 3, p. 22 (Oct. 5, 1714).

35. Lines made to direct me in signing the Pound-plate.
    3 lines Latin, Ms.a. MHS, pr. *Diary*, vol. 3, p. 49 (July 5, 1715, on the new issue of paper currency).

36. (On the death of his sister, Mrs. Jane Gerrish.)
    d. Newbury, Jan. 29, 1717, a. 57.
    4 lines Latin, Ms.a. MHS, Sewall almanac leaves, pr. 2 *Proc. M.H.S.*, vol. 8, p. 214.

37. A small Vial of Tears brought from the Funeral of John Winthrop, A very goodly Child.
    d. New London, Feb. 15, 1716/7, a. nearly one year.
    10 lines broadside, MHS, in Winthrop Deeds, etc., p. 99, signed S.S.; Ms.a. MHS, pr. Letter Book, vol. 2, p. 70.

38. (On several deaths in the family.)
    6 lines Latin, Ms.a. MHS, pr. *Letter Book*, vol. 2, p. 84 (c. early Feb., 1717).

39. (On the death of his wife.)
    d. Boston, Oct. 19, 1717, a. 59.
    2 lines, Ms.a. MHS. pr. *Letter Book*, vol. 2, p. 84, with Latin translation by his son Stephen.

40. Salem, Dec. 13, 1717. A specimen of New English Celibacy.
    6 lines, *Boston News-Letter*, Feb. 13, 1721, followed by verses signed J. W. (John Winthrop IV), repr. 2 *Proc. M.H.S.*, vol. 3, pp. 380–1; Ms. in letter to brother Stephen Sewall, Dec. 23, 1717, pr. *New England Hist. Gen. Reg.*, vol. 24, p. 292, preceded by Latin distich (error: "salatior" should be "solatia").

41. (Imitation of a distich of Ovid.)
 2 lines Latin, Ms.a. MHS, pr. *Letter Book*, vol. 2, p. 123 (Nov. 21, 1719).

42. Upon the drying up that Ancient River, the River Merrymak.
 36 lines, broadside MHS, dated Jan. 15, 1719/20, signed S.S., with answer, 38 lines, "Connecticut's Flood, on Merrymak's Ebb," dated March 10, 1720/1, signed Anthropos, repr. *New England Weekly Journal*, June 23, 1735, with second signed J.W. (i.e. John Winthrop IV), repr. 2 *Proc. M.H.S.*, vol 9, pp. 8–10; facsim. Winslow, p. 161.
 Note: *Diary*, vol. 3, p. 240, seems to imply that a first edition of the broadside, with only the first set of verses, was issued Jan. 1720.

43. Upon the downfall of the Papists at Black Friers, London, October the Twenty sixth, 1623.
 14 lines Latin, pr. *Boston News-Letter*, Oct. 24, 1723, repr. *Letter Book*, vol. 2, p. 141.

44. Upon the River Merrimak.
 2 lines Latin, pr. *Boston News-Letter*, Feb. 21, 1723, repr. *Diary*, vol. 3, p. 321 note.

45. Decembris 2. 1722.
 2 lines Latin, pr. *ibid.*, repr. *ibid.* (error: "laqueatus" should be "illaqueatus"); on Daniel Rogers, d. in Black Rock Cove, between Salisbury and Newbury, Dec. 1, 1722.

46. Januarii 14, 15, 16.
 4 lines Latin, pr. *ibid.*, repr. *ibid.*; on the recovery of Daniel Rogers' body (on the background of 45 & 46 see Sibley, vol. 3, pp. 358–9).

47. Upon the Reverend Mr. Samuel Pierpont and Mr. Benjamin Gibson . . . their dying in one and the same night.
 drowned in the Connecticut and Penobscot rivers, March 15, 1723.
 8 lines Latin, pr. *Boston News-Letter*, April 11, 1723, repr. *Diary*, vol. 3, p. 322.

48. Boston, Feb. 1. 1723/4.
 2 lines Latin, Ms. a. MHS, pr. *Diary*, vol. 3, p. 330; pr. *Boston News-Letter*, Feb. 6, 1724 (after the suicide of John Valentine, Esq.).

49. "Dum Cererem et Bacchum meditaris, Ralle Sacerdos."
    2 lines Latin, Ms.a. MHS, pr. *Letter Book*, vol. 2, p. 174 (on Father Ralle and the defeat of the Kennebec Indians).

50. Feria Quinta, Novembris duodecimo, 1724.
    5 lines Latin, Ms.a. MHS, pr. *Letter Book*, vol. 2, p. 178 (on marriage of John Wendell and Elizabeth Quincy).

51. (On the death of his brother, Stephen Sewall.)
    d. Salem, Oct. 17, 1725, a. 68.
    2 lines Latin, Ms.a. MHS, pr. *Letter Book*, vol. 2, p. 193.

52. (On the pall bearers of Mary Cony.)
    2 lines, Ms.a. MHS. pr. *Diary*, vol. 3, p. 375 (after April 12, 1726).

53. In Remembrance of Mr. Samuel Hirst.
    d. Boston, Jan. 14, 1726/7, a. 21 (Sewall's grandson).
    24 lines, broadside, MHS.

SHEPARD, JEREMIAH (1648–1720), b. Cambridge, Mass., H.C. 1669, pastor Rowley, Essex, and Lynn, Mass.

(Calendar Verse.)

"Here grant me leave to rouse the Thespian train."

18 lines in his *An Ephemeris of the Coelestial Motions for the Year . . . 1672*, p. 2.

Note: the prefatory verses in William Hubbard, *A Narrative of the Troubles with the Indians* (Boston, 1677), signed J.S., generally attributed to Jeremiah Shepard (or to John Sherman), were actually written by John Saffin and occur in his Ms. commonplace book (see above, Saffin no. 20).

SHEPARD, THOMAS I (1605–1649), b. Northamptonshire, Eng., Emmanuel College, Cambridge, N.E. 1635, pastor Essex and Yorkshire, Eng., Cambridge, Mass.

'You Roxburough poets take this in time."

4 lines, Ms.c.c., Historical Society of Pennsylvania, in hand of Increase Mather. A garbled version, the only one hitherto known, occurs, in the *Magnalia*, vol. 1, p. 367; Cotton Mather seems to have relied on his memory at this point and to have "revised" the quatrain unconsciously, to the drastic perversion of its original meaning.

SHEPARD, THOMAS II (1635–1677), b. London, Eng., N.E. 1635, H.C. 1653, fellow, pastor Charlestown, Mass.

1. (Calendar Verse.)
   8 lines under each month in his *Almanack* for 1656.
2. An Elegie on the Death of that Eminent Minister of the Gospel, Mr. John Norton.
   d. Boston, April 5, 1663, a. 57.
   13 four-line and 2 six-line stanzas in Morton, pp. 166–8, signed T. S. (see *Magnalia*, vol. 1, p. 271 for attribution).
3. Upon the Death of that most Reverend Man of God, Mr. John Wilson.
   d. Boston, Aug. 7, 1667, a. 78.
   52 lines, in Morton, 188–90, signed T. S. (see *Magnalia*, vol. 1, pp. 288 & 289 for attribution).
4. (Elegy on Jonathan Mitchell.)
   d. Cambridge, July 9, 1668, a. 44.
   apparently lost, mentioned in the prefatory lines of Cotton Mather, *A Poem Dedicated to the Memory of the Reverend and Excellent Mr. Urian Oakes* (Boston, 1682); may have been printed at the time.
5. (Epitaph on Richard Mather.)
   d. Dorchester, April 22, 1669, a. 73.
   apparently lost except for one line in Latin, *Magnalia*, vol. 1, p. 411.
6. (Epitaph on Zechariah Symmes.)
   d. Charlestown, Jan. 28, 1670/1, a. 72.
   on tombstone in Charlestown, 2 lines quoted in *Magnalia*, vol. 1, p. 415; possibly but not certainly by Shepard.
7. (Epitaph on Thomas Gilbert.)
   d. Charlestown, Oct. 28, 1673, a. 63.
   5 lines Latin, 6 lines English translation, on tombstone in Charlestown, pr. *Magnalia*, vol. 1, p. 545; a three line variant pr. in Richard Frothingham, *The History of Charlestown* (Boston, 1845), p. 187; possibly but not certainly by Shepard.
8. (Epitaph on Richard Russell.)
   d. Charlestown, May 14, 1676, a. 64.
   16 lines, on tombstone, pr. Frothingham, *op. cit.*, p. 146; possibly but not certainly by Shepard.

SMITH, THOMAS

N.E. c. 1650, naval captain, portrait painter.

"Why why should I the World be minding."

8 lines, in self portrait, AAS; paper with poem and monogram painted in lower left corner of portrait; pr. in *XVIIth Century Painting in New England* (Worcester, 1935), p. 134, facsim. pp. 136 & 137 (error in transcription).

SOMERBY, ANTHONY (1610–1686), b. Lincolnshire, N. E. 1639, Newbury, Mass., schoolmaster (one year), town clerk.

(The Holy Bible in Verse.)

large fragment, 73 pages quarto, double column, c. 1600 four-line stanzas, Ms.a. AAS, following two prose treatises (the first in another hand; following it, in Somerby's hand, the notice of the birth of his son Abiel in 1641, and the second treatise). The first stanza begins with the letter A, the second with B, and so on through the first 20 letters of the alphabet (omitting J) to U, the poem making a total of about 80 tours through the alphabet, with some omissions and inconsistencies. Alliteration is used as one of the chief literary devices. The fragment extends through the Psalms.

STARKEY, GEORGE (1628–1665), b. Eng. (?), to Bermuda with father, H.C. 1646, to Eng. c. 1650, alchemist and physician, pseud. "Eirenaeus Philalethes," d. London in the Great Plague.

1. *The Marrow of Alchemy, Being an Experimental Treatise, Discovering the secret and most hidden Mystery of the Philosophers Elixer . . . By Eirenaeus Philoponos Philalethes.*

   London, 2 parts, 1654 and 1655; 556 six-line stanzas, preceded by an 18-line Latin poem in the first part, and by William Sampson's commendatory verse in the second part.

2. (Prefatory Poem.)

   Latin with Eng. transl., prefixed to John Heydon, *Idea of the Law* (London, 1660).

3. (Prefatory Poem.)

   Latin, dated May 4, 1663, prefixed to John Heydon, *Theomagia* (London, 1664), signed with both name and pseudonymn.

STEERE, RICHARD (1643–1721), b. Eng., Citizen of London, N.E. c. 1682, voyage to Eng. 1683–84, New London, Conn., defended rights of John Rogers (Rogerenes), to Southold, L. I. c. 1690's, merchant.

1. *The History of the Babylonish Cabal; Or The Intrigues, Progression, Opposition, Defeat, and Destruction Of the Daniel-Catchers; In a Poem.*
   London, 1682, 36 pages (without the additional poems in 3), AAS.
2. *A Monumental Memorial of Marine Mercy . . . in A Late Voyage from Boston in New-England To London, Anno 1683. In a Poem . . . To which is added Another . . . Returning 1684.*
   Boston, 1684, 10 pages, and 2 pages, MHS, facsim. in George Emery Littlefield, *The Early Massachusetts Press* (Boston, 1907), vol. 2, after p. 78.
3. *The Daniel Catcher. The Life Of the Prophet Daniel: In a Poem. To which is Added, Earth's Felicities, Heaven's Allowances, A Blank Poem. With several other Poems.*
   Boston, 1713, 90 pages, AAS, MHS, facsim. *ibid.*, vol. 2, after *A Monumental Memorial.*
   1–53 The Daniel Catcher (no. 1 above in revised form).
   55–73 Earth Felicities, Heavens Allowances. A Blank Poem.
   73–81 Antichrist Display'd. In . . . the Church of Rome (anti-James II, pro-William and Mary).
   82–85 A Poem, Upon the Caelestial Embassy Perform'd by Angels, to the Shepards (in lyric stanzas).
   85–88 A Christian Alphabet.
   89 On a Sea-Storm nigh the Coast.
   90 The Authors Option.

STODDARD, SOLOMON (1643–1729), b. Boston, Mass., H.C. 1662, librarian, fellow, pastor Northampton, Mass.

Utrum Deus puniat peccata necessitate naturae.
   10 lines Latin, in *Quaestiones in Philosophia Discutiendae* (Cambridge, 1665), repr. Sibley, vol. 2, pp. 101–2, and Morison, *Harvard College in the Seventeenth Century*, pp. 600–1.

STONE, SAMUEL I (1602–1663), b. Hertford, Eng., Emmanuel College Cambridge, N.E. 1633, pastor Essex and Northamptonshire, Eng., Cambridge, Mass. and Hartford, Conn.

In obitum viri Doctissimi Thomae Hookeri.

d. Hartford, July 7, 1647, a. 61.

60 lines, the first of three poems prefixed to Thomas Hooker, *A Survey of the Summe of Church-Discipline* (London, 1648).

STONE, SAMUEL II (c. 1640–1683), b. Hartford, Conn., at H.C. during 1659, preached at Wethersfield, Middletown, and other Conn. towns, habitual drunkard, drowned.

William Leet Esq. Governour of connecticot collony.

d. Hartford, April 16, 1683, a. c. 70.

51 lines, Ms.c.c. NYHS, Samuel Sewall's commonplace book, pp. 5–6, signed S. Stone.

T., J. (no satisfactory identification has been found).

A Postscript to the Reader.

7 six-line stanzas, in Philip Pain, *Daily Meditations* (Cambridge, 1668), last 2 unnumbered pages after p. 16, HEHL, facsim. San Marino, California, 1936; 2nd ed. Cambridge, 1670, MHS. In the 2nd ed. the initials have been changed to M. J. "which may represent either a confession or a pretense to authorship by Marmaduke Johnson."

TAYLOR, EDWARD (1642–1729), b. Leicestershire, Eng., N.E. 1668, H.C. 1671, pastor Westfield, Mass., physician.

1. (An acrostic letter to James, Samuel, and Alice Taylor, his brothers and sister.)

   present whereabouts unknown; last mentioned in John T. Terry, *Rev. Edward Taylor, 1642–1729* (New York, 1892), p. 6.

2. (Elegy on Richard Mather.)

   d. Dorchester, April 22, 1669, a. 73.

   apparently lost; referred to by Taylor in the opening line of his elegy on Increase Mather.

   "Nigh Sixty years ago I wept in verse
   When on my Shoulders lay thy Fathers herse."

3. (Verses on the death of children.)

   2 six-line stanzas, Ms.c.c., MHS, in Samuel Sewall's commonplace book, dated Aug. 14, 1686, pr. in Cotton Mather, *Right Thoughts in Sad Hours* (London, 1689), at end of tract

with "Extract of a Letter. Westfield, 14th. 6 M. 1686," signed E. T. Revised and incorporated as stanzas 5 and 7 of his "Upon Wedlock and Death of Children," *Poetical Works* (Johnson ed.), pp. 117–8.

4. *Poetical Works.*

Ms.a., c. 400 pages, at Yale. For an exact description of the Ms., with listing of the c. 250 poems, see Thomas H. Johnson, *The Poetical Works of Edward Taylor* (New York, 1939), which also prints a large selection of the best poems, including the magnificent "Gods Determinations," pp. 31–109. Further publications from the Ms. by Johnson: "Some Edward Taylor Gleanings," *The New England Quarterly*, vol. 16, pp. 280–96.

"The Topical Verses of Edward Taylor," *Publ. Col. Soc. Mass.* vol. 34, pp. 513–54; includes verses on:
Zechariah Symmes, d. Charlestown, Jan. 28, 1670/1, a. 71.
Francis Willoughby, d. Charlestown, Apr. 4, 1671.
John Allen, d. Dedham, Aug. 26, 1671, a. 75.
Charles Chauncy, d. Cambridge, Feb. 19, 1671/2, a. 82.
Elizabeth Fitch (Taylor) 2 love poems, 1674.
Elizabeth Fitch Taylor, d. Westfield, July 7, 1689, a. 38.
Samuel Hooker, d. Farmington, Nov. 6, 1697, a. 62.
Mehetabel Wyllis Woodbridge, d. Hartford, Dec. 20, 1698, a. c. 40.
Increase Mather, d. Boston, Aug. 23, 1723, a. 84.
(also verses on the English language May 5, 1671, and on Pope Joan).

TILESTON, THOMAS (1611–1694), b. Eng., N.E. by 1634, Dorchester, Mass., var. town offices.

Funeral Elegy, Dedicated to the Memory of His Worthy Friend, The Learned & Religious Mr. John Foster.

d. Dorchester, Sept., 9, 1681, a. 33.

104 lines, broadside (lost?), repr. from Ms.c.c., private possession, in Thomas C. Simonds, *History of South Boston* (Boston, 1857), pp. 34–7, and from same Ms. in Samuel A. Green, *John Foster* (Boston, 1909) pp. 38–41. Though both Simonds and Green copied from the same Ms. (error in Ford, see Green, p. 35), the results show about 135 points of differ-

ence, most of them in punctuation and orthography, a few verbal. In general, Green seems to have been more accurate, though at some points, particularly in the third section from the end, he seems to have lapsed and Simonds to offer the correct version. There is apparently no direct evidence of the existence of the original broadside since the advertisement in William Brattle's almanac of 1682.

TILLAM, THOMAS (16 –after 1668), b. Eng. N. E. 1638, ret. Eng., Seventh Day Baptist, Millenarian, Utopian, pastor Hexam, Northumberland and Colchester, Essex, Eng., active 1661–67 in establishing his followers in a communal monastic society in Germany, probably in the Palatinate.

1. Upon the first sight of New England June 29, 1638.
   22 lines, Ms.a. MHS, Davis Papers, vol. 1, p. 15.
2. A hymn celebrating the Lord's Sabbath . . . at Colchester.
   Pr. in his *The Seventh-day Sabbath sought out and celebrated* (London, 1657).
3. The seventh Angel sounding, presents a glimpse of the glorious reign of Jesus Christ.
   16 lines, signed T.T., in Samuel Hutchinson, *A Declaration of a Future Glorious Estate* (London, 1667), p. 3, AAS.
4. More verses Concerning the same Subject.
   8 four-line stanzas, signed T.T., in *ibid.*, pp. 18–9. The T.T. is probably, though not certainly Tillam, who wrote a similar Apocalyptical-Millenarian work, *The Two Witnesses* (London, 1651), and from whom Hutchinson quotes several times after the verses (pp. 27–30).

TOMPSON, BENJAMIN (1642–1714), b. Braintree, Mass., H.C. 1662, school-teacher Boston, Charlestown, and Braintree, Mass., physician.

1. (Satirical lines on the ordination of the Rev. Mr. Samuel Arnold at Marshfield by a farmer and a blacksmith.)
   20 lines in 5 stanzas (4 & 5 irregular), Ms.l.c. Yale, pr. in *Extracts from the Itineraries . . . of Erza Stiles* (New Haven, 1916), p. 55, with the statement "supposed to be made by one Mr. Thompson." Since Samuel Arnold was ordained in 1658, this poem, if it is by Benjamin Tompson, was written

by him at the age of 16, a possibility which the immaturity of the poem does not contradict. The satiric vein is typically Tompsonian.

2. Remarks on the Bright, and dark side of that American Pillar Mr William Tompson.
   d. Braintree, Dec. 10, 1666, a. 63.
   72 lines, Ms.c.c. MHS (elegies of the Tompson family), pr. 2 *Proc. M.H.S.*, vol. 10, pp. 281–3, repr. Howard Judson Hall, *Benjamin Tompson . . . His Poems* (Boston, 1924), pp. 105–7; another version, with a couplet inserted in the *Magnalia*, vol. 1, pp. 397–8.

3. Gulielmi Tompsoni Braintreensis . . . Epitaphium.
   6 lines, Ms.c.c. MHS, pr. *ibid.*, p. 283, repr. *ibid.*; also in Joseph Tompson, Ms., pr. Murdock, p. 20.
   Note: the anagram and poem on William Tompson following in Hall, *op. cit.*, is not by Tompson but by Samuel Danforth I.

4. The Grammarians Funeral, Or, An Elegy composed upon the Death of Mr. John [i.e. Robert] Woodmancy . . . But now Published upon the Death of the Venerable Mr. Ezekiel Chevers.
   a) d. Boston, 1667, b) d. Boston, Aug. 21, 1708, a. 93.
   76 lines, broadside MHS, facsim. and repr. Hall, pp. 115–7, facsim. Winslow, p. 25.

5. *New Englands Crisis.*
   Boston, 1676, 31 pp., HEHL. Contents:
   4–8. The Prologue.
   9–20. New-Englands Crisis.
   21. A Supplement.
   21–25. Marlburyes Fate.
   25–26. The Town called Providence Its Fate.
   26–27. Seaconk Plain Engagement.
   27–28. Seaconk or Rehoboths Fate.
   28. Chelmsfords Fate.
   29–30. On A Fortification At Boston begun by Women.
   repr. Hall, *op. cit.*, pp. 45–71.
   Note: the first two parts were published, with slight variations, in London, 1676, under the title *Sad and Deplorable Newes from New England.* This publication, HEH, has remained unidentified until now. For the London edition of the remaining parts, with new poems added, see no. 6 following.

6. *New-Englands Tears For Her Present Miseries.*
London, 1676, 14 pages, JCB. Contents:
1. "What means this silence of Harvardine Quills" (same as "A Supplement" in 5. above).
1–3. Marlburies Fate.
4. Providences Fate.
4–5. Seaconk Plain Engagement.
5–6. Rehoboth's Fate.
6–8. Upon the setting of that Occidental Star John Winthrop Esq; Governour of Connecticott Colony.
8–9. Chelmsfords Fate.
9–10. Sudburies Fate.
10. Celeusma Militare.
10. Epitaphium (on Major Simon Willard).
11. The Indians threaten to Dine at Boston on our Election.
11–13. M. J. Antonomies the Grand Sachems Death.
13. On the Fortifications began by Women upon Boston Neck.

repr. Hall, *op. cit.*, pp. 75–95.

7. A Funeral Tribute to the Honourable Dust of that most Charitable Christian, Unbiassed Politician, And unimitable Pyrotechnist John Winthrop esq: A Member of the Royal Society, & Governour of Conecticut Colony.
d. Boston, April 6, 1676, a. 70.
88 lines, broadside, private possession, photostat MHS, repr. Hall, *op. cit.*, pp. 99–102.
Note: this elegy has often been confused with the elegy on Winthrop in *New Englands Tears*; the latter has 72 lines and, except for the introductory couplet (above the title), is entirely different.

8. Upon The elaborate Survey of New-Englands Passions from the Natives.
38 lines, prefixed to William Hubbard, *A Narrative of the Troubles with the Indians in New-England* (Boston, 1677), repr. Hall, *op. cit.*, pp. 121–2.

9. The Rev. Man of God Mr Peter Hubbard [Hobart].
d. Hingham, Jan. 23, 1678, a. 74.
80 lines, Ms. owned in 1860 by S. P. Fowler, pr. *New England Hist. Gen. Reg.*, vol. 14, pp. 141–2, signed B. T., repr. Hall, *op. cit.*, pp. 125–7.

10. New-Englands grand Eclips by the withdrawing of . . . Jno Leverett Governour of the Massathuset.
    d. Boston, March 16, 1678, a. 63.
    134 lines, Ms.c.c. MHS, commonplace book of John Leverett II, pp. 1–4, signed B. T.; it may have appeared in a contemporaneous broadside now lost.
11. Upon the Very Reverend Samuel Whiting.
    d. Lynn, Dec. 11, 1679, a. 82.
    94 lines, *Magnalia*, vol. 1, pp. 459–61, repr. Hall, *op. cit.*, pp. 131–4.
12. A short memoriall & Revew of sum vertues in that exemplary Christian Mary Tompson.
    d. Billerica, March 23, 1678/9, a. 37.
    82 lines, Ms.c.c. by Joseph Tompson, pr. Murdock, pp. 3–5.
13. A Short but Sorrowfull memoriall Of my dear Sister Sarah Tompson.
    d. Braintree, Jan. 15, 1679/80, a. 43.
    72 lines, Ms.c.c. CHS, second part of the Sarah Tompson, Ms. (first her religious autobiography, third an elegy by an anon. friend).
    Note: Sarah, wife of Deacon Samuel Tompson, was sister-in-law of Benjamin and mother of Edward the poet.
14. Edmund Davie 1682.
    d. London, 1681, c. 25.
    38 lines, preceded by an anagram, and followed by an Epitaph of 18 lines and 2 lines Latin, Ms.c.c. NYHS, commonplace book of Samuel Sewall.
15. To my Honoured Patron Humphery Davie A Renewing the Memory of Dr Edmund Davie. Who expired at London Anno 1681.
    18 lines, Ms.c.c. NYHS, *ibid.*, signed "Benjamin Tompson Braintry, 29 4 1682."
    Note: the biographical mystery surrounding Edmund Davie, H. C. 1674, M.D. Padua, the brilliant son (not brother) of Humphrey Davie, and elder brother of Sir John Davie, is finally cleared up by the finding of these poems.
16. "My loyalty is still the same."
    4 lines, Ms.a. BPL, letter to Increase Mather, Nov. 25, 1683, pr. 4. *Coll. M.H.S.* vol. 8, p. 635, facsim. Hall. *op. cit.*, facing 16.

17. A Character of the most Exemplary Christian, Mr Samuel Tompson.
    d. Braintree, June 18, 1695, a. 64.
    100 lines, Ms.c.c. MHS (elegies of the Tompson family), pr. 2 *Proc. M.H.S.*, vol. 10, pp. 275–7, repr. Hall, *op. cit.*, pp. 137–40.
18. To Lord Bellamont when entering Governour of the Massachusetts.
    78 lines, Ms.l.c. MHS, commonplace book of Ebenezer Parkman (Lord Bellamont arrived at Boston, May 26, 1699).
19. Celeberrimi Cottoni Matheri.
    6 lines Latin and 12 lines English, *Magnalia*, vol. 1, p. 17, repr. Hall, *op. cit.*, p. 143.
20. (Epitaph on Edward Tompson.)
    d. Marshfield, March 16, 1705, a. 40.
    6 lines, on gravestone, pr. var., e.g. Harriette M. Forbes, *Gravestones of Early New England* (Boston, 1927), p. 35. Here attributed to Benjamin Tompson on the basis of its style and on his relation to his poet-nephew.
21. The Illustrious Fitz-John Winthrop Esqr Governr of Quinecticott Colony.
    d. Boston, Nov. 27, 1707, a. 68.
    62 lines, Ms.a., MHS, Winthrop Deeds, etc., p. 100, pr. 2 *Proc. M.H.S.*, vol. 10, pp. 369–71, repr. Hall, *op. cit.*, pp. 147–9.
22. (Epitaph on Moses Fiske.)
    d. Braintree, Aug 10, 1708, a. 66.
    8 lines, gravestone, pr. *New England Hist. Gen. Reg.*, vol. 9, p. 151. Here attributed to Benjamin Tompson on the basis of its style and location.
23. A Neighbours Tears dropt on the grave of an Amiable Virgin . . . mrs Rebecka Sewal.
    d. Brookline, Aug. 4, 1710, a. 6.
    28 lines, Ms.c.c. MHS Winthrop Papers, pr. Hall, *op. cit.*, pp. 156–7.
24. A Cloude of Tears, sprinkled on the Dust of the Amiable Virgin mrs Rebecka Sewel.
    46 lines, Ms.c.c. *ibid.*, pr. *ibid.*, pp. 157–9.

24a. A Neighbour's Tears Sprinkled on the Dust of the Amiable Virgin, Mrs. Rebekah Sewall.

32 lines, broadside MHS, repr. *ibid.*, pp. 155–6 (with facsim), "made up wholly of couplets from the other two versions"; facsim. Winslow, p. 27.

25. The Translation by death, of that Holy Man of God, Reverend Mr. James Allen.
    d. Boston, Sept. 22, 1710, a. 78.
    52 lines, in Benjamin Wadsworth, *Death is Certain* (Boston, 1710), repr. Hall, *op. cit.*, pp. 163–4.
26. The Amiable virgin memorized—Elizabeth Tompson. . . .
    d. Boston, Aug. 24, 1712, a. 24.
    72 lines preceded by anagram, Ms.c.c. of Joseph Tompson, pr. Murdock, pp. 9—11.
27. The following Verses were made by Mr Benjamin Tompson Roxbury June 20th. 1713. being some of his last lines.
    10 lines, Ms.c.c. MHS (elegies of the Tompson family), pr. 2 *Proc. M.H.S.*, vol. 10, pp. 277–8, repr. Hall, *op. cit.*, p. 167.

TOMPSON, EDWARD (1665–1705), b. Braintree, Mass., H.C. 1684, school-teacher Newbury, Mass., pastor Simsbury, Conn., Newbury and Marshfield, Mass.

1. An Elegiack Tribute to the Sacred Dust of the Reverend and Worthy Mr. Seaborn Cotton. . . .
    d. Hampton, April 20, 1686, a. 52.
    90 lines, Ms.a. (?) MHS, Winthrop Papers, vol. 7b, p. 36; broadside MHS with three additional lines of Latin at end.
2. Hypomnemata Schemuelis Tompsoni. or A small Testimony of my Great Love and Duty to my Deare Father. Samuel Tompson.
    d. Braintree, June 18, 1695.
    4 lines Latin and 99 lines English, Ms.c.c. (elegies of Tompson family), pr. 2 *Proc. M.H.S.*, vol. 10, pp. 278–81.

TORREY, SAMUEL (1632–1707), b. Devonshire, Eng., N.E. 1640, H.C. during 1653–56, pastor Weymouth, Mass.

Upon the Death of Mr William Tompson.
    d. Braintree, Dec. 10, 1666, a. 68.
    30 lines, Ms.l.c. of Joseph Tompson, pr. Murdock, pp. 18–9.

VINCENT, PHILIP (1600–after 1637) b. Yorkshire, Eng., Peter House, Cambridge, pastor in Surrey, Eng. till 1629, to Guiana c. 1632, traveller and physician in Italy, Germany, and Netherlands c. 1634–1636, M.D., N.E. 1637 in Pequot War, ret. Eng. 1637.

Ad Lectorem Authoris carmen ἐυχαρίστικον de Victoria hac Nov'-Anglica, 1637.

20 lines Latin, signed P. Vincentius, prefixed to his *A True Relation of The Late Battell fought in New-England, between the English and the Pequet Salvages* (London, 1638), repr. 3 *Coll. M.H.S.*, vol. 6, pp. 29–43, verse p. 31.

WAKEMAN, SAMUEL (1635–1692), b. Eng., H.C. 1655 (not grad.), pastor Fairfield, Conn.

(Early Verses.)

Letter to John Cotton of Plymouth (on the latter sending him the elegies on Thomas Walley and Noah Newman) Fairfield, April 16, 1680 (Ms. BPL, Cotton Papers, vol. 8, p. 18): "& were not that little poeticall fancy I once had lost through disuse . . . such an occasion would have tempted me to have returned you something. . . ." His early verses, if they still exist, have not yet been located.

WALKER, PHILIP (c. 1628–1679), b. Eng., N.E. by 1643, Rehoboth, Mass., weaver, saw-mill owner, deacon, and town official.

Captan Perse and his coragios Company.

456 lines, mostly in four-line stanzas, Ms.a. AAS, 18 pages taken from a bound volume of pamphlets which once belonged to George, John, and Samuel Curwin (Ms. perhaps from Walker to pastor Noah Newman, to latter's brother Antipas Newman, to Antipas' brother-in-law John Curwin of Salem); poem signed: " by a friend to his Cuntry and Frinds P. Walker." Internal evidence about the historic events recorded places the writing of the work about April, 1676. The work is divided into several parts, as follows:

1. Captan Perse and his coragios Company.
   (on the tragic ambush of Captain Pierce, March 26, 1676, and on the New England Indian policy, 5 pages.)
2. The Stragamen off the Indians.
   (in prose, in the form of a proclamation from Satan to his servants, the Powwahs, 1½ pages.)

3. The First smile of god in this land.
(The contrast between the ideals of the founding fathers and the present forgetfulness and abandonment of them, with God's consequent punishment of New England, 11 pages.)

WALTER, NEHEMIAH (1663–1750), b. Cork County, Ireland, N.E. 1679, H.C. 1684, fellow, pastor Roxbury, Mass.

An Elegiack Verse, on the Death of the Pious and Profound Grammarian and Rhetorician, Mr. Elijah Corlet.
d. Cambridge, Feb. 24, 1687, a. c. 78.
81 lines, blank verse, broadside HCL, facsim. in Walter Eliot Thwing, *History of the First Church in Roxbury* (Boston, 1908), facing p. 87. Perhaps the earliest New England poem in blank verse, though Steere's "Earth's Felicities" may have been written about this time.

WARD, JAMES (c. 1624–16), b. Elbing, Germany, or London, Eng. (?), N.E. 1634, H.C. 1645, ret. Eng. Dec. 1646, fellow Magdalen College, Oxford, M.A., and Bachelor of Physic, 1649.

1. (A Latin Poem.)
in *Musarum Oxoniensium* Ἐλαιοφορια (Oxonia, 1654), signed "J. Ward, A.M., ex Aede Christi"; HCL copy (the only one available to me) defective at this point, containing only the last 12 lines of the poem on p. 22.
2. "Caesar! securus pelago committe fideli."
40 lines in *Britannia Rediviva* (Oxoniae, 1660), sign. H[1]verso-H[2]recto, signed as above (see Sibley, vol. 1, p. 122).

WARD, NATHANIEL (1578–1652), b. Suffolk, Eng., Emmanuel College, Cambridge, Lincoln's Inn, barrister, pastor Elbing, Germany, London and Essex, Eng., N.E. 1634, pastor Ipswich, Mass., ret. Eng. 1646, satirist.

1. Mr. Ward of Anagrams thus.
7 lines, Ms.l.c., MHS, Thomas Weld III, commonplace book.
2. "When bootes and shoes are torne up to the lefts."
4 lines (last in Latin), in his *The Simple Cobler of Aggawam in America* (London, 1647), var. ed., on title page.
3. "Gray Gravity it selfe can well beteam."
4 lines, *ibid.*, repr. Boston, 1843, p. 26.

4. "These whimm Crown'd shees, these fashion-fansying wits."
   2 lines, *ibid.*, p. 27.
5. "When States dishelv'd are, and Lawes untwist."
   2 lines, *ibid.*, p. 33.
6. "Where clocks will stand, and Dials have no light."
   2 lines, *ibid.*, p. 40.
7. Halfe a dozen distichs.
   12 lines, *ibid.*, p. 47, on the English Civil War.
8. "The crazy world will crack, in all the middle joynts."
   2 lines, *ibid.*, p. 49.
9. "The body beares the head, the head the Crown."
   2 lines, *ibid.*, p. 50.
10. "Subjects their King, the King his Subjects greets."
    2 lines, *ibid.*, p. 55.
11. "A peace well made, is likeliest then to hold."
    2 lines, *ibid.*, p. 56.
12. "King Charles will joyne Himselfe to bitter Griefe."
    2 lines, *ibid.*, p. 62.
13. "They that at stake their Crownes and Honours set."
    2 lines, *ibid.*, p. 69.
14. "Grace will dissolve, but rigour hardens guilt."
    4 lines, *ibid.*, p. 72.
15. Half a dozen plaine honest Country Hobnailes.
    6 four-line stanzas, plus another "The Church," *ibid.*, pp.85–6.
16. "The world's a well strung fidle, mans tongue the quill."
    4 lines, *ibid.*, p. 87.
17. "He that to tall men speakes, must lift up's head."
    4 lines, *ibid.*, p. 88.
18. "When Kings are lost, and Subjects cast away."
    4 lines, *ibid.*, p. 89.
19. "The world is growne, so fine in words and wit."
    4 lines, *ibid.*, p. 90.
20. "Poetry's a gift wherein but few excell."
    4 lines, *ibid.*, p. 91.
21. "Coblers will mend, but some will never mend."
    4 lines, *ibid.*, p. 91.
22. "Poore Coblers well may fault it now and then."
    4 lines, *ibid.*, p. 91.

23. "So farewell England old."
3 four-line stanzas, *ibid.*, p. 92.

24. Postscript.
8 lines, *ibid.*, p. 92.

25. (Verse in *Mercurius Anti-Mechanicus*, London, 1648.)
Much of the text is in verse form.

26. "Mercury shew'd Apollo, Bartas Book."
18 lines, first of prefatory poems in Anne Bradstreet, *The Tenth Muse* (London, 1650); repr. 2nd ed. *Several Poems* (Boston, 1678), and in Ellis ed. (Charlestown, 1867), p. 85.

WELDE, EDMUND (1631–1668), b. Essex, Eng., N.E. 1632, H.C. 1650, pastor Inniskean, Ireland.

Dialogue between Death, the Soul, the Body, the World, and Jesus Christ.
19 ten-line stanzas, Ms.a. or c.c., apparently lost, pr. Timothy Alden, *A Collection of American Epitaphs* (New York, 1814), vol. 3, pp. 42–9.

WELDE, THOMAS I (1595–1661), b. Suffolk, Eng., Trinity College, Cambridge, pastor in Suffolk and Essex, Eng., N.E. 1632, pastor Roxbury, Mass., ret. Eng. 1641 as agent of colony, pastor Newcastle, Durham, Eng.

The Whole Booke of Psalmes Faithfully Translated into English Metre.
Cambridge, Mass., 1640. He collaborated in this translation with John Eliot and Richard Mather.

WELDE, THOMAS III (1653–1702), b. Roxbury, Mass., H.C. 1671, pastor Dunstable, Mass.

1. (Elegy on the death of Samuel Danforth.)
d. Roxbury, Nov. 19, 1674, a. 48.
excerpt of 8 lines in *Magnalia*, vol. 2, p. 51. The whole elegy, if still extant, has not yet come to light.

2. (Verses and Epigrams.)
Ms.a. MHS, commonplace book of Thomas Welde, 1669 ff.; though most of these verses are apparently derived from English and American authors, a few of them may be of his own composing.

WETHERELL, WILLIAM (1600–1684), b. Yorkshire, Corpus Christi College, Cambridge, N.E. 1635, schoolmaster Charlestown, pastor Scituate, Mass.

1. On the piously affected Matron, Mrs. Sarah Cushing.
   d. Scituate, March 9, 1678/9, a. 38.
   Ms. or broadside (?), in 1831 in the possession of the Moody family in Newbury, Mass.; last immediate ref. in Samuel Deane, *History of Scituate* (Boston, 1831), pp. 192 & 398.

2. Upon the much to be lamented Death of the thrice three times Honoured Josiah Winslow.
   d. Marshfield, Dec. 18, 1680, a. 51.
   129 lines, Ms. or broadside (?), in 1831 in the possession of the Seaver family of Kingston, R. I., pr. Dean, *op. cit.*, pp. 395–7.

WHARTON, EDWARD (–1677), a Quaker merchant af Salem, Mass.

1. "Although our Bodyes here in silent Earth do lie."
   couplet, in his *New England's Present Suffering under their Cruel Neighbouring Indians* (London, 1675). Verses placed by him over the graves of the Quakers executed and buried in Boston.

2. "Beware, beware, and enter not!"
   verses affixed to the meeting house in Salem, 2 lines quoted in the *Magnalia*, vol. 2, p. 566; by "a noted Quaker there," not certainly but very possibly Wharton.

WHITING, SAMUEL (1597–1679), b. Boston, Lincolnshire, Eng., Emmanuel College, Cambridge, pastor in Norfolk and Lincolnshire, N.E. 1636, pastor Lynn, Mass.

1. To the Author, his singular good Friend, Mr. William Wood.
   12 lines, prefixed to William Wood, *New England Prospect* (London, 1634), signed S. W. and attributed to Samuel Whiting in *Publ. Col. Soc. Mass.*, vol. 25, p. 21.

2. (Elegy on John Wilson.)
   d. Boston, Aug. 7, 1667, a. 78.
   apparently lost; ref. Benjamin Tompson's elegy on Samuel Whiting, *Magnalia*, vol. 1, p. 459:

"When Wilson, that Plerophory of Love,
Did from our Banks, up to his Center move,
Rare Whiting quotes Columbus on this Coast,
Producing Gems, of which a King might boast."

WIGGLESWORTH, MICHAEL (1631–1705), b. Yorkshire, Eng., N.E. 1638, H.C. 1651, fellow, pastor Malden, Mass., physician

1. "Christe, Parum doleo quia Te non diligio multum."
   2 lines Latin, in Cotton Mather, *A Faithful Man* (Boston, 1705), "An Appendix . . . from the Reserved Papers of Mr. Michael Wigglesworth," p. 42 (from the time of his long sickness at Malden, c. 1660).
2. "Ira premit, Peccata gravant, afflicto frangit."
   6 lines Latin, 2 lines English, in *ibid.*, p. 43.
3. *The Day of Doom.*
   224 eight-line stanzas, written 1661–1662, pr. Cambridge, 1662 or 63, fragm. NEHGS; 1666 fragm. AAS & MHS; London, 1666, British Museum, earliest complete copy; London 1673 & 1687, Boston, 1701, MHS, NYPL, etc., and numerous later ed. up to Kenneth B. Murdock's, New York, 1929.
4. To the Christian Reader.
   16 eight-line stanzas, prefixed to *The Day of Doom.*
5. A Prayer unto Christ the Judge of the World.
   30 lines, prefixed to *ibid.*
6. A Short Discourse on Eternity.
   22 eight-line stanzas, following *ibid.*
7. A Postscript unto the Reader.
   518 lines, in *ibid.*
8. A Song of Emptiness, to fill up the Empty Pages following. Vanity of Vanities.
   27 four-line stanzas, in *ibid.*
9. "I walked and did a Little Mole-hill view."
   116 lines between "The Day of Doom" proper and "Vanity of Vanities" in the London ed. of 1673.
10. God's Controversy with New-England. Written in the time of the great drought Anno 1662.
   442 lines, and 4 lines Latin, Ms.a. MHS, pr. *Proc. M.H.S.*, vol. 12, pp. 83–93.

11. "When as the wayes of Jesus Christ."
    7 eight-line stanzas, Ms.a. NEHGS, Ewer Mss., vol. 1, p. 9; pr. *New England Hist. Gen. Reg.*, vol. 26, p. 12.

12. Upon the much Lamented Death of that precious servant of Christ Mr Benjamin Buncker.
    d. Malden, Feb. 3, 1669/70, a. 34.
    112 lines in 14 stanzas, Ms.a. NEHGS, Ewer, Mss., vol. 1, p. 8; pr. *New England Hist. Gen. Reg.*, vol. 26, pp. 11–2.

13. *Meat out of the Eater.*
    completed 1669, pr. Boston, 1670, fragm. Yale (two ed. betw. 1670 and 1689 lost), 4th ed. 1689, BPL, NYPL, AAS; revised 1703, 5th ed. 1717, AAS, NYPL, etc., 6th and last ed., New London, 1770, no modern ed. Consists of the introductory "Tolle Crucem," 10 "Meditations," and a "Conclusion Hortatory," pp. 3–50 of 1689 ed., 3–34 of 1717 ed.

14. *Riddles Unriddled, Or Christian Paradoxes.*
    pr. with *ibid.*, pp. 51–208 of 1689 ed., 35–143 of 1717 ed. Consists of nine parts, containing 42 "Songs" or "Meditations," with introductory verses to the various parts.

15. Upon the return of my dear friend Mr Foster with his son out of captivity under the Moors.
    8 stanzas of eight short lines each, Ms.a. once in the possession of John Ward Dean, pr. *American Historical Record*, vol. 1, p. 393.

16. Death Expected and Welcomed.
    12 lines, in Cotton Mather, *A Faithful Man* (Boston, 1705), p. 45; repr. in 1715 ed. of *The Day of Doom* and subsequently.

17. A Farewell to the World.
    68 lines, in *ibid.*, pp. 46–8; repr. in 1715 ed. of *The Day of Doom* and subsequently.

WILLARD, SAMUEL (1640–1707), b. Concord, Mass., H.C. 1659, fellow, pastor Groton and Boston, Mass., Vice-President H. C.

(Epitaph on John Sherman.)
    d. Watertown, Aug. 8, 1685, a. 72.
    10 lines, on tombstone, pr. Convers Francis, *An Historical Sketch of Watertown* (Cambridge, 1830) p. 138.

WILLIAMS, JOHN (1664–1729), b. Roxbury, Mass., H.C. 1683, pastor Deerfield, Mass., captive to Canada 1704.

1. Some Instructions, Written by Mr. John Williams, for his Little Son, when the Child was in danger of taking in the Popish Poisons.
   36 four-line stanzas, in Cotton Mather, *Good Fetch'd out of Evil: A Collection of Memorables relating to our Captives* (Boston, 1706), pp. 23–9.
2. Some Contemplations of the Poor, and desolate State of the Church at Deerfield.
   38 lines, dated Oct. 21, 1704, in his *The Redeemed Captive returning to Zion* (Boston, 1707), pp. 41–3.

WILLIAMS, ROGER (c. 1603–1683), b. London, Eng., Pembroke College, Cambridge, N.E. 1630, pastor Salem and Plymouth, Mass., Providence, R. I., founder of R. I.

1. "The Courteous Pagan shall condemne Uncourteous Englishmen."
   3 four-line stanzas, in his *A Key into the Language of America* (London, 1643), and var. modern ed., incl. the 5th (same pagination as 1st), Howard M. Chapin ed. (Providence, 1936), p. 10.
2. "Course bread and water's most their fare."
   3 four-line stanzas, *ibid.*, p. 17.
3. "God gives them sleep on Ground, on Straw."
   3 four-line stanzas, *ibid.*, p. 21.
4. "Their Braines are quick, their hands."
   2 four-line stanzas, *ibid.*, pp. 26–7.
5. "The Pagans wild confesse the bonds."
   12 lines, *ibid.*, pp. 30–1.
6. "How busie are the sonnes of men?"
   12 lines in 2 stanzas, *ibid.*, p. 48.
7. "Boast not proud English, of thy birth & blood."
   8 lines, *ibid.*, p. 53.
8. "Mans restless soule hath restlesse eyes and ears."
   6 lines, *ibid.*, pp. 61–2.
9. "The Indians find the sun so sweet."
   11 (really 12) lines in 2 stanzas, *ibid.*, p. 64.
10. "The Sun and Moone and Stars doe preach."
   12 lines in 2 stanzas, *ibid*,. pp. 67–8.

11. "God makes a Path, provides a Guide."
    3 four-line stanzas, *ibid.*, p. 78.
12. "When Sun doth rise the Starres doe set."
    3 four-line stanzas, *ibid.*, p. 81.
13. "English and Indians spie a Storme."
    12 lines, *ibid.*, pp. 84–5.
14. "English and Indians both observe."
    3 four-line stanzas, *ibid.*, pp. 87–8.
15. "If Birds that neither sow nor reape."
    12 lines in 2 stanzas, *ibid.*, pp. 93–4.
16. "Yeeres Thousands since, God gave command."
    3 four-line stanzas, *ibid.*, p. 102.
17. "The Indians, Wolves, yea, Dogs and Swine."
    3 four-line stanzas, *ibid.*, p. 106.
18. "They see Gods wonders that are call'd."
    12 lines, *ibid.*, p. 111.
19. "What Habacuck once spake, mine eyes."
    3 four-line stanzas, *ibid.*, p. 117.
20. "O what a Tyrant's Custome long."
    3 four-line stanzas, *ibid.* p. 122.
21. "Two sorts of men shall naked stand."
    12 lines, *ibid.*, p. 139.
22. "Adulteries, Murthers, Robberies, Thefts."
    3 four-line stanzas, *ibid.*, p. 145.
23. "When Indians heare that some there are."
    3 four-line stanzas, *ibid.*, p. 151.
24. "The Indians prize not English gold."
    3 four-line stanzas, *ibid.*, p. 158
25. "Oft have I heard these Indians say."
    3 four-line stanzas, *ibid.*, p. 167.
26. "I have heard ingenious Indians say."
    3 four-line stanzas, *ibid.*, p. 170.
27. "To harmlesse Roes and Does."
    2 lines, *ibid.*, p. 173.
28. "Great pains in hunting th'Indians Wild."
    3 four-line stanzas, *ibid.*, pp. 176–7.
29. "Our English Gamesters scorne to stake."
    3 four-line stanzas, *ibid.*, pp. 181–2.
30. "The Indians count of Men as Dogs."
    3 four-line stanzas, *ibid.*, pp. 190–1.

31. "Truth is a Native, naked Beauty; but."
    3 four-line stanzas, *ibid.*, p. 193.
32. "One step twix't Me and Death."
    3 four-line stanzas, *ibid.*, p. 200.
33. "The Indians say their bodies die."
    4 four-line stanzas, *ibid.*, pp. 204–5.

WILSON, JOHN I (c. 1588–1667), b. Windsor, Eng., King's College, Cambridge, fellow, pastor Suffolk, Eng., N.E. 1630, pastor Boston, Mass.

1. *A Song of Deliverance for the Lasting Remembrance of Gods Wonderful Works.*
   London, 1626, repr. Boston, 1680, NYPL, NYHS, repr. Murdock, pp. 23–75. Contents (Murdock ed.):
   27–31. The Introduction from out of the XXXI of Deuteronomy, 138 lines.
   31–68. A Song of Thanksgiving, 1412 lines.
   69. Deo Bisultori Saxum . . . 1588, 20 lines Latin.
   70. Ad memoriam proditionis Pulverariae Anno 1605, 24 lines Latin.
   71–72. To God our twice-Revenger, 48 lines.
   73. A Pillar Consecrated, 6 lines.
   74. (Verses made by Theodore Beza) Thus Englished, 18 lines.
   74–75. Another Song, 33 lines.
2. In Pientissimum, Reverendissimumq; Virum Johannem Harvardum.
   d. Charlestown, Sept. 14, 1638, a. 31.
   42 lines Latin, *Magnalia*, vol. 2, pp. 27–8, repr. Murdock, pp. 79–80, written later than 1638, some years after the founding of the college.
3. An Anagram of Mrs. Tomson . . . Abigayll Tomson. I am gon to al blys.
   d. Braintree, Jan. 1, 1643.
   62 lines, Ms.c.c. Church Records of Roxbury, vol. 1, pr. William P. Lunt, *Two Discourses . . . on . . . the First Congregational Church, Quincy* (Boston, 1840), pp. 84–5; Ms.l.c. by Joseph Tompson (defective), pr. Murdock, pp. 7–9.

4. An Anagram. Anna Bradestreate Dear neat An Bartas.
   2 anagrams and a couplet, prefixed to Anne Bradstreet, *The Tenth Muse* (London, 1650); Ellis ed., p. 92; unsigned and only possibly by John Wilson.
5. Upon the Death of the first and only Child (being an Infant) of his Daughter Mrs. Danforth.
   d. Roxbury, c. July, 1653.
   excerpt of 14 lines, *Magnalia*, vol. 2, p. 286, repr. Murdock, p. 81; the complete poem has not come to light.
6. A Copy of Verses . . . On the sudden Death of Mr. Joseph Brisco.
   d. Boston (?), Jan. 1, 1657/8.
   4 lines, anagram, and 34 lines, broadside MHS, fasim. in S. A. Green, *Ten Fac-simile Reproductions Relating to New England* (Boston, 1902), and Winslow, p. 5; repr. Murdock, pp. 82–3.
7. Claudius Gilbert. Anagram. Tis Braul I cudgel.
   14 lines, Ms.a. AAS, in Claudius Gilbert, *The Libertine School'd* (London, 1657), presentation copy to his "Reverend Friend Mr. Wilson," t.p. verso. Copy later given by Wilson to Richard Mather.
8. (Poem addressed to Governor Peter Stuyvesant.)
   apparently lost, known from the poetic reply to John Wilson from Henricus Selyns, Ms.a. NYHS, pr. Henry C. Murphy, *Anthology of New Netherland* (New York, 1865), pp. 168–9.
9. Thomas Shepardius. Anagr: Paradisus hostem?
   18 lines Latin, prefixed to Thomas Shepard, *The Church-Membership of Children* (Cambridge, 1663), AAS, HCL, repr. Murdock, p. 84.
10. Thomas Shepard. Anagr: ô a map's thresh'd.
    44 lines, prefixed to *ibid.*, repr. Murdock, pp. 85–6.
11. Thomas Shepard. Anagr: More hath pass'd.
    24 lines, prefixed to *ibid.*, repr. Murdock, pp. 86–7.
12. Thomas Shepard. Anagr: Arm'd as the Shop.
    44 lines, prefixed to *ibid.*, repr. Murdock, pp. 87–8, signed at end: John Wilson Senior.
13. Johannes Nortonus. Anagr. Nonne is Honoratus?
    36 lines Latin, prefixed to John Norton, *Three Choice and Profitable Sermons* (Cambridge, 1664), AAS, HCL, repr. Murdock, pp. 89–90.

14. Anagr. 2 . . . Anagr. 3.
    2 lines Latin and 6 lines English, prefixed to *ibid.*, repr. Murdock, pp. 90–1.
15. To the same purpose. John Norton. Anagr. Into Honnor.
    196 lines, prefixed to *ibid.*, repr. Murdock, pp. 91–7, signed at end: John Wilson Sen.
16. (Upon the death of Mr. William Tompson.)
    d. Braintree, Dec. 10, 1666, a. 68.
    2 parts of 80 and 92 lines, Ms.l.c., NYHS, commonplace book of Samuel Sewall; Ms.l.c. by Joseph Tompson, pr. Murdock, pp. 12–7. The two Mss. exhibit numerous differences, both are imperfect and supplement each other.
17. Anagram . . . on, and for himself.
    2 anagrams and 2 lines Latin, *Magnalia*, vol. 1, pp. 289–90.

WILSON, JOHN II (1621–1691), b. London, Eng.. H.C. 1642, pastor Dorchester and Medfield, Mass., schoolteacher and physician.

1. A poeticall Epistle sent from my Father Wilson to my wife after her Shoulder bone was set, composed on Lords day evening.
   32 lines, Ms.c.c. MHS, commonplace book of Thomas Welde III (1669 ff.), pp. 172–3 (his wife Elizabeth was the daughter of John Wilson II).
2. (Elegy on the Rev. Ralph Wheelock.)
   d. Medfield, Mass., Jan. 11, 1684, a. 84.
   Ms. in the possession of Mrs. Benjamin Pomeroy, Hebron, Conn., in 1781; one stanza quoted in Ezra Stiles, *Literary Diary* (New York, 1901), vol. 2, p. 535.

WINSLOW, JOSIAH (c. 1629–1680), b. Plymouth, Mass., H.C. during 1650–53, military and civil leader, governor of Plymouth Colony, d. Marshfield, Mass.

William Bradford. Anagr. I made Law for Bridl'. For Law I made Bridl."
   d. Plymouth, May 9, 1657, a. 69.
   15 four-line stanzas, 1 of six lines, 1 of seven, and 1 of eight, the last two stanzas forming an acrostic, in Morton, pp. 146–8.

W., W. (believed to be Wait Winthrop [1642–1717], b. Boston, Mass., at H.C. 1659, physician, Major General, and Chief Justice of Mass.).

Some Meditations Concerning our Honourable Gentlemen and Fellow-Souldiers, In Pursuit of those Barbarous Natives in the Narragansit-Country.

32 four-line stanzas, broadside, original ed. apparently lost, repr. New London, April 4, 1725; dated and signed at end: December 29, 1675. W.W., MHS, facsim. Winslow, p. 113. Generally attributed to Wait Winthrop, a likely choice, though no evidence as to his authorship has come to light.

WISWALL, ICHABOD (1637–1700), b. Dorchester, Mass., H.C. 1651 (not grad.), pastor Duxbury, Mass., astronomer.

1. (Elegy on the death of Governor Josiah Winslow.)

   d. Marshfield, Dec. 18, 1680, a. 51.

   broadside (?), in private possession 1826, present location unknown, ref. John Davis ed. of Nathaniel Morton, *New Englands Memoriall* (Boston, 1826), p. 467 note.

2. *A Judicious Observation of that Dreadful Comet, which appeared on November 18. 1680.*

   London, 1683, 409 lines, MHS; at end: "Sic Cecinit. J. W. March 6. 1680/81." On attribution see *Publ. Col. Soc. Mass.*, vol. 11, pp. 403–8.

3. A Small Testimony of that great Honour due to that Honourable Servant of God and his Generation John Alden Esq.

   d. Duxbury, Sept. 12, 1687, a. 89.

   66 lines, broadside BA & MHS, "Printed in the year, MDCLXXXVII," facsim. *The Mayflower Descendant*, vol. 9, facing p. 129, and Winslow, p. 13; Ms.c.c. NYHS, commonplace book of Samuel Sewall. Anonymous, but here attributed to Wiswall, Alden's pastor at Duxbury; the neighboring pastor, John Cotton II, also wrote an elegy on Alden.

4. Upon the Death of that Reverend and Aged Man of God, Mr. Samuel Arnold.

   d. Marshfield, Sept. 1, 1693, a. 71.

   22 four-line stanzas, followed by an anagram and 36 lines, broadside Library of Congress, facsim. Winslow, p. 15; signed Ichabod Wiswell (in third column, followed by a fourth column with Arnold's own verses).

WOOD, WILLIAM (1606–after 1637), b. Eng., N.E. early 1629, Lynn, Mass., to Eng. 1633, ret. 1635, to Sandwich, Mass. 1637, when he disappears from the records.

1. "Trees both in hills and plaines, in plenty be."
   20 lines, in his *New Englands Prospect* (London, 1634), repr. var., e.g. by Eben Moody Boynton of West Newbury (1898), p. 17.
2. "The kingly Lyon, and the strong arm'd Beare."
   12 lines, *ibid.*, p. 20.
3. "The Princely Eagle, and the soaring Hawke."
   28 lines, *ibid.*, pp. 28–9.
4. "The king of waters, the Sea shouldering Whale."
   18 lines, *ibid.*, p. 34.
5. Kinds of all Shel-fish.
   "The luscious Lobster, with the Crabfish raw."
   6 lines, *ibid.*, pp. 34–5.

WOODBRIDGE, BENJAMIN (1622–1684), b. Wiltshire, Eng., N.E. 1634, H.C. 1642, Magdalen Hall, Oxford, S.T.D., pastor Salisbury and Newbury, Eng., ret. N.E., pastor Amesbury, Mass. 1666–1669, ret. Eng.

1. Upon the Author; by a known Friend.
   12 lines, signed B.W., the third of the prefatory poems in Anne Bradstreet, *The Tenth Muse* (London, 1650), and in subsequent ed.
2. Upon the Tomb of the most Reverend Mr. John Cotton.
   d. Boston, Dec. 23, 1652, a. 68.
   66 lines, broadside, apparently lost (Cambridge, c. 1667), repr. Morton, pp. 137–9 and *Magnalia*, vol. 1, pp. 258–9 (with several differences).

   Note: That the first printing of this elegy was in the form of a broadside and about 1666 or 1667, can now be proved by the finding of a letter from Thomas Chisholm to his "sister," Mrs. Margaret Witchfield, of Windsor, Conn., dated Cambridge 27–2–67 (April 27, 1667), Ms. CHS, Wolcott Papers, vol. 1, no. 7, the postscript: "I have sent you a small token namly 3 papers of verses made by on[e] doctor woodbridg that was one of the first that did come up at our colledge upon the reuerant mr John Cotton one for your self and one for each of your daughters." Woodbridge had only recently returned to N.E.

WOODBRIDGE, BENJAMIN (c. 1650–1710), b. Eng., H.C. (not grad.) pastor Windsor, Conn., Bristol, R. I., Kittery, Me., Portsmouth and Newcastle, N. H., and Medford, Mass.

(Epitaph on his wife, Mary Woodbridge.)

d. Bristol, Oct. 11, 1685, a. 36.

4 lines, on gravestone (defective), pr. *New England Hist. Gen. Reg.*, vol. 23, p. 475.

WOODBRIDGE, JOHN (1613–1695), b. Wiltshire, Eng., Magdalen Hall (?), Oxford, N. E. 1634, pastor Andover, Mass., to Eng. 1648, pastor in Wiltshire, ret. N.E., pastor Newbury, Mass. 1663–1670, var. civil offices in town and colony.

To my dear Sister, the Author of these Poems.

74 lines, the second of the prefatory poems in Anne Bradstreet, *The Tenth Muse* (London, 1650), and in subseq. ed.

WOODBRIDGE, MERCY DUDLEY (1621–1691), b. Eng., N.E. 1630, sister of Anne Bradstreet and wife of the Rev. John Woodbridge, Newbury, Mass.

(A Poetic Epistle addressed to her sister upon the subject of her volume.)

Ms.a. (?), last direct reference in Samuel Kettell, *Specimens of American Poetry* (Boston, 1829), vol. 1, pp. xxvii–xxviii.

WOODBRIDGE, TIMOTHY (1656–1732), b. Wiltshire, Eng., H.C. 1675, pastor Kittery, Me., and Hartford, Conn., founder, trustee, and fellow Yale College.

To the Reverend Mr. Cotton Mather on his History of New-England.

36 lines, *Magnalia*, vol. 1, p. 18.

WORTHINGTON, WILLIAM (1670–1753), b. Hartford, Conn., resided Norwich and Colchester.

(Epitaph on Sunseeto, the Son of Uncas.)

buried Mohegan burying ground, Norwich.

4 lines, copied by Erza Stiles, with attribution, but no indication of date, *Extracts from the Itineraries* (New Haven, 1916), p. 143.

ANONYMOUS POET of Boston or Vicinity (fl. 1669–1675).

1. A description of fallen man, or fallen man described.
   Ms.a. (?) in a large folio book containing about 100 pages in Ms. of poetry c. 1670, present location unknown. In 1859 the volume apparently belonged to Dr. J. P. Fessenden, of Lewiston, Maine; ref. *New England Hist. Gen. Reg.*, vol. 13, p. 207, communicated by John G. Locke (w. pr. of no. 5); "titles of several of the pieces" communicated by *ibid.* (J.G.L.) in the *Historical Magazine*, vol. 2, pp. 182–3. "Notwithstanding the orthography, the author was a man of considerable mind and genius, and his writings are full of quaint ideas and forms of expression." On the basis of the inadequate external evidence given, as well as of the style and expression of the one published poem, one could hazard the guess that the author might have been Joshua Scottow (1618–1698).
2. The affect of man's fall, or what man's fall hath affected.
   Ms.a., *ibid.*
3. Upon the death of that worthy servant of the Lord, Mr. William Woodward.
   d. Dedham, June 27, 1669.
   Ms.a., *ibid.*
4. Upon the death of Mr. John Minot, Sen'r.
   d. Dorchester, Aug. 12, 1669.
   Ms.a., *ibid.*
5. Upon the death of Mr. Zacheriah Sims.
   d. Charlestown, Jan. 28, 1670/1, a. 72.
   74 lines, Ms.a. *ibid.*, pr. *New England Hist. Gen. Reg.*, vol. 13, p. 207, but with the title: "An epatha upon the Death of Mr Zechariah Sims."
6. Upon the death of Mr. James Pen, elder of the first church in Boston.
   d. Boston, Sept. 30, 1671.
   Ms.a., *ibid.*
7. An epitaph upon the death of that Honnorabal and most worthy to be very highly esteemed Mrs. Mary Whitingham.
   d. Boston, Nov. 1671.
   Ms.a., *ibid.*

8. These lines weare written upon the Death of Thomas bridg of Cambridge.
   d. Cambridge, March 21, 1673, a. 17 or 18.
   Ms.a., *ibid.*
9. The last words and dying word of Lydia Stevenson.
   Ms.a., *ibid* (cf. below no. 14).
10. These lines were ocasunaly writen upon the Death of a young maid ho died on the eaigh of the 7th month (1671) of a [word blotted] desese with and which to home I wished well, was visited and throw God's grace recovered.
    Ms.a., *ibid.*
11. These vearses were written upon the Death of Joseph Grene of Bostoun (ho died three weeks after his wedding in the spring), son to Ensin Grene of Cambridge.
    Ms.a., *ibid.*; the author adds "1672 as i remember," thus this Ms. was apparently an autograph copy of a somewhat later date.
12. Another theme on Joseph Greane.
    Ms.a., *ibid.*
13. These lines were occasionied upon the prevalency of the indians at Sudbury.
    Ms.a., *ibid.*, c. 1675.
14. On the death of Lydia Stevenson.
    d. Cambridge, March 1, 1675, a. 27.
    Ms.a., *ibid.*
15. Concerning Death and trioumph over Death gained by a wright improvement of the gospel, painfully written and freely given to his much honnered and most worthy to be hi-ly esteemed (E B).
    Ms.a., *ibid.*

ANONYMOUS (arranged chronologically)

1. Our Forefather's Song.
   46 lines (originally apparently an introductory couplet and 6 eight-line stanzas, of which the last 4 lines of the fifth stanza have been lost); a popular ballad, handed down by word of mouth, first recorded late in the 18th century, pr. *Massachusetts Magazine*, vol. 3 (1791), pp. 52–3; repr. 3 *Coll. M.H.S.*, vol. 7, pp. 29–30, repr. Edward E. Hale, *New England History in Ballads* (Boston, 1903), pp. 16–8 (Hale here

says that the ballad was first printed in 1773, but gives no further reference). The internal evidence places the ballad in about the 1630's; in style, spirit and humor it bears some resemblance to Edward Johnson's Woburn verses and to the *Good News* of 1648.

2. "Abel his Offering accepted is."
   4 lines, on the gravestone of a boy (surname unknown), 1644, Dorchester North Burial Ground, pr. *New England Hist. Gen. Reg.*, vol. 2, p. 381, and *History of the Town of Dorchester* (Boston, 1859), p. 656.
3. (Epitaph on Ephraim Huit.)
   d. Windsor, Sept. 4, 1644.
   4 lines on gravestone, pr. Charles W. Elliott, *The New England History* (New York, 1857), vol. 1, p. 422.
4. 1645. aboute the 16th of 5th month was this anagram sent to mr Dudley then govnor by some namelesse author.
   anagram and 10 lines, Ms.c.c. by John Eliot in his records of the Church in Roxbury, pr. *New England Hist. Gen. Reg.*, vol. 33, p. 64.
   Note: judging from the technical quality of the contrapunctal pattern, this poem may be by John Fiske, though Charles M. Ellis, *The History of Roxbury Town* (Boston, 1847), pp. 103–4, attributes it to John Eliot.
5. "Submite Submited to her Heavenly King."
   4 lines, on the sister of Abel (see no. 2 above), d. 1648, a. 3, same gravestone, pr. *New England Hist. Gen. Reg.*, vol. 2, p. 381, and *History . . . of Dorchester*, p. 656.
6. "Here lie three Clarkes, their accounts are even."
   2 lines, on gravestone of Joseph, Thomas, and Bray Clarke of Dorchester (dates of death unknown), pr. *History . . . of Dorchester*, p. 46.
7. "Resplendent studs of heaven's frame."
   34 four-line stanzas, Ms.a. (?) BPL, Mellen Chamberlain Collection; there attributed to the younger John Rogers of Ipswich (1666–1745), though the handwriting does not in the least resemble his (nor his father's), but seems to be of an earlier period. It seems to have been designed as an almanac poem, though it is of greater length even than Samuel Danforth's of 1648, and it may be the verse for one of the lost Cambridge almanacs, 1651–1655 or 1658.

8. (Epitaph on Edward Winslow.)
   d. at sea between St. Domingo and Jamaica, May 8, 1655, a. 61.
   6 lines, pr. Morton, p. 143, written by "One of the Company who was imployed in taking notice of the Particulars of that Tragedy."
9. (Lines on the exile of Nicholas Upsall to Rhode Island, 1657.)
   pr. "in a note in an English edition of George Fox's Journal?"; ref. and repr. of 14 lines (on Indian hospitality contrasted to New English cruelty) *New England Hist. Gen. Reg.*, vol. 34, p. 25; possibly an excerpt from George Joy.
10. (Epitaph on Mary Holyoke.)
   d. Springfield, Oct. 26, 1657.
   4 lines on gravestone, pr. John Warner Barber, *Historical Collections . . . Massachusetts* (Worcester, 1839), p. 298.
11. (Elegy on Ralph Partridge.)
   d. Duxbury, May 1, 1658, a. 79.
   52 lines and a 14 line acrostic, pr. Morton, pp. 153–5; written by "one who was a true Admirer of his worth"; possible authors: Nathaniel Morton, Josiah Winslow.
12. (Epitaph on William Paddy.)
   d. Boston, Aug. 24, 1658, a. 58.
   12-line acrostic, pr. Morton, p. 156; written by "One who was well acquainted with his Worth and gracious Endowments"; possible authors: Nathaniel Morton or John Norton I. For the 6 line epitaph on his gravestone see Samuel G. Drake, *The History and Antiquities of Boston* (Boston, 1856), p. 354.
13. Epitaph (on Ezekiel Rogers).
   d. Rowley, Jan. 23, 1660/1, a. 70.
   4 lines English, 2 lines Latin, apparently from his gravestone, pr. *Magnalia*, vol. 1, p. 373.
   Note: the same epitaph, with slight changes, was applied to John Richardson, d. Newbury, Apr. 27, 1696 (Sibley, vol. 2, p. 212).
14. (Epitaph on Major Humphrey Atherton.)
   d. Dorchester, Sept. 16, 1661.
   6 lines, on gravestone Dorchester North Burial Ground, pr. *New England Hist. Gen. Reg.*, vol. 2, p. 382, and *History . . . of Dorchester*, p. 104; possible authors: William Pole, Richard Mather, or Edward Johnson.

15. The Phaethontick ἐκπύρωσις.

    14 lines, in Nathaniel Chauncy's *Almanack* for 1662, signed "Incerti Authoris."

    Note: the lines signed thus in John Richardon's *Almanack* for 1670 are by President Charles Chauncy.

16. The following rural lines were written upon a discourse had with one (about the year 1661) about the whore that rides on many waters.

    18 lines, Ms.a. (?) author's possession, fly leaf of a volume of Protestant tracts of the late 16th century, with marginalia in the same hand. The poem touches on the prophecies concerning 1666 (cf. N. Noyes no. 1 above) and opposes a prevalent Puritan belief that the Antichrist was only at Rome.

17. An Epitaph on Captaine Richard Lord.

    d. New London, May 17, 1662, a. 51.

    8 lines, on gravestone New London Burial Ground, pr. *New England Hist. Gen. Reg.*, vol. 11, p. 22.

18. (Epitaph on John Glover.)

    d. Springfield, Jan. 14, 1664/5, a child.

    4 lines, on gravestone, pr. Barber *op. cit.*, p. 298.

19. Some offers To Emblam the Memory of the Truly Reverend and Renowned, John Wilson.

    d. Boston, Aug. 11, 1667, a. 79.

    59 lines, pr. Cotton Mather, *Johannes in Eremo* (Boston, 1695), pp. 43–5, from a Ms. in his possession; repr. *Magnalia*, vol, 1, pp. 291–2, and *IV. Early American Poetry*, The Club of Odd Volumes, 1896. Here and elsewhere the poem is incorrectly attributed to Cotton Mather (see above under Cotton Mather no. 10). Possible authors are Benjamin Tompson or Nicholas Noyes.

20. Epitaphium (on John Wilson).

    2 lines, pr. *ibid.*, p. 46, repr. *ibid.*, p. 292; this epitaph "was directed for him, immediately upon his death, by an honourable person, who still continues the same lover, as well as instance, of learning and vertue . . . ." (4 lines Latin, are added "from another hand"; whether original or an adaptation from a foreign model is uncertain).

21. Upon the Death of the virtuous and Religious Mrs. Lydia Minot.

    d. Dorchester, Jan. 25, 1667/8.

54 lines (3 anagrams, each with verses, and a concluding couplet), broadside, private possession, facsim. Winslow, p. 7; possible authors: Richard Mather, William Pole.

22. Richard Mather. Anagram. A Third Charmer.
d. Dorchester, April 22, 1669, a. 73.
8 lines, Ms.c.c. (or a.?), Dorchester Church Records, pr. (without title) in *History . . . of Dorchester*, p. 217, title and excerpt *New England Hist. Gen. Reg.*, vol. 40, p. 337; possible authors: Josiah Flynt, William Pole.

23. Epitaph (on Richard Mather).
10 lines, Ms.c.c. (or a.?), *ibid.*, pr. *ibid.*
Note: the first and third couplets, much changed and preceded by 5 lines in Latin, were inscribed on his gravestone, pr. *ibid.*, pp. 217–8.

24. "Welcome, great prophet, to New-England shore."
6-line excerpt from a poem addressed to Urian Oakes upon his arrival from England in 1671, *Magnalia*, vol. 2, p. 97.
Note: in a greatly changed form this is incorporated into Cotton Mather's elegy on Oakes of 1682 (cf. under Cotton Mather no. 10, the discussion of the attribution).

25. "When Lusher was in office, all things went well."
couplet current during the generation after the death of Major Eleazar Lusher, d. Dedham, Nov. 12, 1672, pr. *New England Hist. Gen. Reg.*, vol. 34, p. 361 n, and var.

26. An Ellegy on Thomas Prence Esqr. Governour of New Plimouth Colony.
d. Plymouth, March 29, 1673, a.c. 73.
23 lines, unfinished Ms.c.c. NYHS, Samuel Sewall's commonplace book, pp. 33–4; possible authors: Nathaniel Morton, Samuel Sewall.
Note: Sewall's note at the head of the poem, "Begun Nov 28," may refer either to the copying or to the composing.

27. Epitaph (on Thomas Shepard II).
d. Charlestown, Dec. 22, 1677, a. 43.
14 lines Latin, 1 line Greek, on his tombstone, pr *Magnalia*, vol. 2, p. 101.

28. (Elegy on Thomas Shepard II.)
28 lines, pr. *Magnalia*, vol. 2, pp. 101–2; followed by 2 lines from another, Latin elegy on him; the other four couplets quoted on these pages are from Urian Oakes' elegy.

29. (Epitaph on Captain Jonathan Poole.)
    d. Reading, Dec. 24, 1678, a. 44.
    6 lines, on gravestone, pr. Lilley Eaton, *Genealogical History of the Town of Reading, Mass.* (Boston, 1874), p. 568.
30. (Epitaph on Captain Hugh Mason.)
    d. Watertown, Oct. 10, 1678, a. 73.
    8 lines, on gravestone, Watertown Burying Ground, pr. *New England Hist. Gen. Reg.*, vol. 34, pp. 280–1.
31. (Elegy on Daniel Russell.)
    d. Charlestown, Jan. 4, 1678/9, a. 36.
    Ms. or broadside (?), present location unknown; ref. Sibley, vol. 2, p. 285: "An Elegy on his death was in possession of Charles Lowell, H. U. 1800." cf. above under James Allen.
32. To the Memory of his Deseased friend Sarah Tompson.
    d. Braintree, Jan. 15, 1679/80, a. 43.
    120 lines, Ms.c.c. CHS, third part of Sarah Tompson Ms., preceded by her religious autobiography and the elegy of Benjamin Tompson; possible authors: Samuel Torrey, Josiah Flynt, Moses Fisk.
33. (Epitaph on Thomas Kendall.)
    d. Reading, July 22, 1681, a. 63.
    9 lines, on gravestone, pr. Barber *op. cit.*, p. 428.
34. (Epitaph on Urian Oakes.)
    d. Cambridge, July 25, 1681, a. 50.
    14 lines Latin, on tombstone in Cambridge, pr. *Magnalia*, vol. 2, p. 100.
35. (Epitaph on St. Aspenquid, Indian missionary.)
    d. York, Maine, May 1, 1682, a. 94.
    2. lines, pr. Farmer and Moore, *Collections Historical and Miscellaneous* (1824), appendix, pp. 85–6, repr. *New England Hist. Gen. Reg.*, vol. 22, p. 316.
36. (Epitaph on President John Rogers.)
    d. Cambridge, July 2, 1684, a. 54.
    17 lines Latin, 1 line Greek, on his tombstone, pr *Magnalia*, vol. 2, p. 13, repr. Sibley, vol. 1, pp. 169–70 & note; by "one of the scholars in Harvard-Colledge," possibly Samuel Danforth II, Nehemiah Walter, Edward Tompson, or Nathaniel Mather.
37. Epitaph (on Thomas Shepard III).
    d. Charlestown, June 8, 1685, a. 27.
    4 lines, *Magnalia*, vol. 2, p. 127; possibly by Cotton Mather.

38. "New England alarmed."
    Ms. orig. lost, 4 line excerpt pr. Joshua Coffin, *A Sketch of the History of Newbury* (Boston, 1845), p. 150; directed against the Andros government, 1688.
39. (Epitaph on Giles Hamlin.)
    d. Middletown, Sept. 1, 1689, a. 67.
    6 lines, on gravestone in Middletown Burying Ground, pr. *New England Hist. Gen. Reg.*, vol. 2, p. 71.
40. Some few Lines by another Hand, we shall leave to the Interpretation of Time, & the Intelligent Reader.
    4 stanzas of 4, 5, 6, and 7 lines, in Tulley's *Almanack* for 1693, p. (16); on a prophetic theme of which Samuel Sewall was very fond.
41. A General Tribute of Tears: For the Death of her Royal Majesty Mary, Queen of England Scotland France and Ireland.
    d. London, Dec. 28, 1694, a. 32.
    24 four-line stanzas, broadside, Boston, 1695, apparently lost, Ms.c.c. NYHS, Samuel Sewall's commonplace book, pp. 17–9, with notation at end: "Printed in Boston 1695;" probably a reprint from an English broadside.
42. (Epitaph on John Hall.)
    d. Middletown, Jan. 22, 1694/5, a. 75.
    6 lines, on gravestone in Middletown Burying Ground, pr. *New England Hist. Gen. Reg.*, vol. 2, p. 71.
43. (Epitaph on Sarah Bacon.)
    d. Middletown, 1695/6.
    4 lines, on gravestone, pr. *New England Hist. Gen. Reg.*, vol. 2, p. 73.
44. (Anonymous verse in Cotton Mather's *Magnalia.*)
    on the many short scraps of verse scattered through the *Magnalia*, see above under Cotton Mather, no. 10.
45. (Epitaph on Capt. William Buswell.)
    d. Salisbury, June 15, 1699, a. 73.
    2 lines, on gravestone in Salisbury, pr. *New England Hist. Gen. Reg.*, vol. 14, p. 164.
46. (On Mrs. Sarah Thyer.)
    excerpt of 3 four-line stanzas, quoted without any ref. in Louis B. Mason, *The Life and Times of Major John Mason* (New York, 1935), p. 147.